BAD COMPANIONS

Engraved for the Ladies Magazine

RYNWICK WILLIAMS,
Commonly called
THE MONSTER!

(From a drawing by Gillray.)

BAD COMPANIONS

BY

WILLIAM ROUGHEAD

WITH AN INTRODUCTION BY

HUGH WALPOLE

"Therefore let men take heed of their companions."
— SIR JOHN FALSTAFF.

NEW YORK

DUFFIELD & GREEN

TO J. B. PRIESTLEY

My dear Priestley,

I feel that some apology is due as well for the perversion of your title, as for the kind of company to which I propose to introduce you. It is, indeed, no fair exchange for the joy your delightful folk afford me, who am but an humble unit in the multitude of your admirers, that I thus invite your countenance for my rascals. What would Miss Trant think of Madame Rachel? How should Mr. Jollifant endure The Monster? Could Mr. Oakroyd away with Mr. Wooler? While as for Fanny and Miss Cumming . . . why, Mrs. Tarvin would simply send for the police! I can but commend them to your charity; and at least beg you to believe that I am not ungrateful.

W. R.

A LITTLE FOREWORD

Good books need no Prefaces. Most certainly this book needs none. But I am glad to have the opportunity of saying publicly wherein I think that Mr. Roughead's treatment of Crime differs from that of anyone else.

In these days Crime is the thing. There are Crime Clubs, Crime Societies, Crime Dinners. As to how many new Crime Novels there are every week only Publishers can say, but if some Publishers grow rich it is on Crime nowadays that they do it.

Our interest in Crime is no new thing. Probably the artists who painted those wonderful boars on the ceilings of the Altimira Caves thirty thousand years ago had a Crime Club, but we have in our time an especial attitude to Crime and Mr. Roughead is our prophet.

The other day I read a most excellent story by Mr. Forrester called "Plain Murder." This story treated with the utmost calmness of a clerk, stout and Hebraic, who ran amuck in a quiet assured way and, having murdered his boss and found it easy, proceeded then to murder a fellow-clerk, and attempt the further murders of a second clerk and the wife of his own bosom. He was a quite ordinary man who found murder, when once he had tried it, as natural as breathing. In the days of Dickens and Jonas Chuzzlewit we were led to suppose that a murderer—any and every murderer—suffered agonies and tortures of remorse after the deed. We have changed all that, or rather the War has changed it for us. Having been commanded for four long years by every clergyman and civil magistrate to kill as many people as possible, it is not strange if human life has, for some of us, lost some of its value.

This is where Mr. Roughead comes in. He does not condone crime: all his books are most strictly moral although never moralising; but he is calm, dispassionate, and often amused. He is sometimes also disgusted, but he never permits his disgust to betray his judgment.

He is therefore an ideal investigator. Entirely normal himself, he is able the more justly to probe the abnormality of others. Indeed, at the end of his investigation, he is inclined to say to us: "I do not call this person abnormal. If he is dangerous to society he must be removed, but it is not for me to condemn." He has a great charity, great patience, and a fine sprinkling of Scottish caution. He has two other very valuable gifts—a love of letters and a sense of the dramatic.

He has a style of his own. I have heard readers complain of it as affected; for myself, I enjoy it greatly. It is instinct with humour, replete with allusion, and stuffed with good reading.

His sense of the dramatic is even more an asset. Any reader of this book who remembers his now classical "Burke and Hare" in the "Notable Trials" Series—and what reader will not?—will recall the magnificent way in which he summons up out of the vasty deep that old grimy, itchy, dusky life of the Edinburgh byways, making you almost scratch yourself as you read. That murky cloud that hangs behind the two terrible central figures can never be forgotten!

In this present work his art of the dramatic is to be seen at its best. They are not on the whole major criminals whom we are invited here to study. The cases are in themselves often slight, but how human and moving he

FOREWORD

makes them, and how full of blood do the most pinched and peevish facts become under his care!

My own favourite in this book is "The Siren and the Sorceress." Here is a subject precisely to Mr. Roughead's hand. The figure and form of Madame Rachel moves before us. We feel that we need to take the merest step to enter the shop in New Bond Street, or to enjoy a bath, like the luckless Mrs. Borradaile, "at Mrs. Hicks's in Davies Street." This is, I think, the gem of the collection; but I have a great fondness also for "Closed Doors" (how tactfully does Mr. Roughead deal with this very difficult subject!), "Pretty Fanny's Way," and many another.

Some say that these interests are morbid. I reply that under Mr. Roughead's hand they become human, eloquent, and instructive.

May he give us many more of these volumes!

HUGH WALPOLE.

BRACKENBURN,
    October 7, 1930.

CONTENTS

ILLUSTRATIONS

THE MONSTER;

OR, PUNCTURES IN PICCADILLY

THE MONSTER;

OR, PUNCTURES IN PICCADILLY.

Ford. You shall have sport; I will shew you a monster. . . . Will you go,
  gentles ?
All. Have with you to see this monster.
  —*The Merry Wives of Windsor*, Act III., Sc. 2.

STUDENTS of the psychology of sex would be apt to
find in the idiosyncrasy of Mr. Rhynwick Williams
grist for their scientific mill. But as I am more interested
in storytelling than in sadism, I shall confine myself to the
simple facts of his case, upon which the psychopathically-
minded reader is at liberty to found whatsoever unpleasant
theories he pleases. The plain tale of these fantastic doings
is good enough for me, and of a quality sufficient for my
purpose.

It so happens that, having become possessed of a copy
of the rare report of The Monster's trial, and also of the
unconvincing vindication of his innocence addressed by his
counsel to the trial judge, I am moved to share with others
the entertainment which their perusal provides. The
title-pages of these tracts are as follows:—(1) *The Trial
at Large of Rhynwick Williams, at the Old Bailey, July 8th,
1790, Before Judge Buller, For maliciously and feloniously
making an Assault on Miss Ann Porter, and cutting her
Cloak, Gown, Stays, Petticoat, and Shift ; with the Pleadings
of the Counsel, and Judge Buller's excellent Charge to the
Jury, verbatim.* By E. Hodgson, Short-hand Writer to the
Old Bailey. London: Sold by R. Butters, No. 79, Fleet-
Street. (Price 1s. 6d.) pp. 55; and (2) *The Monster at
Large : or The Innocence of Rhynwick Williams Vindicated,
in a Letter to Sir Francis Buller, Bart., One of His Majesty's*

3

Judges of the Court of King's Bench. . . . By Theophilus
Swift, Esq. London: Printed for J. Ridgway, No. 1,
York-Street, St. James's-Square. [16th November 1790.]
pp. 213. Such other authorities as I have been able fruit-
fully to consult will be indicated in the course of my
narration.[1]

I.

In the year of grace 1789 the West End of London
suffered a reign of terror less diabolic than, but in some
respects akin to, the appalling outrages in Whitechapel
which well-nigh a century later horrified humanity. The
Annual Register, with reference to the matter, records:
"During the course of the two last and of the present
months, the streets of the metropolis were infested by a
villain of a species that has hitherto been nondescript. It
was his practice to follow some well-dressed lady, whom he
found unaccompanied by a man, and sometimes after using
gross language, sometimes without saying a word, to give
her a cut with a sharp instrument he held concealed in his
hand, either through her stays or through her petticoats
behind. Several ladies were attacked by him in this
manner, and several wounded; and the wretch had always
the address to escape undetected." Among the maids and
matrons in whom this unique miscreant literally had his
knife, and whose names are included in the several indictments upon which he was subsequently arraigned, were
Mrs. Elizabeth Davies, in Holborn, on 5th May 1789; Mrs.
Sarah Godfrey, in Charlotte Street, on 13th May; Miss
Mary Forster, in Maxwell Street, on 26th September; Miss
Ann Frost, in Jermyn Street, on 9th November; Misses
Elizabeth and Frances Baughan, in Parliament Street, on
6th December; and Miss Ann Porter, in St. James's Street,
on 18th January 1790. All these ladies were confident in
their identification of Williams as the wretch who had

---

[1] Another and excellent report of the trial is contained in *Select Criminal
Trials at Justice-Hall in the Old-Bailey*, vol. i. pp. 398-452. Edinburgh: 1803.
There is no report of the case in the *State Trials*.

attacked them; but many others, either owing to the excitement of the assault or the unfavourable conditions of the occasion, failed to recognise him as their assailant.

Such was the extent of the fear induced by The Monster's activities, that a contemporary journalist observes: "It is really distressing to walk the streets towards evening. Every woman we meet regards us with distrust, shrinks sidling from our touch, and expects a poignard to pierce what gallantry and manhood consider as sacred." The wildest rumours prevailed as to The Monster's methods. "Sometimes, as reported, the villain presented a nosegay to a young female, wherein was concealed a sharp instrument; and as he offered them [sic] the flowers to smell, stabbed them in the face. Other tales were told of some being stabbed in the thigh and behind; in fine, there was universal terror in the female world of London." [1] The nosegay story—though the others were true enough—proved but the flower of a too-fertile fancy in the reporter, based upon the following incident. A gentleman met a young lady, whom he persuaded to accompany him to a place of public refreshment. Over an amicable glass, he produced a small bouquet, of which he begged her acceptance. The damsel smilingly acquiesced; and on taking it felt a sharp prick in her hand, which drew blood. She at once raised an alarm; the supposed Monster was seized and conveyed to the watch-house; and only on discovery that the girl had pricked her finger with the wire used to bind the flowers, was her misguided entertainer set at liberty. [2]

From an interesting account of our subject we learn further particulars of The Monster's doings. [3] "In March

---

[1] *The Newgate Calendar.* By Knapp and Baldwin. Vol. iii. p. 161. London: 1828.

[2] *Edinburgh Herald,* 16th June 1790.

[3] *Old Times: A Picture of Social Life at the End of the Eighteenth Century.* By John Ashton, pp. 247–261. London: 1885. Reprinted from an anonymous article, "An Old Story Retold," in *All the Year Round,* New Series, vol. xxvi. p. 324. London: 1881. There are also accounts, more or less reliable, in

1790 a Mrs. Blaney, of Bury Street, was stabbed at her door after she had knocked. Dr. Smith, seeing an account of this outrage in a newspaper, inserted a notice in the *Morning Herald*, and that journal having made some severe remarks on the matter, public opinion began to be awakened, and numerous letters were written on the subject to the newspapers of the day." A subscription was opened at Lloyd's by Mr John Julius Angerstein,[1] to raise a reward for the capture and conviction of The Monster; and the authorities took the matter up in earnest, as appears from the following notice:—

> PUBLIC OFFICE, BOW STREET.
> *Thursday, 29th April* 1790.

ONE HUNDRED POUNDS REWARD.

Several ladies having of late been inhumanly cut and maimed by a person answering the following description, whoever will apprehend him or give such information to Sir Sampson Wright at the above office as may be the means of his being apprehended, shall, immediately upon his committal to prison, receive fifty pounds from Mr. Angerstein of Pall Mall, and the further sum of fifty pounds upon his conviction.

N.B.—He appears to be about thirty years of age, of a middle size, rather thin made, a little pock-marked, of a pale complexion, large nose ; light-brown hair, tied in a queue, cut short and frizzed low at the sides ;. is sometimes dressed in black, and sometimes in a shabby blue coat ; sometimes wears straw-coloured breeches, with half boots, laced up before ; sometimes wears a cocked hat, and at other times a round hat with a very high top, and generally carries a Wangee cane in his hand.[2]

Mysteries of Police and Crime, by Major Arthur Griffiths, vol. iii. pp. 116–118. London : *n.d.* (Special Edition) ; *The Chronicles of Crime* ; *or, The New Newgate Calendar*, edited by Camden Pelham, vol. i. p. 320. London : 1887 (Reprint) ; and *The Book of Remarkable Trials and Notorious Characters*, edited by Captain L. Benson, pp. 265–270. London (1871).

[1] John Julius Angerstein (1735–1823), merchant, philanthropist, and amateur of fine art; underwriter in Lloyd's, 1756; devised systems of state lotteries ; re-established Veterinary College ; acquired collection of pictures which formed nucleus of National Gallery.

[2] Sir Sampson Wright, chief magistrate at Bow Street, was the judge by whom Deacon Brodie was examined and committed to Bridewell on 11th July 1788, pending his removal to Scotland for trial, after he had been apprehended in Amsterdam and brought back to England.—*Trial of Deacon Brodie*, Notable British Trials Series, *passim*.

Servants were instructed to report any man staying at home during daylight without apparent cause; washer-women were requested to note bloodstains upon any man's handkerchiefs or linen, "as the wretch generally fetches blood when he strikes"; and cutlers were desired to watch if any man answering the description "is desirous of having his weapon of attack very sharp."

Prudent folk were not slow to reap benefit from the ill wind then blowing in the West End. Thus we read:—

A new musical piece was produced last night at Astley's called " The Monster," and being brought forward at a time when the attention of all London was engaged in discovering him, cannot fail of producing full houses. Astley seems to have taken up the matter very seriously, as the piece abounds with much satire against the Monster. The songs also are well adapted, and produced unbounded applause. This piece will certainly be a good acquisition to Astley, who is said to be the author.[1]

Less legitimate means were used to exploit the popular excitement. On 10th May a gentleman was beset in Holborn by a gang of pickpockets, who, having robbed him of his watch and money, raised the cry: "That is the Monster; he has just cut a woman!" Immediately a crowd collected, and pursued by yells of "The Monster!" the unfortunate man fled for his life. Overtaken, knocked down, and evil-entreated by the mob, he hardly had escaped alive but for the intervention of some gentlemen, who conveyed him in a hackney-coach to the Brown Bear in Bow Street. The hostile mob beleaguered the house and broke the windows; and only by a stratagem was he safely lodged in the police office. When Sir Sampson Wright heard the facts of the case, he discharged the prisoner, "and lamented that it was not in his power to punish the perpetrators of this daring and alarming assault, but did all he could by giving that gentleman his protection until the mob dispersed."[2] On another occasion, as one Mr. Heather was crossing Tower Hill, he saw a well-dressed woman lying on the ground. Going to her assistance, he

---

[1] *Morning Herald*, 27th April 1790.   [2] *World*, 11th May 1790.

observed blood upon her gown, and was informed by her that she had just been stabbed with a sharp instrument by a very tall man. She asked him to get her a coach to take her home, which he did; and only after the fair object of his compassion had driven off, did the Good Samaritan discover that she had relieved him of his watch and three guineas![1] Divers ingenious damsels about town, by feigning to have been the victims of the ruffian's attentions, contrived to extort money from the compassionate. "This," says our authority, "is a new kind of Monster!"

On 15th March 1790 there was published—fortunately for my purpose, if not for the proprietors—it only survived till 1806—the first number of a new Scots newspaper, entitled the *Edinburgh Herald*, which made a feature of reporting English law cases, much more fully and satisfactorily than had theretofore been done by its conservative local rivals, the *Caledonian Mercury* and the *Courant*. To the columns of this admirable journal I am indebted for an account, sedulously reprinted from the contemporary English Press, of the various criminal proceedings of which The Monster became the subject.

II

On 18th January 1790 a young lady named Ann Porter, returning with her sister and a lady friend to her home in St. James's Street from a ball at the Palace, held in honour of the Queen's birthday, was ascending the steps of her father's house when she was stabbed in the hip by a man whom she knew by sight, having on more than one occasion been verbally insulted by him in passing. On the evening of Sunday, 13th June, Miss Ann, walking with her mother and sisters in St. James's Park, saw a man whom she at once recognised as her assailant. Mr. John Coleman, who was in attendance on the ladies, started in pursuit, and after a long chase ran his quarry to earth, with the result

---

[1] *Oracle*, 17th May 1790.

that on 15th June he was taken into custody. Of all this there will be more to say when we come to the trial.

On 17th June the man, whose name was Rhynwick Williams, was brought before Sir Sampson Wright at Bow Street, on the charge of being the person repeatedly advertised for in the public Press for having at sundry times assaulted and wounded divers gentlewomen.

He is a young man, apparently under thirty, of a middle size, with a face rather long and thin, features sharp, grey eyes, complexion sallow. He was well dressed, had a genteel appearance, and is by profession in the musical line. He was apprenticed to Mr. Gallini; but some time since has, by his own account, abandoned that pursuit, and has employed himself principally in the manufactory of artificial flowers; and in following this business he has been at Weymouth, Brighton, and other places on the coast.[1]

It afterwards appeared that he was a native of Wales, twenty-three years of age, who had been bound apprentice to Sir John Gallini [2] with the view of becoming a professional dancer. "A misunderstanding as to the disappearance of a watch severed this connection, and he then led a very loose life. For some little time he was a lawyer's clerk; but this employment being only temporary, he was reduced to difficulties until he met with M. Aimable Michell of Dover Street, who taught him artificial flower-making, and with whom he remained until his arrest." [3]

In support of the charge, the Misses Porter identified the prisoner as the assailant of Ann, and as a person who had frequently used obscene language to them in the streets. Mr Tomkins, surgeon, testified to the wound sustained by Ann Porter. Misses Elizabeth and Frances Baughan identified the prisoner as a man who had "cut" both of them in Parliament Street; Miss Ann Frost spoke

---

[1] *Edinburgh Herald*, 18th June 1790.
[2] Gallini, Giovanni Andrea Battista, called Sir John (1728–1805), dancing-master; came to England, 1753; director of dances and stage-manager at Haymarket Opera House; created Knight of the Golden Spur by the Pope; built Hanover Square concert-rooms.
[3] *Old Times*, p. 256.

to his perforating her garments at her own door in Jermyn Street; and Mrs Franklin stated that he had repeatedly hurt her feelings by using infamous language, but had not otherwise wounded her. In reply to the magistrate, the prisoner said he worked at artificial flower- and fancy trimming-making in Dover Street at a guinea a week; that he lodged in Bury Street; and that his employer could prove that he was not out of the house on the nights in question. He was, notwithstanding, committed to the New Prison, Clerkenwell, for trial.

The Duke of Cumberland and a great number of gentlemen were present. The street was very much crowded, and it was five o'clock before the prisoner could be got from the office, as the mob were so exasperated that they would have destroyed him, could they have got at him.[1]

Re-examined on the 20th, the prisoner was identified by four of his other victims: Lady Gordon's maid, whom he wounded in the thigh at her mistress's door; a nameless lady, similarly maltreated in Holborn; Miss Foster, who sustained a like injury; and Miss Wheeler, who, though not physically assaulted by him, suffered moral and intellectual damage by reason of certain words addressed to her by him at Ranelagh Gardens, while she was waiting for her carriage. At this hearing the Dukes of Cumberland [2] and York, Prince William of Gloucester, Lords Beauchamp and Essex, "and several other nobility," were present.

At a resumed sitting on the 22nd, Mrs. Sarah Godfrey, "a lady of uncommon beauty," picked out the prisoner without hesitation, "from a circle of thirty gentlemen," as the person who had wounded her in the following circumstances. In May 1789 she was passing along Piccadilly, when the prisoner came up to her and muttered something which she—happily for her blushes—did not

---

[1] *Edinburgh Herald*, 18th June 1790.

[2] Henry Frederick, Duke of Cumberland (1745–1790), fourth son of Frederick, Prince of Wales; P.C. and K.G. 1767; £10,000 recovered against him for Crim. con. with Countess Grosvenor, 1770; married Mrs. Horton, 1771.

understand. He followed her; and in order to avoid him, she called at her upholsterer's. He watched her coming out and again followed her, until she reached her own door in Charlotte Street, Portland Place, when he gave her a violent blow on her left thigh, which knocked her down. She was severely wounded, "and continued in imminent danger for a considerable time after." Mrs. Godfrey was bound over to prosecute, and the prisoner recommitted.

On 8th July the Grand Jury, at the New Sessions House in Clerkenwell Green, found three bills of indictment against Rhynwick Williams, to be tried at the ensuing sessions at the Old Bailey.

III

On 8th July the trial began before Mr. Justice Buller.[1] The proceedings lasted from half-past nine in the morning till five in the afternoon, and the Court, we read, was "uncommonly crowded." Messrs. Piggott, Shepherd, and Cullen appeared for the Crown; the prisoner, who pleaded Not Guilty, was defended by Mr. Knowlys. The case of Miss Ann Porter was taken first, and the charge was as follows:—

That he, on 18th January last, with force and arms, at the parish of St. James, Westminster, in the King's highway, unlawfully, wilfully, maliciously, and feloniously, did make an assault on Ann Porter, spinster, with an intent to tear, spoil, cut, and deface her garments and cloaths, and the same day, with force and arms in the same public street, wilfully, maliciously, and feloniously did tear, spoil, cut, and deface her garments, to wit, one silk cloak value 10s., one silk gown value 10s., a pair of stays value 5s., a silk petticoat value 5s., one other petticoat value 5s., a linen petticoat value 5s., and a shift value 5s., her property, part of the apparel which she had on her person, against the form of the statute, and against the King's peace, etc.[2]

---

[1] Sir Francis Buller (1746–1800), barrister of the Inner Temple, 1772 ; Justice of the King's Bench, 1778 ; created baronet, 1790 ; Justice of the Common Pleas, 1794–1800. On 30th March 1781 Justice Buller presided at Warwick Assizes on the famous trial of Captain John Donellan for the murder of his young brother-in-law, Sir Theodosius Boughton, Bart., of Lawford Hall, near Rugby.

[2] The Crown authorities had some difficulty in framing the indictment, owing

Mr. Cullen having opened the indictment, Mr. Piggott began his speech for the prosecution, which he described as the most extraordinary that ever called for the attention of a Court of Justice: "an unnatural, unaccountable, and, until now, unknown offence." After narrating the facts and circumstances of the assault, and the arrest and identification of the prisoner, counsel said he understood that the defence was an alibi. "Whenever that alibi makes its appearance, undoubtedly it will be the subject of your attention and due examination. Your experience of the world, your knowledge of business and of human affairs, will I dare say have taught all of you long since that it is either the best or the worst defence in the world." It would hardly be believed that all the Crown witnesses were perjured; it would hardly be pretended, on the opportunities they had of observing this person, that they were mistaken in the facts; and it would be for the jury to say, when they had heard it, what sort of credit this alibi deserved.

The first witness was Miss Ann Porter.[1] She stated that she lived in St. James's Street with her papa. On the night of 18th January, accompanied by her sister Sarah and a friend Mrs. Mead, she attended the ball given in honour of the Queen's birthday. They left the Palace at a quarter-past eleven and walked home. "My sister desired me to make haste, and we went as fast as we could; she said something else, but I did not distinguish the words." On arriving at the house, her sister went first up the steps to the door, to ring the bell; Mrs. Mead followed, and witness came last. "Just as I was passing the corner of the rails I felt a violent blow on my hip; I

---

to the novel nature of the crime, but decided to proceed under the statute 6th Geo. I. c. 23, s. 11, whereby it was felony punishable with transportation for seven years to assault any person in the public streets with intent to tear, cut, burn, or deface the garments or clothes of such person or persons, provided the act be done in pursuance of such intention.

[1] "One of the four daughters of Mr. Porter, who keeps a respectable hotel in St. James's Street."—*Gentleman's Magazine*, July 1790.

turned round to see from whom it proceeded, and I saw that man [the prisoner] stoop down." She knew him at once, having seen him three or four times before. On these occasions he had accosted her and her sisters in the street, using very gross and indelicate language. After striking her, he did not run away, but followed her up the steps and stood close beside her at the door. She had then a full and complete opportunity of seeing his face: "it is impossible I could be mistaken; I could never forget him." Her clothes were cut with a very sharp instrument. She saw the man again in the Park on Sunday evening, 13th June, while there with her mother, her sisters, and a friend, Mr. Coleman. "We were walking in the Mall, and that man passed me very close." She recognised him the moment she saw him; "I turned round to look at him, and he was turning back to look at me." The next time she saw him was at her own house the same evening, when he was brought by Mr. Coleman to be identified. She was then "in such a state" as to be practically unconscious.

Q.—Have you had since that time an opportunity of seeing him more than once, and of recollecting whether he is or is not the man ?

A.—I wanted no recollection ; I knew him the moment I saw him ; I knew him the next day at Bow Street.

Q.—When you saw him at Bow Street was he pointed out to you, or did you know him as soon as you saw him ?

A.—I knew him the moment I saw him.[1]

Cross-examined, her sister told her to hurry when they were a few doors up the street; she ran as fast as she could. The man was close to the rails when she turned round after the blow. She saw him clearly: "our house is surrounded with lights." He had on a light coat, and she believed he had another under that.

Q.—Can you be accurate as to the time when this matter happened ?

A.—It was exactly a quarter-past eleven. My father and two friends were to come to fetch us. I was rather anxious, as the Queen retired so

---

[1] *Trial*, p. 12.

early ; and Mrs. Mead desired me to look at my watch, which I did. That was while we were in the ballroom, the instant we quitted the gallery ; and I do not think it was above five minutes before we got to our door.

Q.—All the other times you had seen him, it was in the day time ?

A.—No ; once I saw him at Ranelagh at night, while we were waiting for a coach.[1]

Miss Sarah Porter, examined, said that the prisoner had followed her in the streets on four occasions, "talking the most dreadful language that can be imagined." She saw him standing at the bottom of St. James's Street on 18th January, between a quarter and half-past eleven.

Q.—Are you sure it was him ?

A.—Oh, I am certain it was him ! I knew him before I came up to him. Some chairmen was passing by, who said : " By your leave ! " upon which he started round, stared in my face, looked again, and said : " Oh, ho ! " and instantly gave me a violent blow on the back part of my head. I requested my sister to run. I said : " Nancy, for God's sake make haste ; do you not see ' The Wretch ' is behind us ? "—a name we always distinguished him by.[2]

As she rang the bell she turned round to see whether he had pursued them, and saw him close to her sister, who dropped down. "I saw him strike her with the greatest violence, and I heard the silk rent." The street was well illuminated and there was a good light in the passage, "which gave me particular opportunity of seeing him perfectly." She saw him again at their own house when Mr. Coleman brought him, and afterwards at Bow Street, where she pointed him out among the crowd. She had no shadow of doubt that the prisoner was the man.

Cross-examined, there were not a good many people in the street ; there was no one near but the chairmen, "who passed instantly." She gave no instructions to pursue the man : she was too terrified. Her father and the servants were then in the house.

Miss Rebecca Porter said she was not with her sisters at the ball. She knew the prisoner by sight. He had

---

[1] *Trial*, p. 13.   [2] *Ibid.*, p. 15.

accosted her and her sister Ann several times, using the most horrible language she ever heard in her life. She recognised him on the Sunday evening with Mr. Coleman, and also at Bow Street; she had not the least doubt he was the man who accosted her and her sister.

Miss Martha Porter said she also had been with sister Ann when the prisoner spoke to her.

Q.—In what manner did he accost her—I do not wish you to state the words he used ?

A.—In the most horrid manner possible.

Q.—Then you heard the words he used ?

A.—Yes, sir ; and very dreadful words they were.

Q.—Have you any doubt that is the man that stands there ?

A.—No, sir ; I am positive that is the man.[1]

John Coleman stated that he was walking with Miss Porter in St. James's Park on the evening of Sunday, 13th June. She became much agitated, and said "The Wretch" had just passed her; she pointed him out. The prisoner was the man.

I followed him—and he walked exceedingly fast—out of the rark and out at Spring Gardens gate. He then turned down by Mr. Walter's, the bookseller. From thence he passed down the Admiralty passage. There I am very sure he perceived I was following him. He walked to the bottom of this passage and up Spring Gardens again. Then he went into Cockspur Street, and along into Pall Mall.[2]

The pursuit continued: up St. James's Street, across by the White Horse Cellar, and "down by the Duke of Devonshire's wall." Then into Boulton Street and down St. James's Street, where the man knocked at a door and spoke for a moment to the manservant who answered it. Mr. Coleman asked the servant whether he knew the man; he replied that he did not. Then up St. James's Street again, and along Bond Street.

I did everything in my power to insult him, by walking behind and before him, looking at him very full in the face, and making a noise behind

---

[1] *Trial*, p. 19.   [2] *Ibid.*

him.　But he would not take an insult ; he never said a word.　I followed him close and behaved in this kind of way (peeping over his shoulder and making a clapping with his hands).　I was going to knock him down once or twice.　He crossed Oxford Road and went into Vere Street. He knocked at a door there which had a bill against it.　I was leaning on the rails in a very impertinent manner, and told him :　" Sir, this is an empty house."　He said :　" No, it was not, for he knew the people very well—*their names was Pearce.*"　He knocked three times again, but nobody came to the door.　From thence he went into South Moulton Street, and knocked at the door of Mr. Smith.　I was quite close behind him.　He went into the house.[1]

Mr. Coleman, having also gained admittance, explained to Mr. Smith the purpose of his call, told him that his visitor had insulted some ladies in the Park, and demanded to know his name and address.　Mr. Smith, observing that he, Coleman, "talked very fair," wrote down the address: "Mr. Williams, No. 52 Jermyn Street."　They then left the house, Mr. Williams going first,　Coleman overtook him in Piccadilly, near the top of St. James's Street, and asked him to accompany him forthwith to the ladies' house hard by, when the matter of identity might be set at rest.　Mr. Williams objected that the hour was late, but finally agreed to do so.

We went up to Mr. Porter's door, and I desired the prisoner to walk in.　He looked up at the house, and said :　" Good God ! this is Mr. Porter's."　I introduced the gentleman to the ladies in the parlour, when Miss Sarah and Miss Ann Porter immediately fainted away, exclaiming : " Oh, my God !　Coleman, that is ' The Wretch.' "

Mr. Williams expressed surprise.　"Good God!" said he, "they do not take me for the person about whom there has been so many publications?"　On being assured that such was the fact, he observed more than once that the ladies were "odd" and "prejudiced"; he was then suffered to depart.

Cross-examined, when witness gave to Mr. Smith his

[1] The name assigned by Williams to the apocryphal tenants of the empty house—so peculiarly applicable to his proclivities—may have been an instance of unconscious humour.

reason for wanting the address, the prisoner raised no objection. When confronted with the Porter ladies he was not in the least embarrassed.

Patrick Macmanus stated that by direction of Mr. Addington he visited the George public house in Bury Street, Jermyn Street, St. James's, and searched the room there occupied by the prisoner. He found a lapelled, close-bodied coat, a hat, and a pair of boots, which he now identified as produced. He found no cutting instruments. It being contended for the defence that the address given to Coleman might apply to the Bury Street tavern, Coleman, recalled, stated in reply to the Court that the Jermyn Street address was written down by Mr. Smith at the prisoner's dictation.

Mr. Tomkins, surgeon, deposed to attending Miss Porter professionally after the assault. The blow must have been struck with a very sharp instrument and with great violence. The several layers of clothing were perforated, and the wound in the thigh was three or four inches deep and nine or ten inches long. The blow had been deflected by the stays; had it not been so, it would probably have pierced the abdomen.

This concluded the evidence for the prosecution, and the prisoner was asked by Court: "Would you say anything for yourself?" He thereupon embarked upon a rambling and irrelevant harangue, wherein he protested his innocence of the very shocking accusation made against him.

While I revere the law of my country, which presumes every man to be innocent till proved guilty, yet I must reprobate the cruelty with which the Public Prints have abounded in the most scandalous paragraphs, containing malicious exaggerations of the charges preferred, so much to my prejudice that I already lie under premature conviction by almost an universal voice.[1]

---

[1] Among the many caricatures or satirical prints relating to the case, published both before and after the trial, the most notable are two drawings by Gillray: (1) "The MONSTER going to take his Afternoon's Luncheon," published 10th May 1790, by H. Humphray, No. 18 Old Bond Street; and (2) "Swearing to the

Confining himself strictly to generalities and making no
comment upon the evidence adduced against him, the
prisoner was content to leave his fate "to the decision of a
British Jury."

I most seriously appeal to the Great Author of Truth that I have the
strongest affection for the happiness and comfort of the superior part of
His creation—the fair sex, to whom I have in every circumstance that
occurred in my life endeavoured to render assistance and protection.[1]

IV

The first witness for the defence was M. Aimable
Michell, "who, being a foreigner, an interpreter was
sworn." He stated that he was a fictive flower-maker,
practising his art at No. 14 Dover Street, Piccadilly. For
the last nine months the prisoner had been in his employment; he was at work as usual on 18th January, the
Queen's birthday.

Q.—How long was he at work with you on that day ?
A.—He worked from nine in the morning till one ; he returned at half
after two, and worked till twelve at night ; after that he supped with me
and stayed till half after twelve. We usually only worked till nine
o'clock, but that day we worked till twelve.[2]

Williams left at half-past twelve. Had he been absent for
any space of time during the evening, witness must have
observed it. He could give the prisoner "the best character
a man can have." Williams always behaved with civility

Cutting MONSTER ; or, A Scene in Bow Street," published 20th May 1790, by
Humphray, as above. These drawings, although executed in the artist's best
manner, are unfortunately much too " free " for reproduction in our day. The
curious will find them in the supplementary folio volume of suppressed plates
issued along with *The Works of James Gillray, from the original plates, with the
addition of many subjects not before collected.* London : printed for Henry G.
Bohn, York Street, Covent Garden. 1847.

[1] " One of the most curious circumstances that occurred on the trial of
Williams was that, in the intervals of time between the commission of his public
offences, he frequently saw a young woman home from the place where he lived,
on purpose, as he professed, *to protect her from the Monster !* "—*Edinburgh Advertiser,* 13th July 1790. He seems to have been a waggish, as well as a dirty dog.

[2] *Trial,* p. 26.

and good nature to the young ladies who worked with him in the house.

Cross-examined, witness had been four years in this country, and occupied the ground floor of the house in Dover Street. The prisoner was not introduced to him; "he offered himself to me to work, either in November or December last." He was the only man employed; the other assistants were three women. Every evening for a fortnight they worked late; nearly every night; he would swear that for eight days before, they were working till midnight. In the course of three hundred and thirteen working days, these were the only nights when this occurred. The reason was the extraordinary pressure due to a commission from Ireland. Notwithstanding, he himself went out that afternoon to see the preparations for the Queen's birthday. He was absent from three to six. The extraordinary order—for Mrs. Abington's gown— came after his return to business; but for that order he would not have kept the prisoner so late. The order was brought by one M. Jerso, a Frenchman. "Q.—What is he? A.—A merchant. Q.—Where does he live? A.— I think it is in Castle Street, Leicester Fields." [1] The gown was duly finished and delivered next morning. The three workwomen were, unfortunately, absent on leave; he had allowed them to down tools at one o'clock for the day; so Mrs. Abington's gown was done by himself, his sister, and two girls "who lodge in the house"—Catherine and Molly. The latter nymph "did the household business"; the functions of the former are not defined. During the whole period of the prisoner's employment "he was never in the streets above once or twice," when witness sent him an errand. As to his leaving that night at precisely half- past twelve, "I only know by the maid [Molly] looking at the clock, hearing the watchman cry the half-hour, and telling me how well the clock went, agreeing with the

---

[1] Jerso, as afterwards appeared, was his own brother-in-law!—Evidence of M. Jerso, *infra*.

watchman." Molly let the prisoner out and made the observation on the time. After much fencing, the witness was brought to admit that he himself did not hear the remark, which was made to his sister. Further, that Molly had only disclosed the fact "about a fortnight or three weeks from this time," *i.e.* the trial; and then upon being approached for the defence. The prisoner continued to work for him until the King's birthday, the 4th of June. The cross-examination closed with some questions directed to the credit of the witness. "Was you at home last night?" The witness pleaded guilty to taking a stroll for the benefit of his health. He knew Lord William Gordon's house in Piccadilly; he did not pass it that night; neither did the course of his itinerary lead him to the Green Park.

Q.—And all the rest that you have sworn today is just as true as the last : that you was not in the Green Park yesterday evening ? A.—Just as true.

Q.—Then, not being in the Green Park, I need hardly ask you whether you accosted any ladies in the Green Park yesterday evening ? A.—No ; I did not address any ladies in the Green Park.

Q.—Or near Lord William Gordon's house ? A.—I was not near that way.

Mlle. Reine Michell said she was a sister of the flowery Aimable. She remembered the Queen's birthday; the prisoner worked from dinner time till midnight; he did not go out during these hours. She confirmed her brother as to the order for Mrs. Abington's gown. M. Jerso drew the pattern and her brother pasted on the flowers, the prisoner assisting. The three workwomen desired a day off because of the birthday. Molly let Williams out.

Cross-examined :—

Q.—What makes you think it was so late as half-past twelve ? A.—Because the maid came in and said that, when she opened the door, the watchman went half-past twelve ; and she made a remark that the clock went extremely right, for it agreed with the watchman.

Pressed as to this, witness "did not recollect" whether the maid spoke of the matter at the time; she stated thé fact voluntarily. Finally, witness admitted that "they sent to ask her about it, since the prisoner was apprehended." The matter was not mentioned till then. It was not customary for the maid to let the prisoner out if he stayed late. By the Court, her brother kept books. Mrs. Abington's gown was debited to M. Jerso.

MR. JUSTICE BULLER.—Let an officer go with M. Michell for his books.
M. MICHELL.—My Lord, shall I call on Jerso and bring him with me ?
MR. JUSTICE BULLER.—Yes ; you may if you will.

Catherine Alman stated that she lived in the house of M. Michell. She corroborated that gentleman as to the prisoner's remaining till twelve-thirty on the night of the Queen's birthday. Her sister Molly mentioned the hour at the time. Cross-examined, she had been with Michell three years, during which the prisoner was constantly at work and never went out, except for an hour or two once or twice. Her sister came into the room where they had supped, after she let the prisoner out, "and she said to me: 'It is half-past twelve; I am afraid it will be too late for Mr. Williams to get into his lodgings.'" Mr. Williams remarked next morning "that the clock struck one when he went into bed." She could not say that the prisoner had ever been so late before; his usual hour was nine. M. and Mlle. Michell were present when her sister made the remark about the watchman. It, the remark, was made in English, though the common conversation of the household was in French.

Q.—Now, Miss Alman, recollect yourself : upon your oath, when did your sister make this observation to you ?
A.—After she shut the door. She came straight from the shop-door into the back-shop, where I was, and related the same I now tell you.

Mary Alman, sister of the last witness, stated that the prisoner worked all the Queen's birthday till twelve-thirty, when she let him out. She looked at the clock and "heard the watchman go" as she did so. Cross-examined, she could not swear that Williams ever stayed beyond his ordinary hour except on this fortunate occasion. Williams asked her the hour, and she looked at the clock to tell him. Some three weeks ago she was asked about the matter by her sister and the Michells.

Q.—Did you tell your sister, when she then applied to you, that you had looked at the clock to tell Mr. Williams the hour ? A.—Yes.
Q.—Had you ever told her so before ? A.—No.
Q.—That was the first time you had ever told her it was exactly half-past twelve when he went away ? A.—Yes, Sir. I am sure it was the first time.

That was the only night they worked late during the six months she was at Michells. She did not say to her sister that she was afraid Williams would be too late for his lodgings.

Frances Bowfield said she was working at Michells on the Queen's birthday and left at half-past eleven that night. The prisoner was still there then. She worked at Mrs. Abington's gown along with the others from two till eleven.

Q.—Now, this night you say was the Queen's birthnight; did not you walk down St. James's Street to see the lights ?
A.—No, Sir ; I was afraid my parents would be angry and I went directly home.

Mrs. Abington's famous gown was finished "about a day or two after the birthnight." Typhone Fournier gave similar evidence.[1] M. Jerso stated that he had dealings with M. Michell, and gave him an order "for a trimming for Mrs. Abington" on the Queen's birthday. He remembered the fact "because the streets were quite illuminated." He gave the order at eight o'clock, but did not know to whom it was given. The work was delivered next morning. Cross-examined,

MR. PIGGOTT.—Do you live in the house ? WITNESS.—No ; I married a sister of M. Michell's. The prisoner has come two or three times to my house.[2]

---

[1] It is to be noted that neither the Michells, Catherine, nor Molly refer to the co-operation of Frances and Typhone on the gown.

[2] "The prisoner called several [other] witnesses, some of whom were very handsome women, and all gave him an excellent character for humanity and good nature."—Select Criminal Trials, vol. i. p. 440 n.

The case for the defence being closed, Mr. Justice Buller proceeded to charge the jury. Before dealing with the evidence, his Lordship observed:—

If, after considering the whole case, you should be of opinion that the facts are made out against the prisoner, still I shall reserve his case for the consideration of all the Judges of England, on two grounds : *First*, Because this is undoubtedly the first prosecution that has ever taken place on the statute on which he is indicted ; and therefore, though I cannot profess to entertain the smallest doubt in my own mind on the true construction of that Act of Parliament, yet, being a new case, I think it right that the opinion of all the Judges should be known. And *secondly*, Because I entertain some doubts about the form and sufficiency of the indictment. But these are questions which it is not necessary now to agitate.[1]

In reviewing the evidence of the four Miss Porters, his Lordship pointed out that they had seen the man several times before the assault, and in the day-time; and the circumstances in which they had seen him were certainly such as called upon them to pay particular attention to his person. They saw him again on the night in question, and they had seen him three times since; and upon no occasion did they entertain the slightest doubt as to his identity. The exclamation, "Oh, ho!" used by the man when, having stared at Miss Sarah, he gave her a blow on the head, appeared to his Lordship "to be the expression of someone who had seen her before, and between whom something or other had passed that was not so agreeable." Why should any man do that, who had not seen her before? With regard to the conduct of the prisoner when challenged in St. James's Park, he walked away very fast, and Coleman was positive he must have seen he was pursued. Why should he go from place to place as described? When exhibited at the Porter's, "two young ladies fell into fits and fainted away. One exclaimed: 'That is the Wretch!'" What was the prisoner's conduct upon this? He remarked to Coleman: "The ladies' behaviour is extremely odd.

---

[1] *Trial*, p. 50.

They do not take me for the person advertised?" And being told that was so, he preserved silence and gave no explanation of himself nor any reference to anybody who knew him. These were circumstances arising from the prisoner's conduct that undoubtedly gave great credit to the positive oaths of the four Miss Porters, who swore most decidedly to his person. Against this, the prisoner called seven witnesses to prove that he could not be the man, because he was in another place, namely, Michell's house, at the time. Michell's recollection of the facts was very loose.

You will find, as I state to you the other evidence, that there are many circumstances in which this witness was contradicted, and in which the other witnesses have contradicted themselves; but what effect that ought to have, or may have on your minds, is for you alone to decide. It is not every little circumstance in which witnesses differ, who speak of the transaction, which is sufficient to destroy the credit of each other; but the question is : Whether the facts in which you find they differ are so material and so pointed, so much within the knowledge of each witness, that if they told you the truth and spoke accurately on what passed, they could not vary so much.[1]

His Lordship then examined at length the evidence for the defence, pointing out its manifold discrepancies and manifest contradictions.

What is there, then, that calls upon them to fix with any degree of certainty in the month of July, whether the night in which the prisoner supped with Michell and stayed till after twelve, was on the 18th of January or any other day ? That he might have supped there some night may be very true ; that in the course of that day M. Jerso was there and did give an order for Mrs. Abington's gown may likewise be true ; but does it follow from thence that it was the night in which the prisoner supped there ? And when we bring the case to that point, to be sure the contradictions that are in the testimony of these witnesses are extremely material, particularly in endeavouring to fix the time. Michell and his sister have no other line to go by but that one servant tells them what another servant told her, and these two sisters directly contradicting one another.[2]

---

[1] *Trial*, p. 53.　　　　　　　　　　[2] *Ibid.*, p. 54.

If the jury believed these witnesses, the prisoner could not be the person who committed the crime, and they would of course acquit him. If, on the other hand, they were satisfied, on the very positive testimony of the four Miss Porters, that he was the man whose person they knew so well they could not be mistaken, the jury must give effect to that, and pronounce the prisoner guilty.

"The jury immediately pronounced a verdict, GUILTY." MR. JUSTICE BULLER.—"Let the sentence be respited till December Sessions; and all the witnesses who are bound over on the other prosecutions, their recognizances must be respited till that time."

V.

Hanged by public opinion, drawn by Gillray, and quartered in as many pamphlets, the trapped Monster awaited in Newgate the issue of his doom. His faith in the virtue of an alibi—a form of defence deemed impregnable by Mr. Weller, senior—must have been somewhat shaken on perceiving the poor appearance made by his witnesses in the box. But his spirits were in nowise cast down, as we gather from the fashionable intelligence of the day:—

THE MONSTER'S BALL.

The depravity of the times was manifested last week in an eminent degree in Newgate. The Monster sent cards of invitation to about twenty couple, among whom were some of his alibi friends, several of the prisoners, and others.

At four o'clock the party sat to tea ; this being over, two violins struck up, accompanied by a flute, and the company proceeded to exercise their limbs. In the merry dance, the cuts and entrechats of the Monster were much admired, and his adroitness in that amusement must be interesting, from the school in which he acquired this branch of his accomplishments.

About eight o'clock the company partook of a cold supper and a variety of wines, such as would not discredit the most sumptuous gala, and about nine o'clock departed, that being the usual hour for locking the doors of the prison.[1]

---

[1] *Oracle*, 20th August 1790.

On 15th November the following announcement appeared in the Press:—

Yesterday, at Serjeants' Inn Hall, eleven of the Judges consulted upon the case reserved at the Old Bailey in September Sessions last, respecting the indictment against Rhynwick Williams, the supposed Monster. The questions were, *first*, Whether his having an intention to cut the person of Miss Porter, and in carrying that intention into execution, cutting the garment of that Lady, is an offence within the Statute of the 6 Geo. I. c. 23, s. 11, on which he was convicted : the Jury having in their verdict found that in cutting her person, he had thereby an intention to cut her garments ? *Secondly*, Whether the Statute being in conjective : " That if any person shall assault another with an intent to cut the garment of such person, and shall cut the garment of such person, then the offender shall be guilty of felony " ; and the indictment in stating the intention, not having connected it with the act, by inserting the words that he " then and there." did cut her garment, could be supported in point of form ?

Nine of the eleven Judges were of opinion that the offence, notwithstanding the finding of the Jury, was not within the Statute, and that the indictment was bad in point of form. This determination declares the offence to be only a misdemeanour, for which in all probability Williams will be indicted at the next Sessions at Hick's Hall.[1]

At the Old Bailey Sessions in the beginning of December the prisoner was again brought to the bar. Mr. Justice Ashurst explained to him his peculiar position under the statute, and recommitted him for trial in terms of the Judges' ruling. The prisoner, in addressing the Court, observed that after having been confined for six months, he felt little satisfaction at the interpretation of the statute: "I am only reserved for severer trials; I have suffered prejudice, which arms Justice with new whips to scourge me."

Much as I have been abused and libelled in the public prints and ill as a persecuting world will be disposed to think of me, I will neither bring people to perjure themselves or prove another alibi. My innocence, however, has not wanted an advocate. In the letter addressed to the Justice who tried me the mistake of the witnesses against me is proved ; but I feel no exultation, finding myself doomed to experience greater

---

[1] *Edinburgh Herald*, 15th November 1790 ; *Scots Magazine*, vol. lii. p. 565 ; *Gentleman's Magazine*, vol. lx. Part ii. p. 1143.

malice. My fond attachment to the fair sex is well known to have been near my ruin ; and now a charge of sanguinary designs against them is seemingly to complete my destruction. I should have been glad to have sought that comfort among savages in another country which has been denied me here.[1]

The letter referred to is that addressed to Mr. Justice Buller by Theophilus Swift, counsel for Williams in the subsequent prosecutions, and later published, as I have mentioned, in pamphlet form.[2]

At Hick's Hall, on 13th December, the prisoner was put to the bar once more to take his trial on eight indictments exhibited against him. The first case taken was that of Miss Ann Porter which occupied the whole day, lasting from ten o'clock forenoon till after one the next morning. He was now charged with assaulting Ann with intent to kill and murder her. A second count narrated that he, "holding a knife in his right hand, did wilfully give the said Ann Porter a dreadful wound of great length and depth on the right thigh and hip: to wit, the length of nine inches and the depth of four." A third count charged him with common assault. The evidence for the prosecution was in substance the same as that led upon the former trial. The Crown witnesses successfully withstood the forensic attack of the learned Theophilus; and on this occasion the defence did not avail itself of the resources of the foreign legion, neither were Catherine and Molly, those veridicous virgins, called upon to testify, the prisoner contenting himself with reading a paper declaring his innocence. Rhynwick Williams, after a trial of over fifteen hours, was found guilty on the first indictment.[3]

On 16th December Mr. Williams—who, like that fair litigant Miss Rugg in *Little Dorrit*, may truthfully be said

---

[1] *Select Criminal Trials*, vol. i. p. 451 ; *Edinburgh Herald*, 13th December 1790.

[2] Theophilus Swift (1746–1815), Irish writer ; son of Deane Swift ; B.A. St. Mary Hall, Oxford, 1767 ; barrister, Middle Temple, 1774 ; sentenced to twelve months' imprisonment for libelling the Fellows of Trinity College, Dublin, 1794. See Note, *infra*.

[3] *Old Times*, p. 260 ; *Scots Magazine*, vol. lii. p. 613.

to have had his "trials"—was brought for the last time to the bar upon the remaining seven indictments, charging him with similar outrages on the persons of the several ladies already mentioned, one charge relating to the assault on Miss Sarah Porter. "When the evidence was closed, the chairman asked the prisoner, Whether he had anything to say in his defence? Mr. Swift desiring him to say nothing, he followed his counsel's advice. Verdict, *Guilty*." The sentence of the Court was as follows:—

That for the assault on Miss Ann Porter, you be confined in Newgate for the space of two years. For the assault on Elizabeth Davies, that you be also confined for two years, to commence from the expiration of the former sentence. And that for the assault on Miss Elizabeth Baughan, you also be confined two years, to commence from the expiration of the former four. That at the end of the six years, you shall find bail for your good behaviour for seven years, yourself in the sum of £200, and two sureties in £100 each, and to return to the custody in which you came.[1]

The Monster, appropriately caged at last, passed quickly from the ken of his contemporaries, and survived but as a painful memory in the minds of his former victims, who could now discard the copper petticoats recommended by the caricaturists for their protection. Thus Horace Walpole, writing to Miss Mary Berry on 28th February 1791, only two months after the event, remarks:—

. . . I am sorry to find that it costs above six weeks to say a word at Pisa and have an answer in London. This makes correspondence very uncomfortable ; you will be talking to me of Miss Gunning, when perhaps she may be sent to Botany Bay, and be as much forgotten here as the *Monster*.[2]

As to the further experiences of Rhynwick Williams after he had served his time, history is silent. Whether he continued to indulge, in modified form, his reprehensible foible or became a pure and blameless ratepayer, we cannot tell. The last word of him I find in those public prints

---

[1] *Select Criminals Trials*, vol. i. p. 452.
[2] *The Letters of Horace Walpole*, vol. xiv. p. 381. Oxford : 1905.

which he so frequently deprecated, is contained in the following paragraph, with reference to the severe winter of 1799:—"Another new *Monster* on Wednesday made his appearance in town. His passion is for *biting* the Ladies' *toes* and *finger ends*. They say his name is *Frost*." [1]

With regard to the £100 reward offered for his apprehension and conviction, Miss Ann Porter is stated to have refused to touch a farthing of it.[2] Perhaps Mr. Coleman, who seems clearly entitled to the reversion, was not so nice.

Note.—THE MONSTER'S CHAMPION

Theophilus Swift, by birth, temperament, and experience, was admirably equipped for his task of vindicating the Monster. An Irishman, and constitutionally "agin' the Government," he first saw the light in the doleful year 1746. Both his parents were cousins of the famous Dean of St. Patrick's, and his father's Christian name, strangely enough, was Deane. B.A. of Oxford in 1767 and called to the English Bar in 1774, Theophilus quitted the peaceful precincts of the Temple in 1783 and retired to the more congenial atmosphere of Dublin. In 1789 he had a meeting with Colonel Charles Lennox (afterwards fourth Duke of Richmond and Lennox), arising out of a pamphlet which Swift had published on Lennox's duel with the Duke of York. Wounded alike in pride and person—he had the worse of the encounter—he issued his *Letter to the King on the Conduct of Colonel Lennox.* For his next affair of honour—collegiate this time, and bloodless—his chosen weapon was the press: *Animadversions on the Fellows of Trinity College, Dublin,* 1794. But once again the fortune of war forsook his arms; he was prosecuted for libel and sentenced to twelve months' imprisonment. The last flashings of his fiery pen were directed against a Dublin Doctor of Divinity, whose daughter,

---

[1] *Times*, 20th December 1799.　　[2] *Old Times*, p. 261.

having, for her sins, accepted Swift's addresses, presently
rued her bargain and resiled from the contract. The disappointed swain published the whole story in his *Correspondence with the Rev. Dr. Dobbin*, 1811.

It was no doubt due to the publication of *The Monster
at Large; or, The Innocence of Rhynwick Williams
Vindicated*, most improperly addressed to the Judge
presiding at the first trial, that led to Swift's being retained
as counsel for the Defence in the subsequent prosecutions.
"Cassandra sung in vain," he remarks in his modest
preface, "but her warnings were divine. Method, however,
has not been neglected; for I am persuaded that without
method no work was ever yet good for anything." The
method adopted by him in the present case is simple: a
base and unscrupulous attack upon the character of each
Crown witness, coupled with high commendation of the
purity and candour of M. Michel and the several members
of the foreign legion. Mr. Porter's establishment, which
we know on the authority of the *Gentleman's Magazine* to
have been "a respectable hotel," is pleasantly referred to
throughout as "The Bagnio." His four daughters are
variously described as "Tavern Vestals," "Nuns of Purity,"
and "Beauties of the Bagnio"; "this Sisterhood of Truth,
this new and holy Order of Swearers." Mr. Coleman is
politely termed a liar and a coward; "the Pander of the
Bagnio," "this Haberdasher of Oaths." The prisoner's
shyness of him when pursued is ingeniously explained:
"The fact is Williams took him for a Catamite, and as such
endeavoured to avoid him; as any of you would do, who
would shun the Beasts of Gomorrah." He admits that his
client had previously made improper advances to Miss
Ann Porter, but only because of her relations with an
unnamed "Captain," condemned to death for highway
robbery, though "the prayer of Beauty obtained his
sentence to be reversed into a Voyage to Botany Bay."
The surgeon's description of the alleged wound is inaccurate
and unintelligible.

I have not measured the depth of Miss Porter's thigh ; but I am told it is very delicate, and that it does not contain in the thickest part *four inches* of Solid Flesh. I can only say it is a pity *The Captain* had not been examined as to this circumstance.

The one fair observation on the evidence made by this coarse and violent advocate is the failure of the prosecution to call Mrs. Mead and Mr. Smith. But had the defence deemed the testimony of these witnesses important, they could have adduced it. According to the learned counsel, the more the Michel crew contradicted themselves and each other, the more are they entitled to belief. "Had they all affected to remember the very hour, I should have been inclined to suspect that they had come *prepared*, or had *whispered* in a corner." Finally, for I cannot follow his argument farther, we have this soaring peroration:—

Time is the perpetual enemy of man. At the blast of his breath, as at the sound of the trumpet, the walls of human pride shall tumble. *Beauty*, *Fame*, and *Genius* sink before his destroying hand. The *Beauty* of Miss Porter shall fade away ; the *Fame* of Coleman shall be forgotten ; and the *Genius of Justice*, that sat on the evidence of them both, shall feel his repressing Touch. *Truth* alone shall abide his chilling frost ; and sooner or later will be rent the veil that now covers her from your piercing Eye.

If this outrageous publication did indeed meet the "piercing Eye" of Mr. Justice Buller, one should expect the author to have experienced "*his* repressing Touch." Dr. Kenealy was disbarred because of his behaviour in the Tichborne case, but the Doctor's diatribes were courtesies in comparison with the virulent invective of Swift.

The form of the "Vindication" is interesting, namely, that of an imaginary speech for the defence. "Had I been Counsel for the Prisoner Williams," he observes, "*and permitted to reply to the charge so eloquently enforced by Mr. Piggott*, I should have addressed the Court in nearly the following words." At that date, according to English practice, counsel for the defence were not allowed to address the jury, but had to rest content with cross-examining the Crown witnesses. We in Scotland were more enlightened; as, for example, in 1788 upon the famous trial of Deacon Brodie, when John Clerk made for the defence his celebrated speech that brought him into conflict with Lord Braxfield.—*Trial of Deacon Brodie, Notable British Trials Series, passim.*

THE SIREN AND THE SORCERESS;

OR, "BEAUTIFUL FOR EVER"

THE SIREN AND THE SORCERESS;

OR, "BEAUTIFUL FOR EVER."

It is better to be beautiful than to be good, but it is better to be good than to be ugly.   *—The Picture of Dorian Gray.*

THE susceptibility of mankind to suggestion is as old as the world. Our current fruitarian slogan, for example, doubtless derives from what happened long ago in a certain Garden; for it is possible, nay likely, that Eve's fateful lapse was due to the subtlety of the Serpent in persuading her that apples are good for the complexion. And so throughout the ages men, and especially women, have been led to swallow in the fullest sense whatsoever nostrum quacks confidently offer. There is no more "promising" profession than that of the inventor of a popular remedy. What though a whole-page advertisement in the *Daily Yell* cost a small fortune? If only you shout loud and long enough in so enlightened and patriotic an organ, the credulous vulgar will harken to your cry. The secret of success resides in the magnitude of the pretension. Modesty is fatal; and to seek to cater for a single ill spells failure. The bolder your pledge, the stouter the belief in your ability to implement it. Don't boggle about the business: give your imagination its head. Assert that your pill or potion will cure everything from housemaid's knee to a guilty conscience; that a single application at bedtime will, metaphorically, unbreech Highlanders, draw blood from stones, and convert sows' ears into mercerised-silk purses. If faith can move mountains, it is surely capable of dealing with molehills. I used to lunch upon a time with a man who took two pink pellets before, and two black pellets after that meal. He was obviously robust and blooming; there was nothing wrong with him, so far as I know; but the satisfaction which he derived from the performance was enviable, and alone well worth the money. For the softer sex, however, the lure is commonly less gastronomic than cosmetical. I never take up a ladies' newspaper and read of the infallible aids to loveliness obtainable for ten and six, without marvelling at the multitude of plain women one meets who have wantonly neglected their opportunities. But this may be owing less to lack of enterprise than to scarcity of half-guineas.

Of the countless practitioners who have conducted their operations in strict accordance with those principles which I have ventured.to commend, none has done so with greater impudence or to more striking effect than Madame Rachel, the beauty specialist of Bond Street. This rejuvenator of corrugated charms, who flourished in the congenial atmosphere of the late Sixties and early Seventies—perhaps the ugliest period of the Victorian era, that decade of plush and prudery, of whiskers, chignons, and bustles—undertook, like Trapbois, "for a consideration," to repair the ruin wrought by Nature and to sustain appeals from the harsh arbitrament of Time. A Jewess, grown old in the ways of wickedness and fat upon the proceeds of iniquity, Rachel resembled in appearance—if the image be conceivable— a dissipated Queen Victoria. She is best described in the happy phrase which Andrew Lang applied to the Lady Reres, Bothwell's unwieldy confidante: "a veteran procuress of vast bulk"; for it must regretfully be admitted by her biographer that the art of Madame had its darker side: she dealt in other wares than those exposed to public wonder in her windows. Serjeant Ballantine, who afterwards had twice the pleasure of prosecuting her, writes: "I saw her, without knowing either her name or calling, behind the scenes at Drury Lane Theatre. Her ostensible object was to sell articles of dress to the female employées. Her real business was brought to light by one of them throwing the contents of a glass of porter into her face in response to an insulting proposition."[1] Those were early days; later she flew at higher game.

Rachel sat in her Beauty Parlour in Bond Street like some bloated and obscene spider in the centre of her web, and woe betide such society butterflies as became entangled in its meshes! Her primary purpose, procuration and blackmail, was masked beneath an appeal to a familiar weakness of human nature. There is no grimmer tragedy than that of old age, and the pathos of our inevitable decay has pointed a moral for many a writer from Isaiah to Herman Melville. "Oh, what quenchless feud is this, that Time hath with the sons of Men!" laments the author of *Pierre*—a plaint which applies with even greater force to the daughters. The desire to postpone so long as possible execution of the dread sentence pronounced upon us all alike is natural, and may, with due regard to exercise and diet, be reasonably enough essayed. But some there are who strive by illegitimate means to cheat the common fate, and of such did Madame Rachel make prey. Her *métier* was to lead captive silly women; and an instructive instance of her methods is recorded by Serjeant Ballantine :—

On a certain occasion the wife of Admiral C—— unwarily entered it [the shop] for the purchase of some trifling article. Madame Rachel was singularly plausible, and induced her customer to purchase from time to time other matters to a small amount, and sent in an exorbitant bill for them, which I believe was paid, and Mrs. C—— discontinued her patronage. Upon this happening, a claim arrived amounting to £1000, upon the allegation that Mrs. C—— had been cured by Madame's aid of some skin affection ; dark hints of other matters accompanying the claim. There was not a word of truth in the assertions or insinuations, and the Admiral most properly resisted the claim, which was scouted with disgust and indignation. Madame Rachel, however, was not discouraged, and still professed the power of making ladies beautiful for ever ; and, strange as it may appear, there were many who yielded to the pleasing belief.[2]

---

[1] *Some Experiences of a Barrister's Life*, vol. ii. p. 77. London: 1882.   [2] *Op. cit.*

The story of one such victim of her cozenage—the most amazing known example of her effrontery, cruelty, and craft—it is my present purpose briefly to set forth.

I.

THE WILES OF RABESQURAT.

One would suspect it for a shop of witch-craft,
To finde in it the fat of serpents, spawne
Of snakes, Jewes spittle, and their yong children's ordure :
And all these for the face.
—*The Dutchesse of Malfy.*

Sarah Rachel Russell, daughter of one Mr. Russell, of whom all that has survived is that "he was a man much respected by his neighbours, being of a very congenial [sic] turn of mind and a great humourist," was born in London about 1806. Other authorities distinguish Aughrim, near Ballinasloe in Ireland, as the place of her birth, and postpone that interesting event to 1814.[1] Of her early life and adventures nothing is known, and she first appears upon the stage of history as the bride of an assistant chemist at Manchester. Her next manifestation is as the proprietress of a fried-fish shop in Vere Street, Clare Market, and thenceforth London remained until the end the venue of her operations. Her second husband was James or Jacob Moses, who perished in the wreck of the *Royal Charter*, off Anglesea, in 1859. His relict soon consoled herself by marrying Philip Leverson or Levison, of 25 Dean Street, Soho, as to whose doings nought is recorded save that he co-operated in the production of a numerous progeny. His identity, as is not uncommon with the husbands of famous women, is merged in the predominant personality of his spouse.

---

[1] The chief sources of information regarding my remarkable heroine are "The Life of Madame Rachel," prefixed to *The Extraordinary Life and Trial of Madame Rachel* (London : Diprose and Bateman, 1868) ; the admirable epitome of her criminous career in *Notes and Queries* (8th S. vi.), Oct. 27, 1894 ; and the *Times* newspaper reports of her three trials, *passim.*

It is interesting to note how often a great career owes its origin to mere chance. In the neighbourhood of King's College Hospital, Lincoln's Inn Fields, where she then happened to live, Rachel was stricken down with fever, was taken to that infirmary, and there lay long and severely ill. Her head had to be shaved, and grief for the loss of her beautiful and abundant hair became an obstacle to her recovery. Her physician, to assuage her woe, gave her a lotion which he promised would produce a further and more copious crop; and whether by reason of the leech's skill or the fecundity of the soil, the patient was soon repossessed of tresses even finer and fuller than of yore. She begged for a copy of the prescription, which the doctor, flattered by the triumph of his art, gladly gave her. We shall see how, from this inconsiderable seed, the genius of Rachel raised the mighty upas tree beneath whose malefic boughs she so long discreditably flourished.

In 1860, under the style and title of Madame Rachel, she opened a shop in New Bond Street for the sale of cosmetics and other toilet requisites, and devoted her personal attention to "enamelling" and the removal of wrinkles. The venture proved unsuccessful; in 1861 her altruistic project led her to the Insolvent Court, and in 1862 she became an inmate of the debtors' prison in Whitecross Street. The sequel shows the irrepressible quality of true greatness and the elasticity of a really powerful mind. On obtaining her discharge, the philanthropic dame, returning to the scene of her defeat, began again at 47 New Bond Street; and undismayed by her previous failure, launched out upon a grander scale.

With the flair for publicity which, as is the way of genius, she possessed in a measure far in advance of her time, Rachel issued her celebrated pamphlet, *Beautiful For Ever*;[1] an epoch-making work, destined to lay the

---

[1] For the satisfaction of bibliophiles I quote the title: *Beautiful For Ever. By Madame Rachel. London : Madame Rachel, 47a New Bond Street. 1863. Price Half-a-Crown.* 8vo., pp. 24.

foundations of the writer's fortunes. As her biographer states that "she certainly received but a very limited education, as *she was never at any time able to write her own name*," this literary achievement is in itself remarkable. But when one considers the nature of the contents, the feat becomes astounding. Rowland of Kalydor fame had hitherto held the field; but this rousing manifesto so out-puffed him as to drive him and his remedy into the limbo of exploded specifics, and even the brilliancy of the famed Macassar suffered a temporary eclipse. The gifted authoress begins with a rhapsody on the female sex which would have delighted old Mr. Turveydrop:—

Lovely as the bright sunshine at morning's dawn; beautiful as the dew-drops on the flowers; so beautiful is lovely woman. Poets have praised her, artists have portrayed her, bards have sung her praises. She is the sculptor's beau ideal; volumes have been written of her, volumes still are to be written of her!

She reviews throughout the ages the regiment of fair women, from Mother Eve to Her Majesty the Queen; and has a heartening word for the penitent frail, who are "led on to repentance by the beautiful." "It is our pleasing duty to embellish and add to their personal charms."

Of the means whereby this amiable purpose was performed, none was more potent than the "Magnetic Rock Dew Water of Sahara," of which we shall hear again, costing but £2, 2s. a bottle. This priceless preparation, brought fresh from the interior of the Great Desert, the sole right of importation having been purchased by the vendor from the Sultan of Morocco "at an enormous outlay," was guaranteed "to increase the vital energies, restore the colour of grey hair, give the appearance of youth to persons far advanced in years, and remove wrinkles, defects, and blemishes." Thus assured that there was balm in Gilead, desiccated spinsters and suropulent matrons alike sought salvation in the wondrous water, and the beneficent importer had the satisfaction to combine good business with pleasure.

Another of her leading features was the "Arabian Bath, composed of pure extracts of the liquid of flowers, choice and rare herbs," and other ingredients equally harmless and efficacious. Rival cosmetics, she points out, are compounded of deleterious drugs and deadly leads; her preparations are made solely from the purest, rarest, and most fragrant products of the East—which may mean, as Serjeant Ballantine subsequently observed, either Arabia or Wapping. Finally, and in peroration, she invites such ladies who are past their youth to place themselves under her hands, and tells them that she can remove all personal defects and put a bloom on old faces, so as to make them look young again as in their youthful prime; and all this upon the reasonable terms set forth in her advertisements.

The "List of Preparations" supplied by Rachel embraces some sixty articles, the average price of which is £2, 2s., and is divided into eight sections: Washes for the Complexion, Powders for same, Dentifrices and Mouth Washes, Hair Preparations, Creams for the Face, Royal Arabian Soaps, Perfumes, and Special Treatments. Of these last the most interesting and expensive is: "The Royal Arabian Toilet of Beauty, as arranged by Madame Rachel for the Sultana of Turkey, the facsimile of which is used by the Royal European Brides, from 100 to 1000 guineas." For modest purses there are "Bridal Toilet Cabinets, arranged from 25 to 200 guineas," "Souvenir de Marriage [sic] from 25 to 100 guineas," and "Venus's Toilet, 10 to 20 guineas." "Jordan Water (per bottle)," at the same price, was a popular and profitable line. Something further of these marvels we shall learn at the trial. Their appeal was equally powerful in Bloomsbury and in Belgravia. Though unable to emulate the Royal European Brides, even stockbrokers' wives might rise to a "Venus's Toilet," and maiden ladies of limited means lay down a dozen or so of "Jordan Water," as a provision against the ravages of Time.

By reason of these spells the traffic throve amain. But our authority discreetly hints at other branches of Madame's trade of which he remarks: "It would not do to enter into the particulars of the various services which Rachel rendered to some of her clients, in addition to selling them enamels and perfumes." Some light is thrown upon the nature of these esoteric mysteries by the criminal prosecutions of which their priestess was afterwards the subject. So well was virtue and a strict application to business in her case rewarded, that she was presently in a position to take, and elegantly furnish, a house in Maddox Street; and in 1867 she had a pit-tier box at the Opera, which cost her £400 for the season!

II.

THE BEWITCHMENT OF MRS. BORRADAILE.

> Sad is that woman's lot who, year by year,
> Sees, one by one, her beauties disappear,
> When Time, grown weary of her heart-drawn sighs,
> Impatiently begins to dim her eyes!
> Compelled, at last, in life's uncertain gloamings,
> To wreathe her wrinkled brow with well-saved combings,
> Reduced, with rouge, lip-salve, and pearly grey,
> To " make up " for lost time as best she may!
>
> —*Patience.*

Mary Tucker Borradaile had been a beauty in her day; but the day was far spent, and her state that of the sort so often satirised by the ungallant Gilbert. Relict of a colonel of distinction in the Indian army, she had been a fearless wife for over twenty years and an irreproachable widow for seven. Well born and well connected—her father was an army officer and Lord Kensington her kinsman—she moved in good society as a lady of condition and of the highest respectability. Like the Hon. Mrs. Skewton, she was "all heart"; but unlike that astute dowager, lamentably lacking in brains. Her age is one of the many mysteries of the case. "I hope you will not think me guilty of impertinence if I ask your age?" was the opening question of her cross-examiner at the first trial in 1868. "It is a very rude question, and it is of no use your pressing me upon the subject," was the petulant reply. "I was married in 1846. The age of the bride is a question I shan't answer." She was in receipt of a military pension, she had investments amounting to some £4000 in the funds and other property, she possessed certain family plate and jewellery, and altogether was worth, pecuniarily, about £5000. But Mrs. Borradaile, though an ancient siren, valued herself far above rubies; the bald present was for her wreathed in the fair ringlets of the past, and she clung to the pretence of youth with a tenacity at once ludicrous and pathetic.

Imagine, then, what it meant to one in her desperate situation when in the autumn of 1864 her failing sight descried in her daily paper the following advertisement:—

Madame Rachel, whose talents have gained for her a world-renowned fame for preserving and enhancing youth, beauty, grace, and loveliness, and whose Royal Arabian and Circassian baths, spices, and perfumes render the hair, teeth, and complexion beautiful beyond comparison, giving the appearance of youth and beauty to persons however far advanced in years, have caused her name to stand a marvel of the age, of which delicate and costly arts she stands the sole possessor.—47A New Bond Street.[1]

She hastened to consult the sorceress, above whose door the Royal Arms and the legend "Purveyor to the Queen" were calculated to inspire loyal hearts with confidence. Of her case Madame Rachel formed a hopeful prognosis, and asked the pertinent question, "How much money she [the patient] had to spend." Reassured upon this point, she guaranteed the adequacy of her process to effect a complete and lasting cure. "On my first visit," says the victim, "I spent £10," and in the ensuing twelve months

---

[1] Quoted by Serjeant Ballantine in his opening speech at the first trial.—*Times*, 21st August 1868.

she was induced to part with £170. "I paid her various sums of money for cosmetics, etc., during the latter part of 1864 and the commencement of 1865. Before purchasing these articles I asked her to do something for my skin; and she promised that, if I would follow out her course of treatment in every particular, she would ultimately succeed in making me beautiful for ever."

Whether or not the arts of Madame, so accurately described in the advertisement as delicate and costly, were in the end so sure as she predicted, they were unquestionably slow, for by the spring of 1866, despite all the baths, soaps, and powders supplied, Mrs. Borradaile's complexion was unimproved. In May of that year the lady had become restive and intimated that she was averse from making further payments: "I told her I expected her to do something for my skin for the £170 I had already laid out at her shop." The sorceress perceived that the time was ripe for the exhibition of her most potent spell. She informed the astonished lady that a certain nobleman of rank and fortune, to wit, Lord Ranelagh,[1] had seen and loved her, and that, subject to the completion of the beautiful-for-ever process, he proposed to make her his wife. Apart from the unflattering testimony of her looking-glass, the inherent improbabilities of the tale should have given this mature gentlewoman pause; but unfortunately her belief

---

[1] Thomas Heron Jones, Viscount Ranelagh and Baron Jones of Navan in the peerage of Ireland ; born 9th January 1812 at Fulham ; succeeded his father, the sixth viscount, 3rd July 1820 ; was when a minor at the siege of Antwerp, and subsequently served as a volunteer in the Carlist camp in the Spanish war of succession ; was also some time an officer of the 1st Life Guards and was one of the earliest promoters of the Volunteer movement in England ; Lieut.-Col. 2nd South Midx. Volunteers, 1860–85 ; Sheriff of Norfolk, 1868 ; K.C.B. (civil), 1881 ; many years Chairman of the Conservative Land Society. He died unmarried 13th November 1885 at 18 Albert Mansions, Victoria Street, Westm. aged 73, when the peerage became extinct. He was buried (with military honours) on the 21st at Fulham. The family estates in 1883 consisted of 3043 acres in Co. Norfolk, worth £5691 a year. Principal Residences : Mulgrave House, Fulham ; and Horsham St. Faith, near Norwich.—*Complete Peerage of the United Kingdom, extant, extinct, or dormant.* Edited by G. E. C. [George Edward Cokayne], vol. vi. p. 326. London : 1895.

in her superannuated charms was such as to defy the
evidence alike of sense and senses. His lordship had seen
her, as appeared, both before and after her marriage; but
though he had lost sight of her for a time, her impression
was still imprinted on his heart. He was, Madame added
as an additional recommendation, "a very good man and
very rich." She undertook to bring about an interview.
The following is the account of this interesting meeting
given by the lady herself:—

Next day I called at Maddox Street, where the prisoner lived. The
house is a corner one, being partly in Maddox Street and partly in New
Bond Street. Madame Rachel opened the door and said : " I will now
introduce you to the man who loves you." She then introduced me to
a man whom I believed, and still believe to be Lord Ranelagh. I said
to him, " Are you Lord Ranelagh ? " and he answered, " Yes ; here is
my card." He then handed me a card, which I returned to him. The
gentleman who gave me the card is the gentleman I now see in Court
[Lord Ranelagh]. Some conversation took place between us, and then
Lord Ranelagh retired. I afterwards went with Madame Rachel to her
room, and she told me that Lord Ranelagh would make me a good
husband. . . .

I saw Lord Ranelagh there on several subsequent occasions. On
one occasion Madame Rachel told me to go and take a bath. The baths
were at a Mrs. Hicks's, in Davies Street, Berkeley Square, close by. I
took the bath, and on my return to the shop I found Lord Ranelagh
there. Madame Rachel again introduced me to him. He made a bow
to me, but I forget the conversation. Lord Ranelagh then again retired,
and I had a further conversation with Madame Rachel. She again told
me he would make me a good husband.[1]

"Was ever woman in this humour woo'd?" The
retiring nobleman, being dissatisfied with the pitch of
perfection thus far produced in his prospective bride by
Madame Rachel's treatment, that expert was by his
lordship's "express desire" instructed to proceed with
the rejuvenating process as quickly as possible. This
meant, as she explained to Mrs. Borradaile, an immediate
outlay of £1000, to which the lady justly excepted as "a

---

[1] Evidence of Mrs. Borradaile at the first trial, 20th August 1868.

large sum of money." But, seeing that she could not be put upon a par with the Royal European Brides at a lower figure, the future peeress reluctantly agreed to foot the bill. Madame obligingly introduced her to an attorney, one Mr. Haynes, through whose good offices £1300 stock was sold, which realised £980, whereof £20 went in expenses and the balance into Rachel's pocket, the consideration being "for bath preparations, spices, powders, sponges, perfumes, and attendance, to be continued till I (Mrs. B.) am finished by the process."

Further, this singular wooer stipulated that the courting was "*to be done by letter writing*" and that the parties were, on the conclusion of the correspondence, "to be married by proxy." In pursuance of this unusual arrangement the lady began to receive a series of love letters. Whether owing to his lordship's parsimony or to his predilection for devious ways, these did not come through the common channel of the post-office, but were delivered by Madame personally to the fair recipient. They were signed "William," which the lady thought odd, the writer's Christian name being Thomas; but Rachel ascribed this foible to his lordship's desire for secrecy. One letter, accompanied by a vinaigrette and a pencil-case, was as follows:—

MOUNT STREET.

MY ONLY DEARLY BELOVED MARY,—The little perfume-box and pencil-case belonged to my sainted mother. She died with them in her hand. When she was a schoolgirl it was my father's first gift to her. Granny has given the watch and locket to me again. Your coronet is finished, my love. Granny said you had answered my last letter, but you have forgotten to send it. I forgot yesterday was Ash Wednesday. Let old Granny arrange the time, as we have little to spare. My dearest one, what is the matter with the old woman ? She seems out of sorts. We must manage to keep her in good temper for our own sakes, because she has to manage all for us, and I should not have had the joy of your love had it not been for her. Darling love ; Mary, my sweet one, all will be well in a few hours. The dispatches have arrived. I will let you know all when I hear from you, my heart's love. Bear up, my fond one. I shall be at your feet—those pretty feet that I love—and you may kick

your ugly old donkey.   Two letters, naughty little pet, and you have not
answered one.   You are in sorrow about your brother.   With fond and
devoted love,   Yours till death,
                                                                    WILLIAM.[1]

"Granny" bore affectionate reference to Rachel, the
Fairy Godmother of their loves.   His lordship had caused
his affianced to deliver up to Madame all her jewels, as un-
worthy of his wife's wearing;   other more suitable and
costly gems were in due course to be provided.   Meanwhile, according to Mrs. Borradaile, "she [Rachel] said
it was necessary I should have diamonds to marry Lord
Ranelagh";   and a coronet and necklace were ordered
from, and delivered by Mr. Pike, a jeweller of New Bond
Street.   "She put them on me and asked me how I liked
them."   The price was £1260.   "I had not at that time
£1260, but I had some property at Streatham," which, by
the friendly aid of Mr. Haynes, was sold for £1540.   Of
this sum Madame Rachel received £1400, "to pay for the
diamonds."   On being asked what had become of the
money, Madame explained "that it was required for
'William,' for the purposes of the Volunteers," with which
movement, as we know, his lordship was intimately concerned.   The future viscountess saw no more of her
diamonds, which, unknown to her, had been returned to
the dealer, who accepted £100 to cancel the bargain;   but
she was consoled by the promise that she should have those
which had belonged to Lord Ranelagh's mother;   in token
whereof Rachel exhibited "an old-fashioned coronet, which
she said would be altered."

Mrs. Borradaile found that to espouse a peer was an
expensive business.   £32 for ornaments for the hair, £160
for dresses, a like amount for linen, and £400 for lace for
the wedding gown, were among the outlays severally incurred.   "The articles were all sent to Madame Rachel's
shop;   I never had one of them";   they were all, as appears,
laid up in lavender by the cautelous "Granny" against

[1] *Times*, 21st August 1868.

the great day of the marriage. The only thing that
Madame ever gave the bride was a cigar. "I recollect
her giving me one in February of this year. It was lighted;
and as she gave it to me she said, 'Here comes Lord Ranelagh.' I saw a person pass out of the door at the time,
but I could not see his face. Madame Rachel said the
cigar was as warm as his love." It is a pity that his lordship did not stay to share with his lady-love the symbolic
smoke. Although the noble wooer was thus unconscionably coy, he does seem to have made one attempt to
interview his betrothed:—

MOUNT STREET.

MY DARLING MARY,—One would suppose that all the people in your
house were dead. I was at your door at a quarter to 5, and could not
make anyone hear. My darling, my sweet love, I was more grieved than
you were. Will you keep up your spirits? I have been very much
fagged, but I leave everything to you to-morrow evening or Wednesday
morning. Did Rachel tell you of the scene to-day? She is an old fox,
but you quite understand each other. My own sweet love, I am worried
to death about money matters, but it will be all settled before we leave
town. With my fondest love and many kisses. Not one line from you
to-day. You must quiet Rachel a little. I think the little lady has
been talking to her to-day. I have no wish to offend her, sweet love.—
I am, ever yours,   WILLIAM.[1]

It says much for his lordship's foresight that throughout the correspondence he should be so anxious to maintain
the friendly relations, upon which the happiness of both
parties depended, between his fiancée and her guardian
"Granny," to whose claims to veneration, obedience, and
respect he inculcates absolute submission. If the lady
jibbed at the demands made upon her purse, he was down
on her at once. "My own dear Love, my sweet, darling
Mary, I called at Rachel's to-day, and she looks as black
as thunder. What is it, my sweet love, my own dear one?
. . . What have you done to offend Rachel?" Again,
"Mary, my heart's love, Is it your wish to drive me mad?
Granny has my instructions. Do as she tells you"; "My

---

[1] *Times*, 22nd August 1868.

MADAME RACHEL.

(From a photograph in the possession of Mr. Charles Kingston.)

[To face p. 48.

own darling Mary, Why don't you do as Granny tells you, why do you put obstacles in the way of your own happiness? Sign the paper; I will pay everything . . . Granny told me she would arrange everything to our satisfaction"; "Granny has behaved very well with regard to money affairs, and she loves you as though you were her own child," etc., etc.

Certain peculiarities presented by these letters were too marked to escape even the limited capacity of the recipient. They were written in no less than three different hands; the spelling, upon occasion, fell something short of the standard expected of a peer; and in one instance the writer subscribed himself "Edward," instead of the wonted and familiar "William." "When I complained to her [Rachel] about the bad spelling of some of his lordship's letters," says Mrs. Borradaile, "she accounted for it by saying that he had injured his arm and had to employ an uneducated amanuensis." Apparently his lordship himself either appreciated his shortcomings as a correspondent, or was averse from exposing to unfriendly eyes the outpourings of his noble heart, for we find him asking more than once that his love-letters be returned to him or destroyed. For example:—

MOUNT STREET.

MY DARLING MARY,—My own pet, do what I ask. I wish you to burn the letters, and all you do I daresay is for the best. My darling pet and love, many thanks. I know you will keep your promise. My sweet love, I will devote my life and all my love to you. I cannot find words to do so. My devotion in years will tell my heart's fond love for you, darling sweet one. I will tell you all at your feet. My own loved Mary, with fond devotion, ever yours, with lots of kisses, WILLIAM.[1]

As the happy day approached Madame Rachel kindly accompanied her friend to a coach-builder's in New Bond Street. "for the purpose of selecting a carriage for the wedding." "She got into one, and said she thought that would do," provided Lord Ranelagh's arms were blazoned

---

[1] *Times*, 21st August 1868.

4

on the panels. Indefatigable in friendship's cause, she
also found time, amid her manifold avocations, to take
Mrs. Borradaile to inspect a house which she deemed an
appropriate lodging for the noble couple, and of which the
bride approved. "I had a quantity of plate which belonged
to my late husband," says that lady, "and a silver tea
service which I had purchased in Bond Street"; but these
valuables were impounded by Rachel as being unsuited
to her future station. Rings and trinkets, family seals,
her marriage settlement, and even her dead husband's
letters, were all relinquished to Madame "and packed up,
as she said, for the wedding." The owner never saw any
of her property again; and when she ventured to inquire
about certain articles, received from Rachel the cynical
reply: "You must ask the man who loves you for them
back."

Finally, having stripped this poor gentlewoman of every
earthly possession except the clothes she stood in, the
rapacious and insatiate "Granny" caused the victim to
execute a bond for £1600, had her arrested for the debt,
and cast her into Whitecross Street Prison, whence she
could only obtain release by making over to her "creditor,"
for the residue of her days, her exiguous pension of £350!

III.

A Sorceress Ensorcelled.

Harke! harke! now rise infernall tones,
    The deep-fetch'd grones
Of labouring spirits that attend
Erictho.
                    —*The Wonder of Women.*

The three several judges, their respective juries, and
the phalanx of counsel on both sides of the bar, who were
called upon successively to deal with the machinations of
Madame Rachel, must have had cause to anathematise
the birth day of that mistress of illusions. Even more
exasperated would be the feelings of Mrs. Borradaile's

relatives, when they learned what a fool had been made of
their fond relation and the state of destitution to which
she had been so unconscionably reduced.

Proceedings were forthwith instituted against the con-
triver of her ruin; and in due course of law, at the Central
Criminal Court, before the Right Hon. Russell Gurney,
Q.C., Recorder, on 20th August 1868, commenced the
celebrated cause, *The Queen* v. *Leverson*.[1] The accused
was charged with obtaining from Mrs. Borradaile by false
pretences £600, and conspiring to defraud her of £3000.
Mr. Serjeant Ballantine, Mr. Montague Williams, and Mr.
(afterwards Sir Douglas) Straight appeared for the prosecution; Mr. Digby Seymour, Q.C., Mr. Serjeant Parry,
Mr. Serjeant Sleigh, and Mr. Butler Rigby conducted the
defence. After a trial lasting two days the jury failed to
agree. The defence offered no evidence, and Mrs. Borradaile was the principal witness for the Crown. "The folly
she had exhibited and her childish mode of giving evidence,"
in the opinion of Serjeant Ballantine, "probably led some
of the jury to distrust her, and they were discharged without
a verdict."[2] Of the personal appearance of the prosecutrix we have from the pens of Crown counsel two contemporary impressions, which present the sometime siren
in an equally unalluring light. "The quondam beauty,"
says Ballantine, "a skeleton encased apparently in plaster
of Paris, painted pink and white, and surmounted with a
juvenile wig, tottered into the witness-box."[3] "She was
a spare, thin, scraggy-looking woman, wholly devoid of
figure," says Montague Williams, who examined her in
chief; "her hair was dyed a bright yellow; her face was
ruddled with paint; and the darkness of her eyebrows was
strongly suggestive of meretricious art. She had a silly,
giggling, half-hysterical way of talking, and altogether gave

---

[1] Cox's *Criminal Cases*, 1867–71, vol. xi. p. 152 ; *Times*, 21st–22nd August
1868.

[2] *Some Experiences of a Barrister's Life*, vol. ii. p. 79.

[3] *Ibid.*

one the idea of anything but the heroine of such a romance."[1]
Verily, viewed as a sample of Madame Rachel's art, Mrs.
Borradaile fell something short of the advertisements.

As regards the abortive result of the trial, Montague
Williams tells us that the deliberations of the jury occupied
five hours; and the *Daily Telegraph* states: "It was matter
of notoriety that she [Rachel] owed her temporary escape
simply and solely to the obstinacy of one of the jury who
tried her." Perhaps his wife had been made "Beautiful
For Ever." From the *Times* report of the proceedings it
appears that the learned Recorder's charge was unfavourable to an acquittal. He deemed it remarkable that *all*
the letters in the case were produced by the *prisoner*, and
that no account was given of how she came by them.
Further, that there was no evidence of the existence of
"William"—whom the defence maintained to be a real
person, quite distinct from Lord Ranelagh; and that if he
did exist, the prisoner must have known him. The *Times*,
in a leading article strangely hostile to the prosecution,
impolitely styled Mrs. Borradaile "a self-confessed idiot,"
and refused all credit to her tale.

It of course now became necessary that the trial should be proceeded
with *de novo*. To go on with the case that session was found to be un-
desirable, and it was accordingly adjourned for a month, the prisoner
being admitted to bail in two sureties of £5000 each.[2]

The second act of this tragi-comedy was begun on 22nd
September 1868, and played to crowded houses for four
days. Scene, cast, and programme were the same; but
on this occasion the performance took place under the
direction of Mr. Commissioner Kerr.[3] Serjeant Ballantine,
in opening the case, covered the ground which we have
already traversed, and stated thus the foundation of the

---

[1] *Leaves of a Life.* Being the Reminiscences of Montague Williams, Q.C.,
vol. i. p. 227. London : 1890.

[2] *Ibid.*, p. 246.

[3] Cox's *Criminal Cases*, vol. xi. p. 153 ; *Times*, 23rd, 24th, 25th, and 26th
September 1868.

defence: it was not denied that Rachel had received every halfpenny of the money:—

The defence was, that it [the money] was obtained because Mrs. Borradaile was a woman of loose habits, who was willing to prostitute herself, who carried on an intercourse for months with a man, and that the sums of money handed to Rachel were so handed to her for the purpose of being used by the person calling himself " William." . . . This presented the prisoner in this position—as a person allowing her house to be used for interviews between ladies and gentlemen, and herself promoting those interviews by all the means in her power, and sharing with one of the persons carrying on the interviews the profits of the transaction. There were certainly places of that kind in London, but they were called by a less savoury name than that of a " perfumer's shop." [1]

On this he, counsel, would take his stand: that no such person as "William" ever existed; that Mrs. Borradaile had never departed from the path of honour; that she had never carried on any intrigue with anyone; and that, on her solemn oath, she would swear that the whole thing was a wicked fabrication.

After keeping the Court waiting for three-quarters of an hour the prosecutrix entered the box, and—better late than never—told in detail the story of which I have given an outline. "Miss Rachel and Madame Valeria were both in the shop with Lord Ranelagh," she said, on the occasion of the introduction. "Madame Valeria must have seen the card." [2] Neither of these ladies was invited by the defence to controvert this statement. With regard to the "William and Mary" correspondence, witness stated that Madame always told her that the "William" letters had come from Lord Ranelagh. "The letters never came to me through the post; they were always given to me by the prisoner. The letters produced—written by me, as I

---

[1] *Life and Trial, supra*, p. 9.

[2] Lord Ranelagh, while admitting the introduction, denied the card. Miss Rachel was the prisoner's eldest daughter ; Madame Valeria, a sister of Fechter, the actor : Evidence of Lord Ranelagh at the first trial.—*Times*, 22nd August 1868.

believed, to Lord Ranelagh—were handed by me to Madame, upon the understanding that she would give them to his lordship. All the letters I wrote to him were dictated to me by Rachel, who always said they would be delivered by her to him." *She always made witness return to her the "William" letters.* Witness often asked what had become of the numerous purchases made on account of the wedding; Madame's official answer was that "Dear William" had them. At neither of the trials, it should be noted, did the defence make the least attempt to provide "Dear William" with a local habitation, although he must have had some address to which the jewels, plate, apparel, lace, and linen were consigned; and Rachel, on her own showing, was in constant touch with him. Personally, I have no doubt as to his domicile: he lodged with one Mrs. Harris, whose abode, as we know on unimpeachable authority, was situated "through the square and up the steps, a turnin' round by the tobacker shop"; but like his famous landlady, he was more frequently heard about than seen.

Mrs. Borradaile was ruthlessly cross-examined by Mr. Digby Seymour, but notwithstanding her age and manifest infirmities, physical and mental, she managed to put up a very fair fight. Some of her letters to "William," though all written, as she swore in Rachel's shop, and to her dictation, were dated from No. 4 Francis Street, Paddington, an hotel with the significant legend "Beds" inscribed upon the lintel, which counsel contended was a hostelry of sinister repute; but witness said that on her arrival in London from Cheltenham she could not get a room in the Great Western Hotel, and was recommended by a railway porter to the Francis Street establishment, where she only remained four days, removing thence to lodgings at No. 28 George Street, Hanover Square, where she had since resided. She wrote no letter while in Francis Street, neither did anyone visit her there. "I always addressed my letters as Madame Rachel directed me," she explained; "I was so foolish. She is a wicked and vile woman, and you [Mr. Seymour] are bad too!" One letter, dated 3rd September 1866, was as follows:—

MY OWN DEAR WILLIAM,—If you knew what I have suffered since Saturday night on your account, one unkind word would never escape your lips to me. My brother-in-law went to the Carlton to see Lord Ranelagh. They told him he was out of town, and they said he would not be back for a week. My brother then went to New Burlington Street, and a servant told him there that his lordship had been out of town for three weeks, and that all his letters had been sent to Lowther Castle. . . . You would have been amused at the frantic manner in which he was running about town looking for the invisible person who could not be found, thanks to our lucky stars. Not content with that, he took us to Regent Street and bought a photo of his lordship, whose nose he did not admire. Mr. Cope [her brother-in-law] made me promise to leave my present lodgings, that he was under the belief that the people at the house and poor Rachel were in league together in fooling me into a marriage with Lord Ranelagh. Mr. Cope and my sister made me promise I would not see Rachel again, as I led them to suppose she had been the promoter of his lordship in intriguing with me. . . .[1]

That letter, said witness, was certainly written by her in the belief that she was addressing Lord Ranelagh, who was "the invisible person" referred to. "Do you consider marriage and intrigue the same thing?" asked counsel. "I really do not know much about intrigues; I don't think they are equivalent expressions," was the reply. In another letter occurred the phrase: "But you seem to know the overland route to my heart." "It is a very happy expression," commented Mr. Seymour; "and you have been to India and back, you know?" "It was not mine," said the witness; "it was she [Rachel] that suggested it to me."

Witness.—Madame Rachel told me on one occasion, in a friendly manner, that she was 80 years of age.

Q.—And did you believe her? *A.*—I did not. I told her I was 68 myself. (Laughter.) [2]

In a letter of 29th September the words: "I am surprised

---

[1] *Life and Trial,* p. 22.
[2] *Ibid.,* p. 26. Probably her figures were nearer the mark than Rachel's.

at Madame Rachel's impertinence; she had no right to be impertinent to you": were, said witness, written by her to Lord Ranelagh at Madame's dictation, as was the further passage: "Tear yourself away from the little lady with the golden hair who is in the habit of scratching your face." Apart from what Rachel told her, she knew nothing of this blonde virago. In her next letter witness wrote:—

One of your kind friends and your bosom companions has informed me that you have been, and are now keeping a woman. Not one member of my family will hold any intercourse with me for forming such a degraded connexion, as it is well known in Pembrokeshire that I have been living with you for some months. When I receive a letter from my daughter it is full of insults. You cannot be, and are not surprised at this, considering the life we have been leading. Am I to believe that the woman you travelled with, and whom you introduced to me as your sister, is your mistress ? [1]

Pressed as to how she came to write in these terms, which she now swore were utterly false, witness replied: "I accepted Madame Rachel's dictation. Trusting to that wicked woman—that foul, wicked woman in the dock —I wrote whatever she dictated. I had *not* been leading an immoral life: I had been living in George Street, Hanover Square, for months." The next letter reads as follows: "My own dear William,—Your letters are safe in my possession, and I am rejoiced to read them over very often. I have no one to care for now but you, and I love you all the more for it. Therefore you must not doubt me. I have given you all a woman holds dear." Questioned as to what she meant by that expression, witness said: "That I had given him all my money." It will be noted with what ingenuity of guile Rachel was in these letters gradually strengthening the meshes of her net, to the end that the captive's reputation should be entirely at her mercy. Witness could not remember writing in another letter that "Rachel growled like a bear"; but she did

---

[1] *Life and Trial*, p. 27.

recollect writing that "she was like a witch, because there was nothing that she did not know."

Q.—The letter goes on : " Your sister ought to see that your stockings are mended. I cannot see why she cannot mend them herself, and put some buttons on your shirts. It would be better than gossiping with the woman next room to her. Send all your clothes that want mending to me." Now did Rachel really tell you to write to a nobleman like Lord Ranelagh with instructions that he should send his tattered garments to you to be mended ?

A.—She did ; she meant that all his clothes that wanted mending were to be sent to me.

Q.—" As you want boots, we shall go to a maker in Oxford Street and get a pair. I am surprised to find that your flannels should be worn out though you have not had them more than six weeks. It is the result of bad washing. There is a man living in a court off Regent Street who mends coats cheaply, and I think that you might give him a job." Now I ask you on your solemn oath, did you, when you wrote that letter to this shirtless, buttonless, stockingless, bootless, flannelless, hatless individual, think that you were writing to Lord Ranelagh ?

A.—I did. At that time I had found out that he was not a rich man.[1]

I pretermit the "roars of laughter" with which this passage in the original is punctuated.

Re-examined by Serjeant Ballantine, Mrs. Borradaile gave an account of the several lodgings which she had occupied in London. She had no idea that the Francis Street hotel was other than respectable. She had one room there for four days, for which she paid two shillings a day. Rachel kept all the "William" letters. Her replies were all written to Madame's dictation in the shop parlour in the evenings, after business hours, or at No. 50 Maddox Street, Rachel's private address. Madame's daughters, Rachel and Leonte, were sometimes present. She never saw anyone represented as "William," except Lord Ranelagh. With a view to alleviating the aridity of these literary exercises, says witness, "she [Rachel] generally gave me whisky before I wrote the letters. Not that I think that there was anything in the whisky. It

---

[1] *Life and Trial*, pp. 31–32.

was proper whisky; because I saw her take it herself. Madame said it had done her a great deal of good." Personally, witness preferred brandy and soda, of which she was in use to partake sparingly, "by a doctor's advice."

Mr. Haynes, the attorney who had conducted in behalf of Rachel the delicate financial operations before mentioned, whereby Mrs. Borradaile was despoiled, made a poor appearance in the box. I am not conversant with English legal practice, but the actings of this gentleman strike me as unusual. He was described by Serjeant Ballantine in his closing speech as "a disgrace to his profession." As "mortgagee" of the premises occupied by Rachel, who was behindhand with her rent, Haynes admitted that out of the funds of Mrs. Borradaile he recouped himself in the matter of rent due, and also deducted the quarterly rent of £62, 10s. during the whole period in question. He alleged that a "violent scene" occurred between the ladies in his office, when Rachel remonstrated with Mrs. Borradaile as to her general extravagance, and she became very angry. Rachel retorted: "You know you have been spending your money recklessly upon your paramour." He kept no cash accounts of the transactions referred to, the only record of which was contained in a "paper" handed by him to Rachel, which was not forthcoming. He understood it was to her cousin, Captain William Edwardes, that Mrs. Borradaile was going to be married, and that the money had been advanced to him. Witness's attention being called to an item in his bill of costs, dated 28th September 1866: "Attending you when you stated that Madame Rachel had deceived you by stating that she had paid £1400 on your account to Lord Ranelagh, and advising you thereon"—Haynes said that his lordship's name "might have been mentioned."

James Minton, a lad employed by a linen draper in Holborn Bars, said that he was engaged by Madame Rachel to come into her famous parlour in the evenings, after his day's work was done. His duties consisted in writing letters to her dictation, and sometimes copying drafts thereof. "She sat beside me and told me what I was to write." He recognised as his handiwork certain of the letters produced. On one occasion, in January 1867, Madame, being dissatisfied with his current performance because, as she complained, "the writing was like a schoolboy's," showed it to a young man named Edward, then present, who remarked that "he could make a better one himself," and put it in his pocket to that end. Witness identified the letter in question as the note signed "Edward." An ugly episode, which reflected little credit on the conduct of the defence, appeared upon the cross-examination of this witness. Certain pages of pencil writing were put to him by Mr. Seymour, whose point was that these were the lad's notes of what he was prepared falsely to swear; but Minton stated—and was corroborated in this by his mother, who followed him in the box—that the notes were merely memoranda of the evidence which he gave at the police court, and that "a gentleman" called at their house while he was at work, and asked his mother for a specimen of his handwriting. "*He told her that he could get me a good situation.*" The mother shewed the visitor the pocket-book, from which he tore out these pages, returning the book to her. Needless to say, the boy heard nothing further from his benefactor. Mr. Seymour, of course, had no knowledge of the disgraceful means whereby the MS. had been obtained.

Colonel—formerly Captain—William Edwardes, Mrs. Borradaile's cousin, denied that he had ever received from Haynes or anybody else one shilling of her money; and Mr. Cope, her brother-in-law—who had "not admired" his lordship's nose—described a visit paid by him to Rachel with a view to finding out what had become of his relative's property, when Madame declared she knew nothing at all about it. She made no mention of Haynes nor of any lover other than Lord Ranelagh. Thomas William O'Keefe said that in April of that year he presented to Mrs. Borradaile, then in Paris, "a letter of introduction." He recommended her to go to London "and contradict certain scandalous rumours that had been spread about her." In cross-examination, it appeared that he had been found guilty in that court fifteen years before of obtaining money from a lady under promise of marriage. Miss Sarah Sutton said she made the acquaintance of Mrs. Borradaile while they were fellow-prisoners in Whitecross Street. Mr. O'Keefe was an old friend of hers and she introduced him to that lady, who had consulted witness regarding her own fiscal entanglement. On obtaining their release, the enfranchised fair ones arranged to call together upon Madame Rachel, for the purpose, if possible, of getting something out of the fire. Miss Sutton thus describes the interview:—

Mrs. Borradaile said to her [Rachel]: "When are you going to get me that money Lord Ranelagh owes me?" Madame Rachel said, turning to me, "Lord Ranelagh has not had any of her money; her William has had her money, and he will not allow her to leave town. He has been walking backwards and forwards outside for the last two hours." I asked Mrs. Borradaile what it all meant. She replied: "That horrid wicked woman has been deceiving you. There is no William; Lord Ranelagh is the man." Madame Rachel appeared confused, and said: "Oh, no; it's your William." I said: "I think you are both in love with Lord Ranelagh—one lending him her money, and the other screening him from payment." [1]

To settle the question, Miss Sutton sensibly suggested that William be invited to step inside. "Oh, my dear madam," exclaimed the scandalised Rachel, "I cannot do that; I never tell my ladies' little intrigues." So William was left out in the cold. When the ladies went empty away, Miss Sutton looked about for him; but William, whose patience was presumably exhausted, had vanished. Joseph Pike, jeweller, No. 136 New Bond Street, deposed to the purchase of the diamond necklace and tiara, as before narrated. He got £100 for cancelling the transaction. Other tradesmen having spoken to purchases respec-

---

[1] *Life and Trial*, p. 64.

tively made from them by Rachel on account of the trousseau, Lord Ranelagh entered the witness-box. Examined by Serjeant Ballantine, his lordship said that he remembered meeting Mrs. Borradaile on two occasions. He was introduced to her by Rachel. He never had the slightest intention of marrying her, and never sent her a vinaigrette or any other article. He never heard of "William." "Every single word in the letters read in this case, so far as I am concerned, is false." Cross-examined by Mr. Seymour, he most solemnly declared that he never gave Mrs. Borradaile his card. He had no conversation with her, beyond wishing her "Good morning." The case for the prosecution closed with the evidence of Mrs. Borradaile's landlord, who said that she had occupied his rooms in George Street, Hanover Square, for the last two years. She was a most exemplary and quiet tenant, and was never visited by gentlemen "of any kind."

For the defence, the demoiselles Rachel and Leonte Leverson, daughters of the prisoner, were called. Miss Rachel said she was twenty-seven, and the eldest of the seven children of her mamma. She remembered Mrs. Borradaile frequenting the maternal shop; she was constantly there, but beyond so seeing her, witness knew nothing about her. She could not recollect the introduction to Lord Ranelagh. She wrote none of the "William" letters. The boy Minton was never employed by her mother to write letters. Cross-examined, she was not called at the former trial. Her mamma could not write; *Leonte generally wrote for her.* Mrs. Borradaile was never in the parlour of an evening; she always came as an ordinary customer by day. Sometimes Leonte used to remain in the shop later than witness. Shown an account rendered by her mother to Mrs. Borradaile, purporting to contain a list of alleged sums paid by Rachel to her, and bearing to be receipted by Mrs. Borradaile—which that lady denied—witness said that *it was in the handwriting of Leonte.* She never knew any "William" except a shop boy of that name, who left their service before the last trial. She was well acquainted with the business conducted by her mamma. The several liquid soaps—Royal Nursery, Royal Palace, Victoria, Princess's, Alexandra, Prince of Wales's, Honey of Mount Hymettus, Peach Blossom, etc.— sold at two guineas a bottle. A flask of Jordan Water cost from ten to twenty guineas, according to size.

Q.—Now I ask you, Miss Leverson, did you believe this Jordan Water was a reality or a sham ? *A.*—I believed it to be a reality.

Q.—You mean to tell the Court and jury on your oath that you believe that water came from the river Jordan ? *A.*—I believe it is brought from the East.

Q.—From the East ! Well, but that is very indefinite, for the East may mean Wapping. What I ask you is, do you mean to say it came from the river Jordan ? *A.*—Yes. Of course, I did not see it brought.

Q.—How do you know that ? *A.*—Because it was consigned to us.

Q.—By whom ? *A.*—Oh ! I cannot expose our professional secrets. If you will come to our shop and buy a bottle, I may tell you.

Q.—Where is the river Jordan ? *A.*—Is it not near Jerusalem ?

Q.—And you say you have an agent there ? *A.*—I don't know whether he is at the Jordan, but I say he consigns the Jordan Water to us.

Q.—Who is he ? *A.*—I'll not tell you.

Q.—Here is another pamphlet of yours ; who wrote that ? *A.*—My sister and myself composed it.

Q.—Listen to this extract : " In the interior of Sahara, or the Great Desert, is a magnetic rock, from which water distils sparingly in the form of dew, which is possessed of extraordinary property. Whether a latent electricity be imparted by magnetism, or an additional quantity of oxygen enters into its composition, it is not easy to say. But it appears to have the property of increasing the vital energies, as it restores the colour of grey hair apparently by renewing the circulation in its capillary tubes, the cessation of which occasions greyness ; and it gives the appearance of youth to *persons of considerable antiquity*. This water is brought to Morocco *on swift dromedaries* for the use of the Court, and its virtues are much extolled by their physicians. It might be called the antipodes of the Lethean Styx of ancient times." [1]

The reading of this extract was accompanied by "roars of laughter," applause which the witness smilingly acknowledged.

---

[1] *Life and Trial*, pp. 71-72.

Miss Leonte Leverson said she was the younger sister of the preceding witness, and assisted her mamma in the business. She often saw Mrs. Borradaile in the shop during 1866 and 1867. She did not write any of the "William" letters produced. The boy Minton was discharged for impertinence. Cross-examined, she knew nothing of any payments by Mrs. Borradaile to her mother; on the contrary, "I often saw mamma lend Mrs. Borradaile money, but I never saw Mrs. Borradaile return what she borrowed. She was always borrowing money, sometimes £100, sometimes £200. I do not know where the money was got from. Mamma had no banker; she kept her money in the house." She never saw Mrs. Borradaile in the shop in the evening, after business hours. "My father is alive, but he and mamma are not on very good terms." If Rachel's marital relations were unfortunate, at least she was blessed in her daughters; unlike her well-known namesake, she had no cause to weep for her children.

The case for the defence being closed, Mr. Digby Seymour addressed the jury on the part of the accused. Varying the proverbial line adopted by counsel who have no case, the learned gentleman abused the Press, whose attitude he held had unfairly prejudiced his client. He scouted Mrs. Borradaile's tale, and maintained that that lady had an intrigue with some man called "William"; that on this paramour she had squandered all her money; that in order to divert the suspicions of her friends, she had concocted a baseless story of an engagement with Lord Ranelagh; that Rachel had assisted her in deceiving her relations and in prosecuting the intrigue; and that in the end Mrs. Borradaile had turned upon her accomplice and accused her of having purloined the money lavished upon the paid adorer. It was, he admitted, "a very dirty story"; but that was the best he could make of it. Serjeant Ballantine, in his reply for the Crown, had little difficulty in disposing of the argument of his learned friend. The failure to produce the slightest proof of "William's" existence, coupled with the production by the prisoner of *both sides of the correspondence*, the form and character of the letters, and the whole history of the monetary dealings between the parties, left no shadow of doubt as to the guilt of the accused. With regard to the appearance presented in the witness-box by Rachel's daughters, respecting whose education, beauty, and propriety of manner Mr. Seymour had been loud in praise, he (counsel) ventured to say that never were there two young ladies in that box who, in the comparatively short time they occupied it, had told more lies than they did. He argued that some of the "William" letters were plainly the work of the younger sister. Mr. Commissioner Kerr, in charging the jury, left them in little doubt as to his own view of the truth of the case. He introduced a fresh point—afterwards the subject of much newspaper correspondence—namely, that many of the letters from the different parties *bore the same watermark*. The jury, after an absence of a quarter of an hour, returned a unanimous verdict of guilty, and the prisoner was sentenced to five years' penal servitude.

While the verdict was generally approved by the Press, the *Times* remained intransigent; and the *Saturday Review* denounced poor Mrs. Borradaile as a "senescent Sappho," remarking that if Rachel in fact concocted and coloured the plot, she had missed her true vocation: such gifts would have won for her high rank among "the purveyors of fornicating literature." "She was," says Serjeant Ballantine in taking leave of her, "one of the most filthy and dangerous moral pests that have existed in my time." [1]

The veteran Sir Harry Poland, who at the third trial was of counsel for the prosecution, tells us in his reminiscences that Rachel did not accept her fate.

She obtained a *fiat* for a writ of error from the Attorney-General on the ground that the Court by which she was tried was not properly

---

constituted throughout her trial. The judge—Commissioner Kerr—was present all the time, but the second "Commissioner" who was necessary to the proper constitution of the Court, under the Act of Parliament, was not continuously present. [As this learned person was an Alderman, he may have occasionally adjourned for refreshment.] When the appeal came on in the Court of Queen's Bench, the Court decided against her. The case is reported under the name of *Leverson* v. *The Queen*.[1]

Montague Williams records an instructive instance of Madame's methods, in a case which did not come to trial. A lady of position and wealth, being a client of Rachel, entered on a course of the famous Royal Arabian and Circassian Baths. One day she left in a drawer in the dressing-room at Maddox Street her diamond ear-rings and several very valuable rings, before proceeding to emulate the Sultana of Turkey by entering the wondrous waters. On leaving the bath, she found that her gems had vanished. Rachel, informed of the fact, waxed furious, and denied that any jewels had been placed in the drawer.

It's no use your giving yourself airs here. I know who you are. I have had you watched. I know where you live. How would you like your husband to know *the real reason for your coming here, and about the gentleman who has visited you here?* [2]

The horrified victim fled, and told her husband what had happened. After consultation with counsel, on his advice the husband refrained from prosecuting, in view of the inevitable scandal, so Rachel got away with the "swag." The episode occurred shortly before her first appearance at the Old Bailey.

---

[1] *Seventy-two Years at the Bar*. By Ernest Bowen-Rowlands, p. 71. London: 1924.

[2] *Leaves of a Life*, vol. i. p. 249.

IV.

THE RETURN OF RACHEL.

Still o'er the door the Royal Arms
May lure within our Circe's arms
The fools who'd by cosmetic charms
Be Beautiful For Ever !

.   .   .   .

Still dropping character and cash
Fools will risk palsy, pimple, rash,
In hopes to rise from paste and wash
As Beautiful For Ever !
                    —*Punch*, 27th June 1868.

From Major Arthur Griffiths, who was officially charged
with the custody of the convict during the period of her
incarceration, we obtain a glimpse of Madame Rachel in
her compulsory retreat.[1] She was not a popular prisoner,
and everyone rejoiced when she left Millbank. She made
no friends "inside," despite liberal promises to "beautify"
the matrons on her release. Soon after her discharge she
had the effrontery to call upon the Governor, and, "dressed
in satin and ostrich feathers," was ushered into his office.
If the visit were meant as showing that she forgave her
enemies, persecutors, and slanderers, it failed to turn their
hearts. The Major has another anecdote concerning his
involuntary guest. A cast of a person's head being required, Madame, as an expert, was employed to perform
the operation; "but the wax was put on so hot that it
injured him for life." [2] The incident forms a fitting
prelude to the last record of Rachel's artistry, with which
we are now to deal.

By what means the "veteran procuress" was enabled
to reface the world in affluence can only be conjectured;
but in December 1876 we find her, under the style and title
of "Arabian Perfumer to The Queen," established at No.
153 Great Portland Street, where she was openly playing

---

[1] *Secrets of the Prison-House*, vol. ii. pp. 11–12. London : 1894.
[2] *Memorials of Millbank*, p. 381. London : 1884.

her old game. Her sign caught the eye of a young married
woman, Cecilia Maria Pearse, a daughter of Signor Mario,
the great tenor, and the wife of Mr. Godfrey Pearse, stockbroker, of No. 40 Ebury Street, Pimlico. An Italian by
birth and twenty-three years of age, Mrs. Pearse was dissatisfied with the state of her complexion, and in an evil
hour decided to consult the sorceress as to its improvement.
Madame remarked that, being herself related to the incomparable tragédienne Rachel—of whom a bust embellished
her emporium—she would do her utmost for a daughter
of Mario: it created, as she observed, a bond. The daughter
of Mario being hard up, and moreover averse from "enamelling" or even painting, Rachel sold her for £1, 1s. a bottle
of face wash; the "process" was a gradual one and its
effects cumulative, so many more would be required. She
mentioned that at the moment she was engaged in "finish-
ing a countess" by the same means. "Do you happen to
know Lady Dudley?" she asked; but the stockbroker's
wife had no acquaintance with the peerage, though she
was suitably impressed by the grandeur of Madame's
connection.

Now this young lady, being blessed with more brains
than Mrs. Borradaile, put to Rachel the pertinent question:
Why had she not herself benefited by her own arts? Instead
of citing the proverbial reluctance of physicians to take
their prescriptions, Madame explained that after sixty,
even her skill was powerless to arrest our natural decay;
and she, alas, was eighty-five! Further, Mrs. Pearse,
having some hazy recollection of certain notorious proceedings associated with the name of Rachel, ventured to
inquire as to the truth of that matter, when it appeared
that Madame was "the victim of a vile conspiracy; but
the Home Secretary had at last undertaken to clear her
reputation." The Minister had his work cut out for him!

After long months' adherence to the "process"—at
the cost of over £20—by December 1877 the last state of
Mrs. Pearse's complexion was worse than the first: a

virulent and painful rash had been superinduced upon
its pristine imperfections. Rachel regarded as "terrible"
this eruptive condition, and expressed the cheering prognosis that if the "cure" were not concluded, the patient
would be disfigured for life! Faced with this fearful
prospect Mrs. Pearse was in despair, but Madame assured
her that all might yet be well. The completed "process,"
for which the Countess of Dudley was to be charged
£2000, she, as a friend, might have for £500, although
the usual fee for commoners was £1000. Mrs. Pearse's
resources, however, were quite inadequate; and as Rachel,
in her goodness of heart, "could not bear to see" the
state to which the patient was reduced, she was prepared in the circumstances to accept £200. But even this
sum was equally beyond the means of Mrs. Pearse. It so
chanced that Signor Mario's affairs being embarrassed,
a benefit concert was arranged to raise for his behoof a
fund, to which Her Majesty the Queen had been pleased
graciously to contribute. The royal subscription was, as
appeared, obtained through Madame's influence with one
of the ladies-in-waiting, whom she had rendered "Beautiful
For Ever." This fund was lodged in Coutts's Bank; and
Rachel suggested that Mrs. Pearse should draw upon it for
the required amount, which that lady indignantly refused
to do.

Anxious, in every way compatible with business, to
pleasure her friend and client, Rachel now proposed another
expedient. In security for the £2000 fee, Lady Dudley
had deposited with Madame the family diamonds. Her
ladyship had artfully given out that these were stolen,
and had even offered a reward of £1000 for their recovery—
"corroborative detail" which Pooh-Bah would have com-
mended; but as a matter of fact they were then reposing
in Rachel's safe! Mrs. Pearse possessed some jewellery;
as this was all she had, Madame was content to accept it,
in lieu of the £50 to which compassion had now reduced
her price. So the jewels took their modest place in the

safe beside those of the countess. But Mrs. Pearse, having gone into the matter with a moneylender, found that she could herself raise more than £50 upon her gems; she therefore requested their return. Rachel regretted that this could not be done; she needed the cash, and had therefore pawned the jewels. So great was her authority over her young friend that she actually induced Mrs. Pearse to write to the pawnbroker, homologating the transaction, and also to give her a written obligation to pay the money! Mrs. Pearse having at length made to her husband "a clean breast," Mr. Pearse called upon Madame Rachel and insisted on delivery of the jewels. She met his demand with truculence and menaces: his wife owed her £150; "*she knew her private affairs,*" and "would make the city ring with it [the scandal]." Mr. Pearse wisely consulted Mr. (afterwards Sir) George Lewis, the eminent solicitor, with the result that a warrant was issued for Rachel's arrest, on a charge of obtaining from Mrs. Pearse two necklaces and other jewellery with intent to defraud.

The trial took place at the Old Bailey, before Baron Huddleston and a jury, on 10th and 11th April 1878. Sir Harry Poland and Sir Douglas Straight appeared for the Treasury; Mr. (afterwards Mr. Justice) Day, Q.C., with Messrs. Besley, Bennett, and Robert Williams, defended the accused.[1] Mr. and Mrs. Pearse having narrated the facts already known to us, Sabina Pilley, an acolyte in the Temple of Beauty, stated that under Madame's direction she prepared the mystic substances requisite to the ritual. The face washes supplied to Mrs. Pearse at one guinea per bottle were composed of starch, fuller's earth, pearl-ash, and water, with the addition of a secret "something" personally contributed by the subtle hand of the High Priestess—which, we learn from the evidence of the analyst adduced, was hydrochloric acid! It is disappointing to find that the Royal Arabian and Circassian Baths,

---

[1] *Times,* 11th and 12th April 1878; *Annual Register for* 1878, part 2, pp. 37-38.

to which the Sultana of Turkey was so partial, consisted merely of hot water and—bran! Sabina further deposed that she was specially warned by her mistress against using the washes for her own beautification—which exhibits Rachel in a light unexpectedly humane; unless it be that she was actuated by a wish to conserve the stock. Madame wore Mrs. Pearse's jewellery, and told witness "they were a Christmas present." Isabella Scott, Lady Dudley's maid, stated that her ladyship's jewels, valued at between £20,000 and £30,000, were stolen from Paddington Station on 12th December 1874; a reward of £1000 was offered, but they had not been recovered. Lady Dudley never used any face wash. In reply to the Court, witness did not in that statement include soap and water. The countess was then laid up with a bad cold. Charles Sheldrick, pawnbroker, of Duke Street, Portland Place, stated that the jewels in question were pledged with him by Rachel for £50; and Harold Senior, the analyst, corroborated Sabina as to the composition of the salutiferous balms. The jury, after an absence of ten minutes, found the prisoner guilty; and the judge, in passing sentence of five years' penal servitude, expressed his regret that he could not give her more. The jewels were ordered to be restored; but as regards the restoration of Mrs. Pearse's cuticle his lordship made no order.

Rachel did not long endure her second punishment; she died in Woking Prison on 12th October 1880.[1] But she did not all die. Burnt, alive, in effigy on the Festival of St. Guido, 5th November 1868, in death the ashes of her memory were kept warm in the Antipodes. A hot spring, on the shores of Lake Rotorua in New Zealand, we read, became known, not inappropriately, as "Madame Rachel's Bath."[2] Further, I find upon research that a certain fawny shade of face powder, much affected by our brunettes,

---

[1] Surrounded by her disconsolate family : her children weeping for Rachel. —*Times*, 19th October 1880.

[2] *Notes and Queries, supra.*

is still, with equal propriety, termed "Rachel." And if the *Dictionary of National Biography*, that "heavenly enchiridion," has seen fit to deny the entrée to Madame Rachel, she has at least secured a niche in the criminous reredos of renown.

Note.—RACHEL'S FAME

In that admirable "best seller" of the Sixties, *Lady Audley's Secret*, I find that the gifted authoress, Miss Braddon, makes two references to the contemporaneous fame of Madame Rachel. In Chapter xxvi.: "Imagine all the women of England elevated to the high level of masculine intellectuality; superior to crinoline; superior to pearl powder and Mrs. Rachel Levison; above taking pains to be pretty; above making themselves agreeable; above tea-tables, and that cruelly scandalous and rather satirical gossip which even strong men delight in; and what a dreary, utilitarian, ugly life the sterner sex must lead." And again in Chapter xxxiv.: "Amongst all privileged spies, a lady's-maid has the highest privileges. . . . She knows when the ivory complexion is bought and paid for—when the pearly teeth are foreign substances fashioned by the dentist—when the glossy plaits of auburn hair are the relics of the dead, rather.than the property of the living; and she knows other and more sacred secrets than these. She knows when the sweet smile is more false than Madame Levison's enamel, and far less enduring— when the words issued from between gates of borrowed pearl are more disguised and painted than the lips which help to shape them."

THE HEBREW AND THE PUBLICAN;

OR, LIKE AS WE LIE

THE HEBREW AND THE PUBLICAN;

OR, LIKE AS WE LIE.

My gold ! my gold ! and all my wealth is gone !
You partial heavens, have I deserved this plague ?
—The Jew of Malta, Act I. Sc. ii.

VISITORS to Caulfield's portrait gallery of celebrities
will find in the four-volume illustrated catalogue
of that exhibition much matter of entertainment.[1] His
singular collection includes in its comprehensive and
catholic embrace eminent malefactors of divers dye,
quacks, eccentrics, and freaks of nature.

Here may be seen William Atkins, the Gout Doctor,
"whose renovating elixer restored youth and vigour to
the patient, however old or decayed, and whose vivifying
drops infallibly cured imbecility in men and barrenness
in women"; John Gale, *alias* Dumb Jack—"tobacco and
ale were his two grand animal gratifications, and his
highest mental enjoyment was that of witnessing the
public execution of criminals"; Matthew Buckinger, "who
although born without hands, feet, legs, or thighs . . . was
married four times and had eleven children"; Mrs. Christian Davies, commonly called Mother Ross, "that very
extraordinary female," who served as a serjeant in the
French war and was buried with military honours at
Chelsea Hospital; Sarah Pridden, *alias* Sally Salisbury, a
lady of the town, who when she died in Newgate "left
behind her the character of the most notorious woman

---

[1] *Portraits, Memoirs, and Characters of Remarkable Persons*, by James
Caulfield. London : 1819.

that ever infested the hundreds of Old Drury"; Jack
Sheppard, with a charming picture of him in the condemned
cell; Mary Tofts, the pretended rabbit-breeder of Godal-
ming, with a sample of her supposititious offspring in her
lap; my old love Mary Blandy, with whom I flatter myself
I am on better terms than Caulfield; Elizabeth Canning—
a capital account and portrait; Hester Hammerton, the
female sexton of Kingston-upon-Thames, who was herself
buried by the collapse of a grave—hoist, one may say,
with her own petard—and was dug out alive after seven
hours' interment; Captain James Lowry, of whom I have
elsewhere given another, and I trust a more adequate
report; Mrs. Sarah Mapp, the society bone-setter—"Mrs.
Mapp continues making extraordinary cures; she has now
set up an equipage, and on Sunday waited on Her Majesty"
—who practised with acceptance in Pall Mall and died
miserably in Seven Dials; James Maclean, the gentleman
highwayman, called "The Ladies' Hero," who should
have had a part in *The Beggar's Opera*, and "was so much
in favour with the fair sex that many presented him with
money while confined"—the donee, not the donors;
Anne Mills, the female pirate, depicted on her own quarter-
deck in the act of decapitating a captive; and, to make a
long story *short*, Robert of that name, who sustained an
operation for gravel and was safely delivered of a stone
"measuring eight inches in circumference," which presents
in the plate the appearance of a large sea urchin.

But to none of these persons, engaging and attractive
as they are, is it my present purpose to direct attention.
I would have you consider with me for a space the strange
tale of Henry Simons, the Polish Jew, and Mr. James
Ashley, the vintner of Bread Street—both of whom are
portrayed by Caulfield—concerning which I happen to
possess certain scarce contemporary tracts, whereby I am
enabled to deal them ampler justice than our congested
author could afford to do. It is an intricate case of envy,
hatred, and malice, and all uncharitableness; the story of

one fallen among thieves in the unavoidable absence of the Good Samaritan; which must have given the Hebraic stranger within our gates cause to remember the gentility of the Gentiles.

I.

Was ever Jew tormented as I am ?
To have a shag-rag knave to come, force from me
Five hundred crowns !
—*The Jew of Malta*, Act IV. Sc. vi.

Our hero, in the appeal which he afterwards published [1] in his own defence, gives the following account of his personality and pursuits:—

Henry Simons, the Object before you, is a Native of Ostrog in Volinia, near the Ukraine, in Poland, and of a very good Jewish Family, for many Years past settled there, he (being early in Life bred to Trade) about Seven Years ago came into England, and then brought with him upwards of Three hundred Ducats, which he soon expended at London and Bristol, by purchasing the Manufactures of this Kingdom, with which he returned to Poland, where he sold them to Profit. The Advantage arising from his first Expedition induced him to a second Trial, flattering himself with the Hopes of Success equal to his former Undertaking; but, alas! this Journey proved very fatal to him, as will too evidently appear in the following plain Relation of the Hardships and Cruelties he has experienced since his Arrival in this Country.[2]

The narrator, who may truly be said, like Miss Rugg in *Little Dorrit*, to have had his " trials," arrived at Harwich from Holland on 8th August 1751. Before he was allowed ashore he was searched for contraband by the responsible officer. Round his body was found a purse-belt containing 554 ducats, his trading capital. On the 12th he reached London, where, in Houndsditch, he lodged with a co-religionist named Berend Abrahams, with whom he continued till the 20th when he set out for Bristol, "hoping

---

[1] *The Case of Henry Simons, a Polish Jew Merchant ; and his Appeal to the Public thereon. Now publish'd, with the Tryal at Chelmsford, for the Benefit of Him and his unhappy Family.* London : 1753.
[2] *Ibid.*, p. 3.

to purchase Goods there at a greater Advantage than he could do in London." But the weather was bad, his feet were worse, and a little beyond Hounslow he resolved to return to town and postpone his journey for a week. He rested by the way at the house of one Ricketts, "who keeps the Sign of the 'Rose and Crown' at Smallbury Green." While Simons in his Polish garb was standing at the door of this asylum, Thomas Ashley, a gardener at Isleworth,[1] "who was greatly intoxicated with Liquor, came out with a Pint of Beer in his Hand," and made some remark, probably opprobrious, upon which the Jew, not understanding English, "very innocently shook his Head" and made no answer. Whereupon Ashley, construing this as an affront, threw the beer in his face "and pulled him by the Beard," which, as we are told, "is one of the most unpardonable Insults that can be offered a Foreigner of his Religion." But "expecting something worse from a Person of Ashley's Stamp, he thought it most prudent to quit the Place quietly in quest of Hospitality and good Manners," which plainly were not included in the tariff of the "Rose and Crown." Ashley, however, being truculent in his cups, pursued his victim, "cursing and swearing all the Way and calling out 'Stop thief!'" Fortunately for the Jew, four gentlemen on horseback were then approaching the inn, and the fugitive "ventured betwixt the Horses, confiding in their Generosity for Protection and Assistance." One of the party, Mr. Wright of the Temple, asked Ashley what was wrong; the gardener, adding insult to injury, said "that the Villain had robbed him of his Beer." Inquiry at the inn disclosed the truth of the matter, and Simons was permitted to depart in peace.

He lay that night at the house of Mrs. Ridgeway at Brentford, whence he regained his lodgings in London, remaining there till 28th August, when "the Blisters

---

[1] This person is to be distinguished from his namesake *James* Ashley, aftermentioned.

on his Feet being well and the Weather becoming fair,"
he set out again upon his way to Bristol, "with the Five
hundred and fifty-four Ducats in his Belt, which was
round his Body." He dined at the "Red Lion" at Brentford, and was subsequently refreshed by a visit to the
"Coach and Horses" at Hounslow. He paid in English
coin, and the golden girdle was still intact. Seven o'clock
that evening found him at the "White Hart" in Cranford
Bridge, kept by one Joseph Goddard, who, as will presently
appear, could on occasion double the rôles of publican
and sinner. From a young lady in the taproom he called,
either in Dutch or by signs, for "a Pint of Beer, a Penny-
worth of Bread, and a Penny-worth of Butter," an order
which indicates that, like Mrs. Gilpin, he took his pleasure
with moderation and restraint. He proposed to stay the
night; but the landlord, not impressed by his order,
"did not chuse he should stay there." The young lady,
who, as appears, was niece to mine host, was of the same
mind. The uninvited guest then "shewed them his Arm
and Bosom, to convince them that he was clean"; this
demonstration failing of effect, he "turned the purse of
his Belt round, and took out several of his Ducats and
Shewed them, that they might have no Fear of his Inability
to pay the Reckoning." This exhibition proved more
persuasive; a bed was prepared, and the traveller retired
for the night. At the subsequent trial he thus described,
through an interpreter, his nocturnal experiences:—

When it was almost Twelve o'Clock I heard the Door come open,
and saw my Landlord, the Prisoner, come into the Room with a Candle
in his Hand alone. I started up in my Bed, and Ask'd him in Dutch
what was the Matter? He answered, "Sleep, sleep!" There were no
Curtains to the Bed. The Landlord went away, and lock'd the Door.
I did not move out of the Bed but went to sleep; and I believe it was
between three and four o'Clock, some body took hold on me and put a
Hand to my Mouth, and with his Knee squeez'd me to the Bed. I
struggled up, and there were two Men; it was the Prisoner that took hold
on me, I could see his face by the Moonlight. The other Person took
from me my Girdle and Money, and went to the Window and drew back

the Curtain, and shot the Money out into his Hat. I found the Girdle in the Room on the Ground. [The Girdle produc'd in Court, made of Leather like a Purse.]

[Upon being ask'd if he could distinguish the Prisoner's Face before the Curtain of the Window was drawn back ? He answer'd, " No, I could not."] He continued holding my Mouth. When the other had the Money in his Hat I heard him say to the Prisoner, " I have got the Money " ; then he took the Money from the other Person and went down Stairs. I got up and opened the Window, and call'd " I am in Distress ! " once or twice in the German Language ; this was as soon as they were out of the Room. I heard them lock the Door. They came in again directly upon my calling out at the Window. The Prisoner stood behind, the other Person came and knock'd me down, and in the mean Time gave me a Punch in the Face, I don't know with what. Then he took a Knife and held it to my Throat, and said, " Hush, hush,—your Life ! " from which I understood, if I did not hold my Tongue, my Life was in Danger. When they went down, I went to the Door to see if it was fast, and found it shut. I held my Shirt up to the Wound on my Head. [He shew'd a small Scar on the Top of his Head.] I put my cloaths on. . . . I watch'd at the Window. When it was Daylight somebody came and open'd the Door softly.[1]

On going downstairs he found a coach just departing, and the landlord standing at the inn door with two of his servants. According to the host, the guest remarked, "You have my Money when you knock me down: you must be flung by the Naik! " But capital punishment had no terrors for the persons of the house; they "laught" at him. The landlord shook his fist and bade his men hold him fast. "I was affrighted, and took up my Things and went away, crying." He returned to Hounslow, and at the "Coach and Horses" complained of his ill-treatment "and shew'd his bloody Shirt," but owing to his lack of English, could not make the people understand his story. When he reached London he confided his troubles to one Higham Levi, "of whom he had bespoke Watches to the Value of £100," and was in treaty "for some Second-hand

---

[1] *A Narrative of the remarkable Affair between Mr. Simonds, The Polish Jew Merchant, and Mr. James Ashley, Merchant of Bread Street, London,* pp. 5–6. London : MDCCLII.

Henry Simons the Polish Jew.

(*From the frontispiece of* " The Case and Appeal of James Ashley.")

[*To face p.* 80.

Cloaths that came from the Princess of Wales's." His friend took him to Mr. Woodman, "Keeper of the Poultry-Compter," whom they informed of the robbery and begged his aid in bringing the perpetrator to justice. As the complainer, thrice examined through an interpreter, stuck to his story, a warrant was procured from a magistrate for the apprehending of Goddard.

"But as the next Day was the Jews' Sabbath, and Mr. Woodman being desirous of taking Simons with him, he was obliged to defer his Journey till the Sunday following, being the 1st of September, when Mr. Woodman, and his Deputy, and Simons set out early in the Morning for Cranford Bridge." Instead of proceeding straightway to the capture of their prey the party broke the journey at Hounslow, whence the innkeeper, being a friend of Goddard and scenting their purpose, dispatched a mounted messenger to warn his colleague. Whereupon that worthy "made his Escape through his Garden on Horseback," and the officers of the law were received at the "White Hart" by "a Mob of People," supporters of the popular publican, "who insulted and abused Simons very grossly." Proceeding with his inquiry, Woodman learned from Goddard's niece "that the Night Simons was robbed her Uncle went to Bed at Ten o'Clock, therefore he could not possibly commit the Fact"; but a lodger who had been there at the time declared "that Mr. Goddard was with him in his Apartment, where they staid till between One and Two in the Morning playing at Cards, consequently could not be in Simons' Room." These "clashing Avowals" shewed bad staff-work on the part of those responsible for the defence. The niece admitted seeing the golden belt and its contents. Woodman then demanded exhibition of the bed linen used by the Jew, which, when produced, "were with the Pillowbier (then unwashed) in a very bloody Condition." An examination of the bedroom floor shewed it "to be greatly stained with Blood, quite from the Bedside to the Window." These circum-

6

stances satisfied the officers of the truth of Simons'
tale.

The fugitive vintner, on reflection, thought it better to
face the music, and accordingly "surrendered himself at
the House of Justice Fielding." To this sportsmanlike
course Goddard was moved by the counsel of his friend,
Mr. James Ashley,[1] wine and brandy merchant, of Bread
Street, London, with whom he had long had spirituous
dealings, and to whom in his dilemma he wrote as follows:—

Sir,—I am know Lebaring under this most unhappy and Torries
[? notorious] pice of Villineay that had been Lodg'd to my Charge,
witch I Beg the Faver of you and Mr. Leach to mett at the Cannon
Tavern, Chearing Crass, whear will bee meaney worthey Frinds of mine
to serve me in this Destress at thise Time, with abliging me in thise
Request I shall bee your most thenkfull Humble Sert. to Comand,—
Jos. Goddard.

4 Sept. 51. 11 o'Clock.
To Mr. James Ashley.[2]

As the result of the consult at the Cannon Tavern,
the persecuted publican was supported before the Justice
by "a great number of gentlemen of fortune, reputable
tradesmen, and innkeepers, who all declared their opinions
that the said Joseph Goddard was innocent of the crime
laid to his charge." But notwithstanding the united
testimony of the Trade, Mr. Justice Fielding proposed to
commit him for trial, which was duly done.

"In the Seventh Sessions of the Mayoralty of the
Right Hon. Francis Cokayne, Esq., Lord Mayor of London,
which began the 11th of September 1751," Goddard was
indicted at the Old Bailey "for that he, in his own dwelling-
house, on Henry Simons did make an assault, putting him
in corporal fear, and stealing from him one leather girdle,

---

[1] Not to be confounded with *Thomas* Ashley, before mentioned.
[2] *The Case and Appeal of James Ashley, of Bread Street, London.* . . . *Printed
for, and Published by, the Appellant ; and sold at the London Punch-house, on
Ludgate-hill ; at the Brandy Warehouse, in Bread Street,* p. 29. London :
MDCCLIII.

value one penny, and five hundred and fifty-four pieces of foreign coin called ducats, value £250." The Jew, *who could not speak English*, gave by his interpreter the account of the robbery which we have already heard. None of the contemporary pamphlets deal with the trial in detail; the only report of the proceedings I can find is that contained in the *Gentleman's Magazine* of the day, from which I take the following particulars:—

Higham Levi declared he saw the money, as did likewise Berend Abrahams and his wife. Jacob Abrahams, a travelling Jew, said he lay at Hounslow the night that Simons lay at the prisoner's, and there he heard that an outlandish man had been robbed. The prisoner in his defence said that the prosecutor did lie at his house; that he had refused him lodging, but his niece had prevailed upon him to let him have a bed, being pleased with the oddity of the man—they said he was a hermit. In the morning he pretended to be robb'd by two men that came in at the window; that he, the prisoner, was much surpriz'd and went up stairs; the window curtains were drawn and the window as clean as possible—not so much as the print of a cat's foot—and the key was on the inside of the door; that he owned he did threaten him for bringing a scandal on his house, and was about to secure him by a constable, but he made his escape; that all the next day he went in search of him, but to no purpose; that upon inquiry he found that the wound he shew'd he had received above a week before at Turnham Green; and that two or three drops of blood that were found by the bedside appear'd like black blood that had been kept in a bottle two or three days; the bed was not in the least disorder'd. The niece confirm'd every circumstance. William Taylor, who liv'd over-against the prisoner's, was up between three and four that morning, and heard no disturbance. Thomas Ashley declared he was the man that broke the Jew's head a week before; he first took him by the beard in a joke, on which the Jew struck him with his staff; and then he, Ashley, cut him with a stone. A great number of gentlemen appeared to the prisoner's character, and the jury thinking the Jew's story very improbable, the prisoner was honourably acquitted.[1]

On 13th September a bill of indictment for perjury was preferred against Simons, supported by the evidence of Goddard, his niece, and Ashley, the gardener, and a

---

[1] *Gentleman's Magazine*, 1751, vol. xxi. pp. 424–425.

warrant obtained for his apprehension on that charge.
Although the subject of this friendly move remained upon
the scene, "going in the most Public Manner on the
Exchange and about the Streets in his Polish Garb, asking
Alms for his Subsistence and to carry him over to Holland,"
no steps were taken to effect his arrest, the warrant being
for the time "kept dormant in the Pocket of Mr. Ford,
Goddard's Solicitor." As the subsequent happenings
formed the bases of no less than three criminal prosecutions
and a civil action of damages, wherein the most material
matters were stubbornly contested at the cost of much
time, labour, and some very hard swearing, it may be
convenient here to set forth, before dealing with the proof
at large, the uncontroverted facts of the case.

It came to pass that upon the 6th of October Mr. James
Ashley, brandy merchant, returning to town in his chaise
from a business tour among his country constituents,
met upon the road between Ilford and Stratford the
picturesque figure of the Jew, "travelling on foot towards
Ilford." He stopped the chaise "on purpose to have a
full view of him"; what further passed between them is
disputed. On reaching London, Ashley communicated to
Ford the fact of the encounter; it was inferred that the
Jew was making for Harwich in order to escape from
justice; so Ashley, armed with the warrant for his arrest
and accompanied by the solicitor's clerk, Newman, set
out in pursuit of the wayfarer. They ran down their
quarry on the highroad, near Witham, in Essex; they
put him in a passing cart, from out of which—naturally
enough— "Mr. Simons jumped and ran, and endeavoured
to make his Escape"; they recaptured him, and at Witham
delivered him up to Hubbard, the constable, who kept
him in ward all night. Next morning he was haled before
Justice Bragg, who was of opinion "that as the Justices
were setting at Chelmsford, it would be better to carry
him thither," which was done. The Chelmsford bench
recommended that the prisoner be taken to London for

'trial, and pending arrangements to that effect, Ashley, Newman, and Hubbard—the vintner, the clerk, and the constable—removed their prisoner to the "Saracen's Head" in the town. What occurred in the parlour of that hostelry was twice the subject of investigation by judge and jury. It is enough for our present purpose to note that Ashley alleged that Simons assaulted him by putting into his pocket three ducats, with intent to charge him with robbery.

Mr. Ashley now humanely provided a Pair of small Iron Handcuffs, and had them screwed on Simons' Hands, placed crossways, as hard as they possibly could be. This being done, the Constable with two of his Assistants, aided by Ashley and his Companion, guarded the unhappy Prisoner to London, and lodged him at the " King's Arms " in Leadenhall Street ; but though he was so well secured, Ashley had not Mercy or Compassion enough about him to disencumber the poor Wretch of his galling Handcuffs, but kept him in that dreadful Situation all Night.[1]

Next morning they brought the Jew before a magistrate, "and poor Simons, for want of Bail, was sent to the New Prison at Clerkenwell," there to abide his trial for perjury. He was visited in his seclusion by James Ashley and Joseph Goddard, but these gentlemen were not, I regret to say, moved thereto by feelings of Christian charity. They indicated by signs their sure and certain hope that the prisoner would be hanged; "basely pulled the greater Part of his Beard out of his Face; and with an insatiable Malice and vindictive Spirit, beat and kicked him about like a Dog"—which probably accounts for the somewhat sparse appearance presented by the Jew's beard in his portrait.

Of the trial itself few particulars have survived. We read that on Tuesday, 10th December 1751,

Henry Simons, the Polish Jew, was try'd at the King's Bench bar for perjury on an information of his being robb'd by Mr. Goddard, the innkeeper, and another person unknown. But the prosecutors not

---

[1] *The Case of Henry Simons*, p. 34.

producing, or even subpœnaing the interpreter of his information (though they knew where to find him) to be at the tryal, the jury, which was special, acquitted him.[1]

It is stated in *The Case of Henry Simons* that "the Trial came on by a Special Jury of Gentlemen, who very soon saw through the Chicanery and artful Management of the Prosecutor, Mr. Ford his Solicitor, and others; and the Jury, by the Direction of the Right Honourable Judge, brought in their Verdict *Not Guilty.*"

This was at the King's Bench where Mr. Simons was acquitted [writes the author of the *Narrative*]; but Mr. Ashley says, not on full Evidence but for want of Evidence, either thro' the Neglect or Mistake of those who were concerned in that Trial. But upon very mature Deliberation it will, I believe, be concluded that even supposing Mr. Simons guilty of Perjury in swearing Goddard committed that Robbery, it was not so easy for him to be convicted of it. There appeared no Witnesses to prove Mr. Goddard did not commit the Robbery, tho' at the Old Bailey there wanted Witnesses to prove he did.[2]

But the unlucky Israelite, though thus escaping from the innkeeper's frying pan, was forthwith to fall into the fire ingeniously kindled for him by the inflammable vintner. Mr. James Ashley, who if he conducted his own business with the energy and resource which he devoted to the affairs of his neighbour must have driven a brisk trade in Bread Street, "having caused a Detainer to be sent by Mr. Justice Fielding against him [Simons] to New Prison, while he there remained a Prisoner to be tried for Perjury," and "being irritated by this Verdict given against his Friend Goddard," presented in January 1752 to the Chelmsford Quarter Sessions a bill of indictment against Simons for putting three ducats into his pocket and charging him with a robbery of them. "The Bill was found on the Evidence of Ashley himself, the Constable, and Hughes (the run-away Taylor), which was likewise removed into a superior Court."

---

[1] *Gentleman's Magazine*, 1751, vol. xxi. p. 570.
[2] *Op. cit.*, p. 24.

Pending the trial at the ensuing assizes, Ashley—one should think, in gross contempt of Court—obtained and caused to be printed a joint affidavit by "four of his Creatures," confirmatory of the prisoner's guilt, many hundred copies of which were by his direction dispersed throughout the county of Essex and the cities of London and Westminster, with the amiable purpose "to prejudice People in general, and particularly the Inhabitants of Essex"—from whom the jury would be selected—"against poor unhappy Simons." To this egregious document the prosecutor prefixed the following statement:—

As the Affair of Simons the Jew for swearing a Robbery against Mr. Goddard the Innkeeper (for which the said Goddard was tried at the Old Bailey and honourably acquitted) has of late made much Noise and occasioned various Conjectures; the following Depositions having been transmitted to me, for the sake of publick Justice and Satisfaction to the World, I have caused them to be published, submitting to their Consideration whether there can be the least Reason *now* left to believe Goddard Guilty on the single Evidence of so wicked a Jew, or that the said Jew was ever robbed at all.

JAMES ASHLEY.[1]

Bread Street, Jan. 19, 1752.

This, the most bare-faced attempt to poison the wells of justice with which I am acquainted, appears to have called forth no judicial comment. Mr. Ashley's "four Creatures" would seem to have enjoyed with their apocalyptic forerunners the advantage of being "full of eyes before and behind," in that they certainly saw more than other people. As we shall hear them later in the witness-box it is unnecessary now to consider their broadcast testimony.

On Thursday, 12th March 1752,

Henry Simons, the Polish Jew, was try'd on an indictment (found by the grand jury at the last quarter sessions at Chelmsford, and afterwards remov'd by certiorari into the King's Bench) for an assault on Mr. James Ashley and putting 3 ducats into his pocket with an intent to charge him with a robbery. After a trial which lasted till 9 at night

---

[1] *The Case of Henry Simons*, p. 43.

the jury withdrew, and at two the next morning deliver'd their verdict
to the judge in his bed at his lodgings, that the defendant Simons was
guilty of the indictment.[1]

The adverse verdict was intended by the jury to be
construed in a Pickwickian sense: "We find him Guilty,
but of no Intent," that is, that the prisoner put the ducats
into the prosecutor's pocket, but without design to charge
him with theft. "This Verdict, as taken down, being
contrary to the Direction of the Honourable Judge in
Point of Law, and the [subsequent] Declaration of the
Jury,[2] it was resolved that a new Trial should be applied
for"; and on 28th April the Court of King's Bench was
moved accordingly, and a rule obtained for the prosecutor
to shew cause why a new trial should not be granted.

Meanwhile, "in the Fourth Sessions of the Mayoralty
of the Right Hon. Thomas Winterbottom, Esq., Lord
Mayor of London, which began the 8th of April 1752,"
Thomas Ashley, the gardener, who, as the reader may
remember, had claimed to have caused Simons' injuries,
was himself indicted for perjury, "in swearing for Goddard
at his tryal that he threw the Jew into a ditch, threw a
stone at him, broke his head, and thereby caused the
blood to flow, in contradiction to what the Jew had sworn:
that his head was broke by the persons that robbed him.
Several witnesses deposed that he [Ashley] was at that
time drunk at a distant place." [3]   Found guilty, the intem-
perate horticulturist was sentenced to stand in the pillory,
opposite the Sessions House in the Old Bailey, "but"—
one regrets to read—"was not pelted," the popularity of
Mr. Goddard extending, as appears, to his false witness.
He was, however, further ordained "to be Imprisoned
in Newgate for One Year, and afterwards Transported for
Seven Years," so that the Jew was amply avenged.

---

[1] *Gentleman's Magazine*, 1752, vol. xxii. p. 139.

[2] The affidavits of the twelve jurymen are printed at large in *The Case and
Appeal of James Ashley*, pp. 1–22.

[3] *Gentleman's Magazine*, 1752, vol. xxii. p. 190.

"The Manner of detecting the Wickedness of Thomas Ashley," we read, "was very singular." It so chanced that Mr. Wright of the Temple, who had rescued poor Simons from the clutches of the intoxicated Thomas at the "Rose and Crown," was present in the Old Bailey upon business, at the same time as the Jew, then in compulsory attendance there; and that unhappy victim of the law recognised his Good Samaritan. "The Moment he cast his Eye on Mr. Wright he knew him, and told his Interpreter that he was one of the Gentlemen who had so generously protected him on the Road." The evidence given by Mr. Wright and his companions upon the trial of Thomas Ashley materially contributed to the exposure and conviction of the accused.

An interesting sidelight on the Goddard trial is provided by the testimony of another witness.

Richard Strickland deposes, that he heard [Thomas] Ashley say that he had been a Witness at the Old Bailey for Mr. Goddard, and that Goddard was cleared, and that he took him down to his House to be paid for his Trouble. That after he had made him Welcome, he took him by the Hand and led him to the Door, and said, " Mr. Ashley, I shall have a Respect for you all the Days of my Life, for you actually sav'd my Life, though I deserve to die, for I actually robb'd the Man. Then he took him in again to pay him for his Trouble, and asked him what he must have ? He answered he would trust to his Honour. Then Goddard throwed him down Half a Guinea and asked if that would satisfy him. He grumbled ; and then he threw down a Crown more, and at last he made it up to a Guinea. Then as he went away he told him to come again such a Day : there would be some Gentlemen there. He went, and said he thought there were a hundred Gentlemen at the Table ; that they called for a Plate to gather Money for him ; that a Gentleman had gave a Shilling, then Mr. Goddard came and took the Plate out of his Hand, seized Ashley by the Collar, and turn'd him out at the Door, saying he was a Rogue ; so he went away very angry. He deposed further that he had heard Ashley grumble about it many Times, that he was not paid enough ; that had he known as much as he then did, he would not have spoke till he had been better paid.[1]

The incident reflects but little credit on Mr. Goddard,

---

[1] *Narrative*, pp. 14, 15.

who should have known that the perjurer is worthy of his hire.

On Friday, 17th July 1752,

Was tried at the assizes at Chelmsford, Essex, the remarkable cause between [James] Ashley and Simons the Jew, relating to the three ducats said to be put into Ashley's pocket by Simons, with an intent to charge him with a robbery. The trial lasted near 13 hours, and the jury, after retiring about 8 minutes, honourably acquitted Simons; and it is said that several persons will be indicted for perjury on the former trial.[1]

II.

How liberally the villain gives me mine own gold !
—*The Jew of Malta*, Act IV. Sc. vi.

We are now to consider at closer range the evidence adduced upon the two trials, which resulted respectively in the conviction and acquittal of the much-prosecuted object of those proceedings; the first at the Lent Assizes before Mr. Justice Forster, the second at the Summer Assizes before Mr. Justice Dennison, both upon the same indictment, at Chelmsford, in the year 1752. By the care and consideration of the respective parties we are furnished with full reports; Mr. Ashley naturally devoting most space to the former trial,[2] Mr. Simons to the latter.[3]

At the first trial the prosecutor unfolded the following plain, unvarnished tale. He attended the trial of Goddard on 5th September. On 6th October, being in his chaise, he met the defendant on the road, near Ilford. He crossed over to get a better view of him, *but did not speak to him.* Next day he reported the matter to Mr. Ford, who "earnestly pressed" him to take the warrant and pursue the Jew. He consented to do so "with great reluctance," and started with Newman, Mr. Ford's clerk, in a postchaise. Near Witham they were informed by a

---

[1] *Gentleman's Magazine*, 1752, vol. xxii. p. 334.
[2] *The Case and Appeal of James Ashley*, pp. 4–15.
[3] *The Case of Henry Simons*, pp. 49–115.

boy on horseback that the Jew was "not far before."
He "encouraged" the boy to give chase. They captured
Simons, and put him in a passing cart. He jumped out,
ran off, and was retaken. They delivered him, with the
warrant, to Hubbard, the constable, who kept him all
night. Next day he was carried before Justice Bragg,
then to the justices at Chelmsford, and thence to the
Saracen's Head. While they were waiting in the parlour
there, he saw Simons pull out a green purse and count
his money; among it were some gold pieces. Simons
desired to speak with him, and as he stooped down to hear
what he had to say, the Jew called out: "My gilt! my
gilt! my gilt! my ducats in pocket," and pointed to
prosecutor's pocket. He (witness) took out his pocket-
book "and asked if that was his?" Defendant cried:
"Ne, ne, not dat pocket; toder pocket," whereupon he
[Ashley] took out his handkerchief, and there dropped out
a ducat, "which much surprised this witness." On further
examining his pocket he found two more ducats, "among
some walnuts." Mr. Alderman Gascoyne, who had signed
the warrant for the Jew's arrest, happened then to be in
the house, and being informed of the incident, ordered him
to be searched; "but there was no more money found
about him than one shilling and ninepence halfpenny."
Witness then took the defendant to London, and carried
him before Mr. Justice Fielding, who committed him to
the New Prison for perjury in the matter of Goddard's
case.[1] Cross-examined, when he met Simons on the
road, *he neither spoke to him nor shewed him any ducats.*
Witness had never seen a ducat in his life until he pulled
one out with his handkerchief at the Saracen's Head,
"tho' he dealt for some thousand pounds a year." He
did not tell the boy that he had a warrant to apprehend
a highwayman. Asked why he was so zealous in hunting
down the defendant, who had done him no injury, witness

---

[1] It should be noted that Ashley preferred on this occasion no charge against
Simons in regard to the affair of the ducats.

said that the Jew was a very bad man, and his only motive for acting as he did was "for the sake of publick justice." He admitted having circulated the four affidavits, but with no idea of prejudicing the defendant; it was done "to satisfy the world, who were in doubt concerning Goddard's innocence."

Mr. Ashley was succeeded in the witness-box by his "four Creatures," whose affidavits he had so sedulously and improperly published before the trial. Richard Taylor, of Boreham, Essex, peruke-maker, said that in the parlour at the Saracen's Head he saw Simons put his hand into Ashley's left-hand pocket; witness pulled his hand out, and asked "if he designed to pick the gentleman's pocket?" Simons then put his hand into Ashley's right-hand pocket, and presently cried out: "Oh, my God! me robbed!" pointing to Mr. Ashley's coat pocket. When that gentleman took out his pocket-book from his left-hand pocket, Simons exclaimed: "Ne, ne, ducats!" and pointed to the right-hand pocket, from which Ashley pulled out his handkerchief, and there fell a piece of gold; also two more, "with some walnuts." Then the Jew said: "Me rob! one great rogue cut me," indicating his head and neck. Witness confirmed Ashley as to the search and its result: "there was no other money about him than one shilling and sixpence in silver, and threepence halfpenny in halfpence." Cross-examined, he was sure he saw the Jew's hand in *both* pockets.

Daniel Hughes, of Witham, tailor, said he acted as assistant to Hubbard in warding the prisoner. He sat up all night with him, "and saw him [the Jew] telling his money"; among it were three pieces of gold like half-guineas, "which he verily believes were the same" as those taken from Ashley's pocket. In cross-examination, he could give no grounds for that belief.

Eleanor Brown, cook at the Saracen's Head, saw Simons' hand in Ashley's pocket, heard him cry: "Mine gilt, mine gilt, robb'd of mine gilt!", and "Dare be de gilt!" on the discovery of the ducats. Ashley remarked: "The villain has put them into my pocket." Cross-examined, there were eight or nine people in the room at the time; Ashley was leaning on his elbow, and the Jew stood on his right side.

Isaac Hubbard, constable of Witham, said he received the Jew under Mr. Gascoyne's warrant. He heard Simons charge Ashley with robbing him: "You have mine gilt!" —"Here be mine gilt!"—"Mine ducats, me robb'd, mine ducats!"; from these phrases he inferred the charge. Cross-examined, at the time of the arrest the warrant was not "backed" by an Essex justice; he thought Mr. Gascoyne was such. Next morning Ashley got it "backed" by the Rev. Mr. Tindal, one of the justices of the peace for that county. Being referred to his affidavit, wherein he swore that the warrant as received by him was signed and sealed by both Gascoyne and Tindal, he replied, "that he should not have sworn it if Mr. Ashley had not requested him to do so."

John Newman, clerk to Mr. Ford, described the pursuit and arrest of Simons. Either Ashley or the boy called: "Stop, highwayman!" He was present when the Jew charged Ashley with having stolen his "gilt." Simons cried: "Dare be my ducats; me robbed of mine ducats!" and greatly rejoiced. Witness thought that Mr. Gascoyne was a verderer of Epping Forest, and he therefore added the words "Essex and" to the word "London" on the warrant after it was issued. Daniel Gains, "that keeps the 'Star,'" deposed that being at the "Saracen's Head" that day, he heard and saw all that happened in the parlour, as to which he corroborated the other witnesses. The proof for the prosecution was here closed.

Hyam (or Higham) Levi, called for the defence, said that he came from Holland in the same ship with Simons. At Harwich on 8th August they were searched; Simons had a belt that would hold above a thousand ducats, which was half-full. Witness advised him to have his

money sent to London, but he said he would not trust
anyone with it, "not his own father." As Simons was
too strict to travel on the Sabbath, they parted company.
Israel Levi, also a fellow-voyager, corroborated. After
the loss of the ducats he saw Simons in London "in great
necessity," and lent him money. Simons had been
obliged to pawn his veil, "which is a thing the religious
among Jews never do, but at the last extremity." William
Payce, "searcher of the customs at Harwich," testified
to the existence of the belt of gold. Sarah Abrahams,
with whom the Jew lodged, while in London, said that
she helped him to count the money in his belt before
he left for Bristol; there were 554 ducats. Her husband,
Berend Abrahams, confirmed her evidence; he accompanied
Simons "as far as Piccadilly," to shew him the way out
of town. Thomas Woodman, keeper of the Poultry-
Compter, said that on 29th August the Jew came with an
interpreter, and complained of being robbed and assaulted
by Goddard at Cranford Bridge. He then appeared to
have been wounded, "and was very bloody." A warrant
was obtained, but Goddard was found to have fled. Henry
Keys, the interpreter, corroborated. Several London
Jews, including officials of the Synagogue, deposed that
after the robbery Simons was destitute and subsisted on
their charity. When he left to return to the Continent he
got half-a-guinea out of the poor-box, and one sympathiser
gave him three shillings.

Joseph Isaacs deposed that on 6th October, as he and
Simons, with whom he had foregathered, were on their
way to Ilford, they met in a chaise a gentleman whom
he now knew to be Mr. Ashley. Ashley stopped and
asked Simons, "Are you the man that swore the robbery?"
to which the Jew replied, "Na fas stand." Ashley then
pulled out a handful of ducats and said, "These; these
ducats?" He then shook his fist at them and drove on.
On the 8th witness again saw Simons in custody near
Witham and was told he was a highwayman, but was not

allowed to speak to him. [Newman and Hubbard, confronted with the witness, both denied that they had ever seen him before.] Cross-examined, he was close to the side of the chaise when Ashley pulled out the ducats. He lived in Rosemary Lane, and his business was "to make women's pockets and carry them about to sell." [Ashley, confronted with the witness, said that Simons was alone on the road, that he never saw the man, nor had he ever seen a ducat till those discovered in his pocket at the inn.] Hyam Levi, recalled, said that shortly after the Goddard trial Ashley came to him in Duke's Place, Aldgate, where he was living with his brother-in-law, Jacob Abrahams, and asked for "Mr. Levi." "Fearing to be arrested for some hair that he had bought," witness said that he was not at home. Ashley left a message for "Mr. Levi" to go to the Punch House in Ludgate Hill; but having consulted a friend,[1] he did not accept the invitation. Ashley called again, and asked "if he came from Holland with Simons and whether Simons brought over any ducats with him?" He added that the Jew was a perjured villain in swearing (a) that Goddard robbed him, and (b) that his ducats were worth 9s. 6d. apiece. "He then pulled out a pair of scales and weighed *a ducat that had a hole in it,* and said, 'You see this weighs no more than 8s. I am a silversmith and deal in ducats.'" [Ashley, confronted with the witness, said he never saw Levi in his life, and that he had not been in Duke's Place for many years.] Moses Jacob said that Simons pawned his veil with him for 30s., and redeemed it the day he left London. The Jew said he had then but 2s. 6d. in the world; witness gave him 5s. to help him on his way to Harwich.

Mr. Alderman Gascoyne [2] said that happening to be at

---

[1] Moses Franks, an eminent Jew, distinguished in the report by the style of "Esquire." Mr. Franks confirmed Levi's evidence, so far as concerned the consultation.

[2] Sir Crisp Gascoyne (1700–1761), afterwards Lord Mayor of London, who took so prominent a part two years later in the famous affair of Elizabeth Canning.

the Saracen's Head when Simons was brought there, he
was called down, as a magistrate, to the parlour. Ashley
said: "That damned villain the Jew has put some ducats
in my pocket and has charged me with robbing him."
Witness asked the Jew in Dutch whether this were true,
and whether the ducats were really his? to which the Jew
answered in Dutch: "They are none of my ducats; Goddard, Goddard, Goddard's ducats!" He denied putting
any ducats into Ashley's pocket or charging him with
robbery. Upon this evidence the defendant was found
guilty in the Gilbertian terms before related.

Here endeth the first trial.

On the revival of that popular Jewish comedy, *The
Enchanted Ducats*, as produced at Chelmsford in the
summer season without regard to expense (of truth),
there were several changes in the cast, together with an
entirely new and improved finale. Of those who had
sustained the parts of "the four Creatures," only the cook
and the constable occupied their former rôles. Actions of
damages having been brought in behalf of Simons against
Taylor and Hughes, in respect of the irregularity of the
warrant upon which he was apprehended and imprisoned,
the peruke-maker and the tailor found themselves "obliged
to quit the country," so their testimony was not available.
Another absentee was Newman, the clerk, who for reasons
best known to himself "was no more to be seen." Fortunately Mr. Ashley, the producer, was in a position to
secure the services of other artists equally capable—of
anything. He himself, as before, played lead; and his
performance was marked by the robustness that characterised the original rendering.

On this occasion the versatile and altruistic vintner
fared more hardly at the hands of cross-examining counsel.
He swore that when he encountered Simons on the road,
the Jew was alone: "On the last Trial there was a Person
declared he was with him; he gave a very romantick

JAMES ASHLEY.

(From a drawing by George Cruikshank in "Caulfield's Portraits.")

[To face p. 96.

Account about pulling out a Handful of Ducats.   I suppose
we shall have him now."   The supposition was, as we shall
find, well founded.   With regard to his part in the arrest
of Simons: "I thought it was for Justice, public Justice,
that Mr. Ford ought to know it; it was to serve the Public
only; I went out of a friendly Motive for the sake of
public Justice."   We shall hear Mr. Ford's version by and
by.   Counsel was unkind enough to suggest that private
profit, rather than public justice, was the "friendly Motive"
upon which the witness acted.

Q.—I will put you in mind whether you did not tell him [Mr. Johnson
of Ingatestone, a witness for the defence] it was for your Interest to
pursue Simons ?
A.—I do not know I said so ; I believe this I did say, that as I deal
with most of the Inns between London and Bath, it would be highly
satisfactory to them to have him brought to public Justice.
Q.—Whether you did not declare that if you served your Friend
Goddard, you should serve all the Inns on the Western Road with
Spirituous Liquors ?
A.—I said it would be a general Satisfaction to all the Innkeepers
on the Road, knowing Goddard was an honest Man, to have the Jew
brought to Justice.[1]

He admitted having travelled in Holland for business
purposes, but denied that he ever saw a ducat while in
that country.   He admitted being present when the Jew
was searched at Witham, the night before the doings at
the Saracen's Head; but swore "there was no Search for
any thing but Snicker-snee Knives"—a weapon pleasantly
reminiscent of *The Mikado*.   Upon this point Hubbard,
the constable, deposed: "I asked Mr. Ashley whether it
was proper to search him for Knives, which he might do
us a Mischief with?   I ordered two Men [Hughes and
Mayhew] to search him.   *They searched him*; but not for
Money; I never enquired for Money, for my part."   Of
course, had the Jew been then possessed of the famous
ducats, this search should have disclosed them.   When

---

[1] *The Case of Henry Simons*, p. 66.

the ducats were found in Ashley's pocket, Simons exclaimed: "God stroaken!" Witness made no answer.
"*Q.*—Did not you say 'God damn you! God Almighty
hath nothing to do with such a Villain as you?' *A.*—I
cannot tell whether I did or not say so."

Thomas Mayhew, a new witness, said that he and
Hughes, "the runaway Taylor," who had testified at the
former trial but was now, like De Quincey's Toad-in-the-
hole, "Non est inventus," were charged by Hubbard with
warding the prisoner. *He was not searched.* Mayhew was
with the party at the Saracen's Head, and professed to
describe how he saw the Jew put the ducats into Ashley's
pocket, giving the same account as his vanished colleague.
He was subpœnaed at the last trial, but was not called.
When the incident occurred, "They [Ashley and Simons]
were close to the Fire." The "four Creatures," it may be
mentioned, all placed them by the window.

Eleanor Brown, the cook, repeated her evidence.
She heard the Jew say, "You robbed me, you got my
Gelt, you have got my Ducats!" He spoke "very plain,"
and she understood every word he said. On the discovery
of the ducats Simons seemed delighted: "He said 'Ducats,
Gelt, Mooney!' and looked pleasant when he saw Mr.
Ashley had his Money. He was not angry till I came to
speak." This probably in reference to some flowers of
speech which, Gampwise, she had strewn on the accused.
Sarah Penney, her assistant, corroborated: "I heard
Eleanor Brown say she saw his Hand under Mr. Ashley's
Pocket-lid." Sarah Crabb, chambermaid, gave similar
evidence: "I saw Nell Brown hold up her Fist at him and
say she saw his Hand at his [Ashley's] Pocket several
Times." Simons spoke in broken English, "but so plain
as I understood him very well." The two Sarahs were not
examined at the previous trial. Hitherto unproductive,
they here emulate their biblical namesake in being better
late than never.

For the defence, Israel Levi, who came from Holland

with the Jew, swore that Simons could not speak a word of English; "when he wanted Bread or any thing he was forced to make use of Signs." When he set out on his return journey he was penniless, save for 2s. 6d.; witness gave him another half-crown to help him on his way to Harwich. Berend Abrahams, whose wife had counted the ducats in Simons' belt, saw him the next day in Duke's Place, after the robbery at Cranford Bridge; the belt was then empty. "I trusted him with Victuals and Lodging about a Month. He sent me to sell his Silk Gown for him, which I did in Monmouth Street for Seven Shillings. He paid me the Seven Shillings which he owed me, and I gave him a Shilling again. He begged Charity from one House to another, and also pawned his Veil"—which, as we have learned, infers in a Jew the maximum of penury. A body of reputable Hebrews succeeded one another in the box, each bearing witness to the decency and destitution of the defendant. Henry Keys, who acted as the Jew's interpreter in the Goddard case, said: "Then Mr. Simons could not speak a Word of English, and I question if he could speak two Words of English when he set out for Harwich. I am positive he could not express such Words as Eleanor Brown says he did; nor could he understand her [saying] what she hath mentioned in Court."

Joseph Isaacs, "the women's-pocketmaker," repeated his account of how he and Simons encountered Ashley on the road. He gave minute particulars of the interview, describing the production of the ducats, the conversation, the appearance of the chaise, etc., and was unshaken by cross-examination. Whereupon the prosecutor most irregularly intervened: "I declare in the Presence of Almighty God there was no Man with Simons; and every Tittle this Man says, as I hope for Salvation, is false, as there is a God in Heaven! Christ have Mercy upon us! It was not so dark but I could distinguish a Man, if there had been any. As I hope to be saved, I did not produce any Money. I call God to be my Witness my Chaise is a very high

Chaise." Such testimony not being obtainable, the mortal
evidence had the last word: "It is a Single-horse Chaise,
and a very low Chaise." Mrs. Frances Bourne, keeper of
the posthouse at Witham, said that one day in October
last Mr. Ashley came to her house. "I had some Conversation with him about meeting the Jew on the Road.
I remember he told me he was going between Ilford and
Stratford; he met the Jew and stopped the Chaise and
talked with him, and asked if he remembered Goddard;
and likewise *either shewed or mentioned Ducats* to him, I
cannot say which; and likewise put his Finger to his
Throat, to signify something about his Throat being cut
by Goddard. And he said the Jew did not seem to understand him, and therefore he drove to London in order to
get a Warrant to take him up." This lady was not cross-
examined, neither did the prosecutor propose to call the
Almighty to confute her; so her evidence must be accepted
as true. It is confirmed by that of Mr. Thomas Foley, a
gentleman who was present at the interview.

Thomas Ford, Goddard's solicitor, deposed that Ashley
came to his house, asked for the warrant, and proposed to
execute it, if one of Ford's clerks would go with him.
"He offered it; and particularly for the sake of public
Justice. I should not have asked him to have went if he
had not offered it; he offered to go as a Friend of Goddard's." All which is in flat contradiction of the account
sworn to by Ashley.[1] Mr. Henry Creswell said he met
Ashley and Newman upon their expedition, and learning
their errand, pointed out that "Goddard was the proper
person to pursue him [Simons], if any. But he [Ashley]
was pretty warm, saying he would follow him to the last
or to the utmost."

---

[1] As Ashley reiterated in his pamphlet that the solicitor " solicited him to
go," promising to defray his expenses, and averred " that his prosecuting Mr.
Simons was by his [Ford's] advice and persuasion," that gentleman wrote a
letter to the Press, giving Ashley on each of these points the lie direct.—*Narrative*,
p. 24.

I saw him again in the Forenoon following; he was sitting at the " Saracen's Head " in this Town. There was Hubbard, the constable, and two or three more bringing the Jew up the Town; they pushed him into the " Saracen's Head "; they went into the back room; I followed them. They had a good many hard Words, calling him Villain and Rogue; the Jew fell a-crying, and lamented his Fate very much.

Q.—Who used those Words to him ?

A.—Hubbard and Mayhew and others. The poor Creature had a good deal of Uneasiness. I took a Turn out, but was backwards and forwards very often in the Room; but was not in the Room at the Time of the Ducats being found, but came in *after they were sealed up.* The People were saying he put Ducats into Mr. Ashley's Pocket, but I heard nothing about charging Ashley with robbing him. The Jew seemed under great Uneasiness that such a Thing should be charged upon him.[1]

William Prior Johnson said that on 7th October, the day before the Quarter Sessions, he met Ashley in the "Red Lion" at Ingatestone. He said he was in pursuit of the Jew. "I took him by himself and said, 'Why do you intermeddle so much?' He said, Goddard was a very honest Man, and that the Jew was a very great Rogue; and as Goddard lived on the Western Road, *he thought it might be of Service to him* [Ashley], *if he was assiduous in it, in his Trade among the Innkeepers on that Road.*" No mention is here made of "public Justice," a phrase which, in Mr. Ashley's mouth, would perhaps be more accurately rendered "public-house Justice." Luke Claxton, the boy on the road, deposed as follows:—

I was going of an Errand for my Master on Horseback. I met Mr. Ashley and Mr. Newman in a Post-Chaise. They asked me if I had met a Jew with a long Beard on the Road. I said I had come up a Lane into the Road. I went my Errand; and as I returned asked them the Reason why they asked me. They told me to ride on and see if I saw him, for he was a Highwayman. I rode on about a Quarter of a Mile and saw him; I turned and asked them if they would swear he was a Highwayman? They said " Yes, a Highwayman, a Highwayman! take hold of him." There was a Lad with a Cart came to my Assistance before they came up with the Post-Chaise. When they came they said he was

---

[1] *The Case of Henry Simons*, p. 103.

a Highwayman. We took him to Witham. Mr. Ashley said he was a Highwayman and we should search him for Knives. I was by when he was searched; they felt in all his Pockets, but I saw nothing taken out.[1]

The Rev. John Tindal told how at the request of Ashley he, as a Justice of the Peace, endorsed the warrant granted by Mr. Alderman Gascoyne for the Jew's arrest.

There was a great Rumour before the Coffee-house Door. . . . I found at the same time the Constable of Witham and other Persons were using him [Simons] in such a Manner as I never saw a Murderer or a Highwayman. I addressed myself to the People, and asked them whether they were Barbarians or not; and told them they appeared like an English Mob, to use a Foreigner so. Then I turned to Mr. Ashley and asked what he wanted with me? He said, " I desire you would commit this Man." The Jew was coming close to the Steps. I said, " I have no Business to commit him; you must carry him to the original Jurisdiction. Said he, " Sir, who is to defray the Expences ? " Said I, " See you to that." [2]

Mr. Tindal then spoke to the prisoner in English, French, and Portuguese: "I found he knew no Language I could understand, and could not make him understand one Syllable."

He appeared in the greatest Agonies that ever I saw or any Man could express. At last he took hold of my Breeches Pocket and said, " Ducats, Ducats, Ducats, Ducats ! " very ,loud. Somebody said, " He is going to swear you robbed him of Ducats." Said I, " He hath just said enough to let me know he is the poor Jew that was robbed of Ducats by Goddard, as we have seen in the public Papers." [3]

Crisp Gascoyne, Esquire, repeated his former evidence. When he asked the prisoner if he spoke Dutch, "he jumped from the Corner of the Room through all the People, rushed upon me with great Eagerness, and still kept on in his own Language with all the Joy he could express, for that Somebody had spoke to him in a Language he

---

[1] *The Case of Henry Simons*, p. 105.
[2] *Ibid.*, p. 106.
[3] This incident throws a suggestive light upon the subsequent happenings in the parlour.

understood. He jumped to me and hugged me; the People cried out, 'Stand away, you Rascal, you want to pick the Alderman's Pocket.'" Witness asked him as to the truth of the accusation and whether he had charged Ashley with the robbery; "he denied it as strongly as a Man could do; he called God to Witness, and most heavily complained, and appeared in great Affliction, and expressed the greatest Innocency in the Affair." Mr. Golding Greggs, who was at the inn at the time, said the prisoner's language was quite unintelligible. "Hubbard acted as Interpreter for the Jew, and at such Times he would address himself to the Company in general. Q.—Did his Interpretations gain Credit? A.—With People that knew as little of that Language as I, it did."

Hyam Levi repeated his evidence regarding Ashley's visit to him in Duke's Place and the weighing of the ducats, as before narrated. Two of these ducats had been pierced. "I went away to the Polander's Lodgings, and asked him if any of his Ducats had Holes in them, seeing that these two had that he [Ashley] shewed me. The Polander said there were about Twenty of them had, which his Wife used to wear about her Neck." One of the three ducats found in Ashley's pocket was proved to have a hole in it.[1] The inference is obvious. Elizabeth Ward said she "lived with Jacob Abrahams in October last in Duke's Place"—but in what capacity was not stated. She corroborated Levi as to the two visits of Ashley there, and the weighing of the ducats. Pointing to Ashley in Court, the witness said that "she knows him very well." Margaret Gough, another handmaid of Abrahams, confirmed her companion. Mrs. Frances Bourne, recalled as to the character of Thomas Mayhew, said she knew him well.

---

[1] " These Ducats were seal'd up and produced in Court on the first Trial of Simons at Chelmsford, and one of them had a Hole in it. H. Levi in his Evidence says the Ducat that Ashley weighed at Jacob Abrahams' House had a Hole in it. This Evidence was given in Court on the first Trial *before the Ducats were opened there*."—*The Case of Henry Simons*, p. 31, *n*.

I know Characters are of great Consequence, and to meddle with them is a tender Point; but as I am called, I must speak the Truth. He is a Man of a very indifferent one. He is of no sort of Business, but is an idle drunken Fellow.[1]

The case for the defence was here closed, and the following "Further Evidence for the King" was led. Two men of Witham who saw the Jew handcuffed said that he cried out, "You hurt my Floish!" Hubbard, the constable, recalled, said the Jew cried, "Oh, my Floish, oh, my Floish!" He also asked for water, wine, and brandy "in his own Language." This officer, as we know, was a specialist in High Dutch. Mr. Ashley, recalled, was given this further and final opportunity of vindicating his fair fame:—

I call Heaven to Witness that it is all as false as God is true in Heaven. I have not been in Duke's Place for, I am sure, six, seven, eight, or twelve Years. I never saw that Man in my life 'til last Assizes. Every Tittle he hath said, I call God to Witness, is entirely false, as God is my Saviour.[2]

Six London publicans having given glowing testimony to the righteous dealings of Ashley, with whom they had all done business, one John Ellice was adduced to attack the character of Abrahams' handmaid:

I live at Dockhead, Surry. I have known Elizabeth Ward about ten Years.

Q.—What is her general Character?
A.—It is a very infamous one.
Q.—Should you credit her on her Oath?
A.—No, I should not; I only happened to see her in Court.

Cross-Examination.

Q.—Did you come down with Mr. Ashley?
A.—I did, but I am an utter Stranger to him.[3]

The prisoner was, in Ashley's phrase of his friend

---

[1] *The Case of Henry Simons*, p. 113. [2] *Ibid.*, p. 114. [3] *Ibid.*, p. 115.

Goddard, "honourably acquitted," the jury arriving at their verdict in eight minutes.

Here endeth the second trial.

The evidence given at these two trials affords one of the most flagrant instances of perjury with which I am familiar—always excepting, of course, the palmary example of the Tichborne Claimant. Each reader may choose for himself that witness whom he deems to be the prettiest liar; personally, my preference is for the prosecutor, Mr. James Ashley, who in his peculiar line seems to me able to give his fellow-false witnesses a stroke a hole. It has been suggested, not without some show of reason, that he was "the other Person" associated with Goddard in the robbery at the "White Hart," which would account for his whole-souled interest in that nefarious business, his virulent persecution of the victim, and his possession of ducats which indubitably formed part of the spoil. That the Jew when he last left London was wellnigh penniless —certainly ducatless—is beyond doubt. Even had he been possessed of the three ducats, the only conceivable motive for putting them in Ashley's pocket must have been in order to charge him with robbery, and so carry the war into the enemy's camp. But this it is proved by Mr. Alderman Gascoyne he refused to do, although interrogated to that end at the time by a magistrate who understood his language. It is probable that the poor man, having seen the day before Ashley, in his chaise, produce from his pocket ducats which he (the Jew) justly believed to be some of those stolen from him by Goddard, did put his hand in the pocket to see if they were still there. Or it may be that, as in the case of the friendly clergyman at the inn door, he merely took hold of the pocket to indicate that he had been robbed.

It is satisfactory to learn that Ashley, though he seems to have escaped a well-merited prosecution for perjury, suffered somewhat in his celebrated pocket. In the account of the affair which he published to vindicate his conduct as a man and a vintner, that indignant brandy-merchant complains:—

> In the mean time actions having been brought against me, as the prosecutor, [Hubbard] the constable, Richard Taylor, and John Newman, on account of Mr. Ford's altering the warrant, as before set forth in the evidence of John Newman, and thereby ignorantly detaining the said Henry Simons illegally in custody, till the warrant was properly backed. This cause was tried before the Lord Chief-Justice Lee, at Guildhall, London, the 9th day of July 1752, where such a number of Jew witnesses were produced, and some others, who swore so very extraordinarily that the jury were induced to give a verdict for Two Hundred Pounds against me, Richard Taylor, and John Newman.[1]

The swearing must have been exceeding hard to surprise such an expert as Mr. Ashley. "The action," we elsewhere learn, "was for an assault and false imprisonment. The ill treatment the plaintiff received being fully proved, the jury, after withdrawing about 10 minutes, brought in a verdict for him, with £200 damages."[2] The costs were taxed at £70. It is pleasant to note that the award was made the day after James Ashley's lying namesake had graced the pillory. As his other accomplices had made themselves scarce, one hopes that the defendant, as the nursery rhyme goes, "had to pay for all."

The case of *Ashley* v. *Simons* was quoted as an authority in 1754 on the famous trial of Elizabeth Canning for wilful and corrupt perjury.[3] Mr. Ashley had at least the satisfaction of establishing a precedent.

"On this decision," we read, "Mr. Ashley published his case and appeal; and having taken a house on Ludgate-hill, opened it as a punch-house, *pro bono publico*, and drew considerable trade by selling that beverage from two-penny glasses to any quantity. The pamphlet, with the portrait of Simons, was sold by Mr. Ashley to his customers

---

[1] *The Case and Appeal of James Ashley*, p. 23.
[2] *Gentleman's Magazine*, 1752, vol. xxii. p. 334.
[3] *State Trials*, vol. xix. pp. 680–692.

at this place, and at his brandy-warehouse in Bread-street, at the price of sixpence. Finding his punch-trade extremely beneficial, he relinquished his other pursuits, and died at Ludgate-hill in 1776, aged seventy-eight years." [1] So altruism turned out a good investment after all.

---

[1] Caulfield's *Remarkable Persons*, vol. iii. p. 27.

CLOSED DOORS;

OR, THE GREAT DRUMSHEUGH CASE

CLOSED DOORS;

OR, THE GREAT DRUMSHEUGH CASE

Tell it not in Gath, publish it not in the streets of Askelon ; lest
the daughters of the Philistines rejoice, lest the daughters of the uncir-
cumcised triumph.   —*The Second Book of Samuel.*

THE fair face of Edinburgh is still her fortune, despite
the fact that her civic wardens have neglected few
opportunities to spoil her beauty.   Poets have hymned her
praises, artists have preserved her features, historians have
chronicled her charms ; but over and beyond such tributes
to her physical perfections does she plume herself on her
respectability.   She sits upon her hills a Cæsar's wife,
above suspicion, and contemplates with complacency the
shortcomings of her sister cities.   Taxed by her enemies—
for who can escape the malice of the froward ?—with being
poor and proud, socially snobbish, and intellectually narrow,
not even her most inveterate rival has ever dared to call
her naughty.   Secure in her monopoly of that singular
attribute a moral sense, she can even spare a sigh for the
wickedness of Glasgow and the knaveries of Aberdeen.

When, therefore, in the year of grace 1810, Auld Reikie
found herself confronted with a blazing scandal, involving
no negligible members of the herd—who are not expected
to behave with propriety—but persons of position and
repute, it is scarcely surprising that she should use every
means to suppress the infamous conflagration; and,
indeed, so capably was this performed that not only was
the fire extinguished, but its very ashes were concealed
from the gaze of a profane posterity, and with a Podsnapian

flourish of her right arm the whole business was swept out
of existence.   The feat is the more remarkable, seeing that
the affair got into the Court of Session, where the proceedings of which it was the occasion engaged the attention of
their Lordships for many years, though actually disposed
of by the House of Lords.   Yet no trace of this prodigious
lawsuit, described by the Lord Ordinary as a *cause célèbre*,
has survived in the official reports or in the legal literature
of the time; no word of it is to be found in contemporary
journals, letters, or biographies; and so far as available
printed records go, the facts of the case are become as
impalpable as the personality of Mrs. Harris.

How comes it, then, in view of the elaborate precautions
taken to ensure oblivion, that I am in a position to frustrate,
more than a century after the event, this so successful
conspiracy of silence? Well, it happened that two at least
of the counsel engaged in the cause preserved their sets
of the printed papers, notwithstanding an order of Court
that twenty copies only should be privately printed for
the use of judges, counsel, and agents, and that these, on
the conclusion of the matter, should be destroyed.   My set
belonged to the celebrated Scots advocate, John Clerk,
afterwards raised to the Bench with the judicial title of
Lord Eldin, and includes the holograph draft of his speech
for the pursuers.   The volume, a handsome quarto, bound
as beseems its price and rarity, and bearing the familiar
bookplate of its late owner, formed No. 8701 of the 8935
lots composing the catalogue of the twenty-eight days'
sale, at Edinburgh in 1886, of the library of John White-
foord Mackenzie, W.S., the well-known collector.   For
some reason, probably puritanic, it was withdrawn from
sale and not exposed to public roup; many years later it
turned up in the hands of an Edinburgh bookseller, from
whom I acquired it—as Trapbois would say, for a consideration—by private bargain.   I fondly imagined my *trouvaille*
to be the sole survivor of the judicial holocaust until I
discovered that a similar set of papers, which had belonged

to James Moncrieff, advocate, also of counsel for the pursuers, was preserved in the Law Library of the Faculty of Advocates in the Parliament House, at Edinburgh.[1] But I doubt if any other copies escaped the vigilance of the custodiers of public morals.

Why, it may still be asked, should I, thus *longo intervallo*, violate the secrecy in which this ancient scandal is enshrouded, and revive for an ignorant, and presumably innocent, generation the shocking facts which their forebears blushed to envisage and did their best to stifle? My reason is twofold: As a conscientious explorer of the dark continent of crime, having discovered this uncharted territory, I feel it my duty to divulge my find; further, frankly I have not the heart to suffer such unique material to remain unused. Increasing scarcity of grist for my criminous mill forbids so wanton a prodigality. I admit that at first sight the subject may appear prohibitive; but I have ripely pondered the matter, and having considerable experience in the negotiation of thin ice, I flatter myself I can execute my delicate task without disaster to the writer or detriment to the reader. Of the legal interest and sociologic value of the essay I am bold to think there can be no question. If Mrs. Grundy does not like the performance, it is open to the dame to lump it. And I hereby formally give her notice that ladies are not admitted. Should she disregard the warning, it is at her proper peril. Shut the door.

I.

REGIMENT OF WOMEN

In the first decade of the nineteenth century there stood, somewhere about the north-east corner of Drumsheugh Gardens in the West End of Edinburgh, a certain genteel establishment for the board and education of young ladies. Hard by the house ran the highway to the north; past the old toll-house that still stands beside the bridge across the

---

[1] *Session Papers*, Moncrieff Collection, vol. xxi. (1811–1821).

valley; thence diving down Bell's Brae to the village of Water of Leith; climbing the northern slope to the hamlet of Dean; and so, by Ravelston and Cramond Brig, to the Hawes Inn at the Queen's Ferry. The school, originally two houses which, by inversion of present-day practice, had been converted into one, faced south, with a terraced garden in front, and consisted of two floors and a sunk storey. On the ground floor were the drawing-room and the schoolroom; on the upper floor, three bedrooms and a dressing-room. At each end of the house a separate staircase led to the bedroom flat, in which there was no passage, the several rooms opening out of one another— an awkward, and as afterwards proved, an unfortunate arrangement.

The priestesses of this scholastic temple, twin tenders of the virgin flames of which it was the shrine, were two gentlewomen of high endowments and fair repute. The senior partner, Miss Marianne Woods, was twenty-eight at the time in question, the daughter of a respectable merchant-tailor in London, and a niece of the famous Edinburgh actor, William Woods, "the Scottish Roscius" of the old Theatre-Royal, and the friend of the poets Fergusson and Burns. From the age of seven she had been adopted by her uncle, and since his death in 1802 her home was with his widow, whom she regarded as a mother.[1] With a view to earning her own bread she was given the best possible education; she assisted her uncle for a time in giving lessons in elocution; and having duly qualified for the teaching profession, she obtained an appointment as assistant mistress in Camden House Academy, a fashionable boarding-school for girls, near London. While attending classes in Edinburgh she made the acquaintance of a fellow-student, Miss Jane Pirie, the daughter of an Edinburgh writer, and a year younger than herself. Miss Pirie also

---

[1] Mrs. Ann Woods herself had been on the boards—*Kay's Portraits*, vol. i. p. 113, wherein she is depicted with Mrs. Siddons in the tragedy of *Douglas*. Her niece was never an actress.

had received a liberal education to equip herself for the post of governess in families of position, and among the situations which she occupied with credit to herself and satisfaction to her employers were those in the households of General Dirom, Captain Lowes, Lord Lucan, Mrs. Campbell of Kailzie, and Mrs. Campbell of Strachur. The close and warm friendship existing between these two young ladies, their mutual esteem, and regard for their respective accomplishments, led them to form the idea of uniting their forces and setting up a boarding-school on their own account.

The house at Drumsheugh, though as a residence small and inconvenient, and singularly ill-adapted to their purpose, was chosen for the scene of their joint adventure, in which were embarked the whole worldly resources of each party. As it happened, despite all their wisdom and learning, neither was a woman of business; the terms of their copartnery were not defined in writing, and were susceptible of misconstruction and dispute. The school was opened by Miss Woods alone at Whitsunday 1809, Miss Pirie's engagement with Mrs. Campbell of Strachur not terminating till Martinmas. When in November of that year Miss Pirie joined Miss Woods, she found that her friend had installed as coadjutrix her venerable aunt, Mrs. Woods, late of the Theatre-Royal, Shakespeare Square. The old lady contributed nothing to the common stock, yet with the acquisitiveness of age she demanded a share of the profits. Beyond looking after the young ladies' wardrobes the matron seems to have been scantily worth her salt. Of the troubles caused by this elderly female drone in the busy and restricted hive there will be much to say in the sequel.

The establishment, as I have said, was a genteel one; only young ladies of the first families were received as pupils; and it was fortunate to enjoy the patronage of Dame Helen Cumming Gordon, relict of umquhile Sir Alexander Cumming Gordon of Altyre and Gordonstoun,

Baronet, and residing when in town at No. 22 Charlotte
Square, Edinburgh. Her ladyship was loud and frequent
in commendation of the merits of the institution and the
virtues of its proprietors, and as the imprimatur of so grand
a dame sufficed for fashionable Edinburgh, the reputation
of the school was made. Perhaps her ladyship, in thus
furthering the fortunes of the venture, had her own axe
to grind. Her son had died in India, bequeathing to his
aristocratic parent a bastard, borne to him by a black
woman. The child, a girl, with the courtesy title of Miss
Jane Cumming, having been at a native school in Calcutta
till she was eight years old, in 1803 was brought to Scotland by a black attendant. She was sent first to a private
school in Elgin, where she remained for six years, until, in
December 1809, her grandmother proposed to enter her
as a boarder at Drumsheugh. Apart from divers physical
and moral drawbacks later manifested, the young lady
was not _ex facie_ a desirable addition to the academic circle.
She was patently what is termed a person of colour—"one
unfortunately wanting in the advantages of legitimacy and
of a European complexion," as the Lord Ordinary later
phrased it; and popular prejudice runs in favour of the
lawful and white variety. The new school mistresses
received her with hesitation and reluctance; their mis-
givings, as we shall find, were only too well founded. But
Lady Cumming Gordon had entrusted to their care her two
legitimate grandchildren, the daughters of Sir Archibald
Dunbar of Northfield, Baronet; she had boomed their
seminary for all she was socially worth; so they agreed to
swallow the black draught, and her ladyship's encomiums
were warmer than ever.

During the brief period of the school's prosperity the
pupils included Miss Sandford, daughter of the Bishop of
Edinburgh ; Miss Cunynghame, daughter of Sir William
Cunynghame of Livingstone, Baronet; Miss Stirling,
daughter of the laird of Kippenross; Miss Anstruther,
daughter of General Anstruther; two Miss Edgars, two

Miss Frasers, the two Dunbars (who were day boarders);
Miss Janet Munro, "daughter of George Munro, Esquire,
residing in Elder Street," and the dusky damsel from the
East.[1] The latter was, in her own words, "going seven-
teen," having been born in 1795; Misses Munro and
Stirling, with whom alone we are concerned, were each
sixteen. Miss Cumming, by reason of her mixed blood,
was much the most mature of the three. The other girls'
ages ranged from fifteen to eleven.

But although the material welfare of the college was
thus assured, the glittering collegiate gold, so attractive to
old Mrs. Woods, was not without its secret alloy. Jane
Pirie, albeit possessed of many amiable qualities of head
and heart, was handicapped by what is euphemistically
termed the artistic temperament. Emotional and highly
strung, she was irritable and petulant, apt to take offence,
and as a friend very jealous and exacting. Miss Woods, of
a milder and more equable spirit, was at once the victim
of her aunt's pretensions and of the exigencies of her
associate. Now, Miss Pirie had not bargained for the
presence at Drumsheugh of the veteran artiste, whom
from the outset she regarded as an incubus. After she
arrived upon the scene of her labours she found that the
tradesmen's bills were made out in the name of the old
lady, who in some sort held herself out as the proprietor
of the business. Further, she had in the pecuniary pie a
finger which Miss Pirie deemed felonious. Poor Miss
Woods, between loyalty to her redundant relative and
affection for her domineering friend, had but a sorry time
of it. Jane Pirie was of a nagging habit, ever worrying
the bone of contention. Mrs. Woods afterwards deponed
that she (Jane) was from her first coming discontented and
unhappy, and behaved "in a very imperious manner" both
to herself and to her niece. Quarrels, disputes and tiffs,

---

[1] There were ten boarders in being, and two more were expected to join at
Martinmas 1811, bringing the company up to full strength; there were also
twelve day-scholars, so that the total number of pupils was twenty-four.

high words and frequent wranglings, punctuated with penitence, reconciliation, tears and kisses, formed the undercurrent of the placid academic stream. For it must always be borne in mind that for sweet propriety's sake, and the due maintenance of their authority, all these unseemly bickerings had to be veiled from the knowledge of the scholars. And when, as may be done from the plan of the house prepared for the trial, the grotesquely limited stage upon which this tragi-comedy was played is visualized, and the twenty watchful eyes—assuming each young lady boarder to be furnished with the usual complement—under which the performance was perforce enacted are not forgotten, it is obvious that the strain upon the chief actors' nerves must have been well-nigh intolerable.

Two servants only were kept, girls of nineteen and sixteen, with whose aid these ladies had to run the house. There were no assistant teachers, so the whole weight of the curriculum by which the pupils profited was borne by the two mistresses alone—Mrs. Woods being at best but an added burden. She who of yore had played Leonora in *The Mourning Bride*, now impersonated to tragic effect the Old Man of the Sea in this extravagant after-piece. But, despite the state of matters behind the scenes, profit the pupils did; for it is clearly proved that their mental, moral, and spiritual needs were carefully, nay, even scrupulously, supplied, to the complete contentment as well of their parents and guardians as of the girls themselves—with one exception, shortly to be noted.

The hours at Drumsheugh were full and strenuous. The young ladies rose at 6.45 in summer and 7.15 in winter, and the labours of the day were ushered in with prayers, which all were required to attend.

Whilst breakfast was preparing the pursuers [Misses Woods and Pirie] heard the young ladies say part of their lessons. After breakfast the writing-master came at nine o'clock ; and from the time of his departure at ten, throughout the whole day the pursuers were constantly employed till between eight and nine o'clock at night in severally teaching

HAND SKETCH of the PURSUERS HOUSE at DRUMSHEUGH

BED ROOM FLOOR

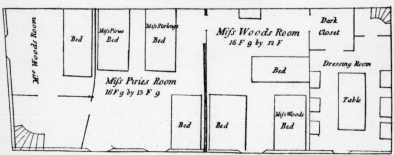

Mr Woods Room

Bed

Miss Piries Bed

Miss Stirlings Bed

Miss Woods Room
16 F 9 by 12 F

Dark Closet

Dressing Room

Miss Piries Room
16 F 9 by 13 F 9

Bed

Table

Bed Bed Miss Woods Bed

DRAWING ROOM FLOOR.

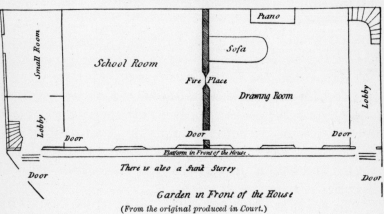

Small Room

School Room

Lobby

Piano

Sofa

Fire Place

Drawing Room

Lobby

Door Door Door

Platform in Front of the House.

There is also a Sunk Storey

Door Door

Garden in Front of the House
(From the original produced in Court.)

[To face p. 118.

the different branches of education to the young ladies, either in classes
or singly, with the exception of an hour allowed for walking and the time
allowed for dinner and tea. The pursuers made it a rule never to allow
the young ladies to be with a master without one or other of themselves
being present. They also, by alternate weeks, walked out along with the
young ladies ; and the one whose turn it was not to walk out remained
at home, and was understood to receive company ; that is, the friends
and relations of the young ladies who chose to inquire about them.[1]

When the business of the day was over, a short interval was
allowed "for playing with dumb-bells and similar useful
relaxations," concluding with evening prayers and the
reading of some sacred history. The young ladies then
.went upstairs to the common dressing-room, "where they
brushed their hair, teeth, &c.," and so to bed.

This must have been more easily said than done.
There were but three bedrooms, one of which was appro-
priated to the peculiar use and single occupation of the
ci-devant Leonora. The other chambers belonged respectively to the two partners. Each contained three beds ;
and we know from the proof that the two elder girls
habitually shared the couches of their mistresses, Jane
Cumming sleeping with Miss Pirie and Janet Munro with
Miss Woods. Thus five of the young ladies lay in each
small room, a fact that would horrify our sanitary inspec-
tors. It was the nightly custom of the partners, having
seen their charges safely abed, to recruit themselves after
the day's travail with a light refection. This was invariably
consumed by Miss Woods in the privy chamber of her aunt ;
Miss Pirie dispatched her solitary repast in the schoolroom.
Hence it is plain, from the structure of the house, that Miss
Woods, having finished her supper and given Leonora a fair
good-night, in order to reach her own room was bound to
traverse Miss Pirie's. On the other hand that lady, "after
having supped below stairs, and adjusted her night-dress
in the general dressing-room,[2] necessarily passed through

---

[1] *Answers for Pursuers*, p. 25.

[2] It is proved that Miss Pirie's night-gear included " a bedgown, wrapper, petticoat, and stockings " ! What would the modern silk-pyjama'd maiden say to that ?

the room of Miss Woods in passing to her own." Now,
what with work, worry, and old Mrs. Woods, this was the
only hour of the four-and-twenty that the two friends were
free to discuss the affairs of their little commonwealth;
and it was at such seasons, when the lights were out and
the pupils were, or should have been, asleep, that the con-
trite Jane was moved to confess her faults of temper and
other failures in discretion, and to receive from the injured
Marianne plenary absolution. But these midnight conferences had to be carried on by the parties in whispers,
one sitting or leaning on the other's bed, lest the slumbers
of the young ladies by whom they were environed should
be disturbed.

If the shepherdesses had their private troubles, the
members of the flock seemed happy and contented under
their strict but salutary sway. Especially did the black
sheep fawn upon them and strive to win their favours. To
drop the woolly metaphor, Miss Jane Cumming, conscious
of the disadvantages from which she suffered in competition
with her fair companions, sought by every artifice to in-
gratiate herself with the principals. She would "bespeak"
the mistress's arm—the place of honour—for the daily walk,
and had been on occasion heard audibly to "bless the day
she came to Drumsheugh." But beneath this outward
seeming the young lady, like her superiors, had her secret
source of bitterness. At her Elgin school discipline was
lax, and she had been allowed to do pretty much as she
liked—the local prestige attaching to the family of her
father doubtless receiving due weight. It was otherwise
at Drumsheugh. Servile protestations of affection were
insufficient to relieve her from the consequences of broken
rules and other misdemeanours. Her punishments were
frequent, she was often in disgrace; and so far from being
chastened by correction, she formed, as appears, a fixed
purpose at all costs to escape from the school and to
wreak signal vengeance upon her taskmistresses. Miss
Woods was wont to say of her that she had no heart;

it was soon seen that she had, and one to match her complexion.

After the summer holidays—June and July—the dissensions by which the government of Drumsheugh was rent became acute. Jane Pirie and Leonora were no longer on speaking terms; Miss Woods, outwearied by incessant warfare, spoke of abandoning her post and leaving them to fight it out—presumably with results similar to those attending the conflict of Kilkenny cats. Less desperate remedies prevailed. By the ghostly counsel and advice of the Rev. Simeon Reid, "Episcopal minister of Edinburgh," specially invoked to that end, the supererogatory dame was persuaded to resign her rôle of titular headmistress (together with the emoluments effeiring to that office), and to retire into private life upon a pension, leaving her adversary and her niece in possession of the stage. Her abdication was arranged to take place in November, when peace and prosperity were expected to reign at Drumsheugh.

II.

Scandal about Queen Elizabeth

It came to pass that on Wednesday, 14th November 1810, Miss Jane Cumming, having obtained leave of absence for the day, set forth from school to visit her grandmamma in Charlotte Square, then the westmost limit of the Modern Athens. Her way would lie by wood and field path, past the great mansion of my Lord of Moray, Drumsheugh House, which then stood on the site of Randolph Crescent. Since her importation from the East the ingenious damsel, if but an indifferent and unprofitable pupil, had made in other respects good use of her time and opportunities. We read of her in the pleadings of her patrician relative:

It was originally intended that she should be bred to business as a mantuamaker or milliner, that she might gain a livelihood by her own exertions in a reputable but inferior station in life. But the increasing esteem and attachment of the respondent [Lady Cumming Gordon] occasioned that plan to be given up, and it was determined that she should be introduced into the world as a daughter of the family.[1]

The youthful immigrant had early appreciated the possibilities of the position, and was well aware on which side her black bread was buttered. The time was now ripe when by a single word she could break in sunder her irksome educational bonds, go home for good, and take her share in the pleasures which Edinburgh society afforded. That day the word was spoken.

"Death and life," says King Solomon, "are in the power of the tongue." Even so astute and crafty a girl as Jane Cumming could hardly be expected to realise the far-reaching effects of her communication; her grandmother, an experienced woman of the world, ought certainly to have done so. The tale—"this most horrible story," as that lady truly termed it—was at once so monstrous and extravagant as to baffle belief. Yet just because it was incredible her ladyship believed it, as told by "a simple, innocent, veracious girl," to whose abominable report she gave "implicit credit." One should have thought that the first action of a lady thus situated would have been to order her carriage and drive to Drumsheugh, with a view to ascertaining by personal enquiry how matters really stood. Common fairness required that people implicated in so grave a charge ought to be given the earliest opportunity to meet, and if guiltless, to refute it. But Lady Cumming Gordon, accepting as gospel the revelations of the half-caste, without the slightest investigation passed sentence upon the traduced gentlewomen, and set about forthwith to compass their destruction. Next day Miss Jane returned to school as usual, the more effectually to blind the victims to the coming blow. Her affectionate, even fawning regard for her mistresses had suffered no abatement, and on her last day she accompanied Miss Woods to tea with the lady of Bishop Sandford. That

---

[1] *Answers for Defender*, p. 4.

night the dowager wrote divers momentous letters, of which the following will serve as samples.

(1)

Lady Cumming Gordon presents best compliments to Lady Cunynghame, and begs to inform her Ladyship that she has, for very serious reasons, taken her grandchildren from Miss Woods' and Pirie's school. As Lady Cumming was one of those who recommended the school to Lady Cunynghame, she feels it her duty very strongly to advise her to the same measure, *as soon as possible.*

(2)

Lady Cumming Gordon presents best compliments to Mrs. Anstruther. She thinks it right to inform her that she has found it necessary to-day, for serious reasons, to take away her grandchildren from Miss Woods' and Miss Pirie's school. As Lady Cumming recommended the school to Mrs. Campbell for Miss Anstruther, she wishes to give her the earliest information. Lady Cumming sent for her children home without assigning any reason but a wish to have them home ; and she will call and give Mrs. Anstruther her reasons for what she has done to-morrow.

(3)

Lady Cumming Gordon presents compliments to Miss Woods and Miss Pirie. She will be obliged to them to send her a statement of the Miss Dunbars' and Miss Jane Cumming's accounts ; as from Lady Dunbar's intending to come up immediately for her children, Lady Cumming does not find it convenient to allow them to return to school any more. She will likewise be obliged to them to send in Miss Jane Cumming's clothes, with the Misses Dunbar's books, music, &c.[1]

So effective were her ladyship's measures that within forty-eight hours all the pupils were one after another removed, "without any cause whatever being assigned," and the busy school, completely abandoned save for its distracted proprietors, became as Tadmor in the wilderness. The amazement and dismay of the schoolmistresses may be imagined. Immediately on receipt of Lady Cumming Gordon's note Miss Woods wrote to her ladyship as follows :—

Miss Woods and Pirie beg leave to address Lady Cumming Gordon. There has been some delay in the execution of her Ladyship's commands ;

---

[1] *Pursuers' Proof,* p. 135.

but as soon as possible they will be attended to. The extreme anxiety
of mind they are in can alone excuse the earnest entreaty they now
make to her Ladyship that she will candidly state to them every particular circumstance which has occasioned her Ladyship's disapprobation, and by its consequences seems to threaten their total ruin.[1]

To this request no answer was returned. Then Miss Pirie,
unable to support the mental agony induced by this unparalleled situation, wrote on 16th November to the
dowager's sixth daughter, Mary Cumming, with whom
she had some acquaintance, this moving appeal:

If ever you expect mercy from the God of mercy, tell what your
niece has said to injure two innocent persons, who have laboured for
nearly twelve months to improve her in every religious and moral virtue,
and who are thus cruelly repaid by her. We never did any thing to
offend her, excepting too rigidly discharging our duty towards her, and
too freely telling her of her faults. You are again implored, for the
sake of that God from whom you hope for mercy, to tell us of what she
accuses us, as the calumny has been traced to her, and she appears to
be the sole author of it. If ever Christian mercy or pity had a place in
your heart, do not delay to state *all* she says against us, as every hour's
delay increases the misery she has already occasioned.[2]

No notice was taken of this petition in which, for my ear
at least, there echoes the authentic accent of truth. If it
be false and feigned, then surely is Jane Pirie the vilest
hypocrite that ever affronted Heaven. I have been thus
careful to set out at length these letters, because I think
they throw light upon the characters of the writers, and
for the further reason that whereas every fact in the case
was fiercely contested, these documents at any rate speak
indisputably for themselves. The two helpless women
then dispatched Miss Pirie's sister, Margaret, who had been
governess to Lady Dunbar's children and was not concerned
in the mystery, to Charlotte Square, in order to find out
what was wrong. The envoy, denied an audience of the
dowager, was sent empty away.

One only of the matrons whose daughters were escaped
alive out of the nameless horrors of Drumsheugh had

---

[1] *Pursuers' Proof,* p. 136.   [2] *Ibid.*

the honesty and fairness to look before she leapt at the
worst conclusion. This honourable exception was Lady
Cunynghame. So soon as she received the dowager's
note, she too went to Charlotte Square upon a similar
errand. More fortunate than Margaret Pirie she was
received, but like her got no information. "What is the
matter?" she asked. "Is it scarlet fever?"—of which, as
appears, her ladyship stood in special dread. Lady Cumming
Gordon said that she was "not at liberty to tell." Lady
Cunynghame told her she most certainly should not take
away her child from school without knowing the reason;
that as there was so much mystery about it, she would go
herself to Miss Woods and state to her the manner in which
she was desired to remove her daughter. Lady Cumming
Gordon said that if her ladyship would call again,
"she would obtain leave to tell her"—presumably from
her secret informer. Lady Cunynghame, having made
enquiries of other parents, whom she found no better instructed than herself, accompanied by two friends, "Mrs.
Professor Dalzell" and Miss Drysdale, drove to Drumsheugh
and saw Miss Woods. "I suppose you know the purpose
of my coming here this morning?" said she; to which
Miss Woods replied, "I too well judge it." Here is her
ladyship's account of the interview:

The witness then said to her, "Miss Woods, I don't know what has
happened, but I am grateful to you for the kindness and attention you
have always shewn to my daughter; there is only Miss Drysdale, you,
and I present: if you have done any thing imprudent, and will disclose
it confidentially to me, you may rely on my advice and assistance to the
utmost of my power to extricate you from the scrape if possible, whatever it may be." That Miss Woods was much affected, and with great
emotion thanked the witness for her kindness, but said she could not
avail herself of it, for she was utterly ignorant of what was laid to her
charge and was not conscious of any thing. That Miss Woods, then in
great agitation, threw her arms round Miss Drysdale, and earnestly
entreated her and Mrs. Dalzell to endeavour to find out of what she and
her partner were accused.[1]

---

[1] *Pursuers' Proof*, p. 128.

So affected was Lady Cunynghame by Miss Woods' distress that she said she could not bring herself to take her daughter away; but Miss Woods said that as nearly all the girls had already gone, her ladyship had better do so. The mother persisted, and left her daughter—till the next day. Having by that time enjoyed the benefit of the dowager's confidence, Lady Cunynghame removed her child. "From her communication with the defender, she thought it improper to shew any more patronage to Miss Woods, and has not seen her since." It says much for the native genius of the Eurasian that she should have so framed her accusation that the mere whisper of its nature was enough to alienate the sympathy and goodwill of the generous Lady Cunynghame. Scarlet fever her ladyship was prepared to face; moral contagion was another story.

And now, like Lady Cumming Gordon, having kept back the secret to the last possible moment, I am compelled reluctantly to indicate the purport of the black girl's blacker charge. Briefly, and with as little offence as may be, it was that these two gentlewomen had conceived for one another an inordinate affection, which they did not scruple wantonly to display in the very presence of their pupils. When the subjects of this foul aspersion at length learned, "by dark and distant hints," what was the nature of the crime imputed to them, they at once consulted their law agent, and were advised to raise an action against the dowager for defamation of character. As, in addition to social damnation, the slander had brought upon them financial ruin, they concluded for damages of £10,000. In view of the high inexpediency of thrashing out such a question in the law courts, proposals were on both sides made for an extra-judicial settlement; but as nothing short of a complete withdrawal of the charge would satisfy the pursuers, while the defender insisted that they must tacitly admit their guilt by leaving the country, it is not surprising that the parties failed to come to terms. The blind obstinacy and rashness of Lady Cumming

Gordon is well-nigh inconceivable. Her ladyship did not scruple to write to Mrs. Stirling of Kippenross in order to induce her daughter to homologate the half-caste's tale, a letter which the Lord Justice-Clerk characterised as "very near subornation of perjury," and of which his Lordship expressed the strongest disapproval. Two features of that story could by the least enquiry have been found demonstrably false, viz. that the mutual relations of these ladies was familiar gossip among their pupils; and that so notorious was their infamy, that during the school walks they were hissed and hooted by the washerwomen at the Water of Leith. Further, she had cited in corroboration of her tale the testimony of Charlotte Whiffin, one of the servants at Drumsheugh who, as we shall see, gives the lie direct to her allegations. Yet the single word of this "simple, innocent, veracious girl" sufficed for the defender and her advisers.

And here I would observe, with reference to my treatment of the subject, I fully realise that I am between two fires: belated Victorians will account me overbold; resolute psychologists will deem me not bold enough. But, in fact, had the accusation been well founded, nothing would have induced me to deal with it. I make no claim to the licence granted to Professor Krafft-Ebing, Mr. Havelock Ellis, and other scientific exponents of such problems. No; my interest in the case resides in the fact that *the charge was false*; also in the astounding audacity of the traducer, and in the long legal duel to which her precocious wickedness gave rise. Further, there are in the evidence touches of local colour that appeal to me as a lover of Auld Reikie; for example, the house of the dowager in Charlotte Square, where the Indian shot her poisoned bolt and the trouble began. How that one day Miss Pirie and her juvenil΄ train, "out upon their walk, at the head of the [Bruntsfield] Links, met a crazy man"—possibly an unsuccessful golfer—"who frightened some of the young ladies." How Miss Woods accompanied Jane

Cumming when that interesting young Christian went to her first Communion "at Bishop Sandford's Chapel"— St. George's Church in York Place, where Sir Walter was wont to worship. How, during the holidays, Miss Cumming did vulgarly "take a walk upon the Castle Hill [1] on a Sunday evening and without the knowledge of the pursuers," and was by them found fault with for such unladylike and unsabbatical behaviour. How, "on a windy night in October," Miss Pirie, having gone to spend an evening with friends in St. James's Square, was forced to stay the night, "and could not return for the violence of the wind"—a veritable Edinburgh vignette. How the women at the village of Water of Leith washed, like the dowager, their dirty linen in public, and in that as yet uncontaminated stream. And how my Lady Cunynghame, "dining one day at Mr. Walker's at Dalry," met Lady Cumming Gordon and asked her what she thought about the new school at Drumsheugh, "when her ladyship gave it the highest character."

III.

THE TEN YEARS' CONTENTION

John Webster has given to his tragi-comedy, *The Devil's Law-Case*, the quaint sub-title, "When Women go to Law, the Devil is full of Business." Though not himself a party to the great cause of *Woods and Pirie* v. *Cumming Gordon*, nor officially of counsel therein, no doubt the Prince of Darkness held a watching brief in the interests of his own. Apart from his presence, it was a very strong Bar. John Clerk, Adam Gillies, and James Moncrieff for the pursuers; the Hon. Henry Erskine, David Cathcart, George Cranstoun, and John Hay Forbes

---

[1] "While dandring cits delight to stray
　　To Castlehill, or public way,
　　Whare they nae other purpose mean
　　Than that fool cause o' being seen."
　　　　　　　　—ROBERT FERGUSSON : *Auld Reikie.*

JOHN CLERK.
(From a drawing by Robert Scott Moncrieff.)

[To face p. 129.

for the defender.[1] The agents were respectively James Balfour and James Mackenzie, both Writers to the Signet.

John Clerk was as powerful an advocate as any then practising at the Scots Bar.[2] Like the late Sir Edward Marshall Hall in England and our own Mr. Craigie Aitchison, he was reckoned the most effective pleader of his day. His first success was his sensational appearance, soon after donning the robe, in the famous trial of Deacon Brodie, when as a forensic David he gave battle to that Goliath of the Bench, Lord Braxfield. His zeal for his client's interests was measureless, records Lord Cockburn. "He did not take his fee, plead the cause, hear the result, and have done with it; but gave the client his temper, his perspiration, his nights, his reason, his whole body and soul, and very often the fee to boot." [3] His colleague James Moncrieff, "a son of Sir Harry, and worthy of the name," [4] was so conscientious in his profession that Jeffrey dubbed him "The Whole Duty of Man." These two counsel were jointly responsible for the written pleadings in which it was then the practice to present to the Court the legal arguments for the parties; those prepared for the pursuers in this case are models of their kind. They were of course supplemented by verbal oratory, when his clients had the further advantage of Clerk's vehement and fiery eloquence.

The summons, dated, signeted, and served on 27th November 1810, by which the action was begun, *inter alia* makes mention "that within these few weeks past the good name, character, and reputation of the pursuers have been unjustly and cruelly defamed and injured by means of false, injurious, and defamatory allegations and

---

[1] All these eminent counsel (except the brilliant but disappointed Harry Erskine) afterwards rose to the judicial Bench, with the respective titles of Lords Eldin, Gillies, and Moncrieff; Alloway, Corehouse, and Medwyn.

[2] The best account of Clerk's personality and achievement is that in *The Scottish Bar Fifty Years Ago*, illustrated with portraits by Robert Scott Moncrieff. Edinburgh: 1871.

[3] *Life of Lord Jeffrey*, vol. i. p. 202.

[4] *Ibid.*, pp. 205-209; see also Cockburn's *Memorials of his Time*, passim.

insinuations," raised and propagated verbally and in
writing by the defender, "to the effect that the pursuers
had been guilty of some very improper or criminal conduct
which rendered them unfit to be trusted with the education
of young ladies"; that upon her advice all the pupils had
been removed by their parents or guardians; and the
school itself, "upon which they solely depended for their
future prospects, has been entirely ruined." The action
was called before Lord Meadowbank, Ordinary, in the
Outer House, on 8th December.[1] After sundry hearings
of counsel "with shut doors," his Lordship ordered the
defender to prepare a written statement, to be transmitted
to him under seal, which was duly done. On 31st January
1811 the Lord Ordinary, "having repeatedly heard counsel
at great length" upon the statement, reported the case,
with his notes thereon, to the Second Division.[2] On 16th
February their Lordships ordered the defender to lodge
a condescendence "of the facts she avers and offers to
prove"; and on 2nd March appointed the pursuers to
give in answers to the same. Both were to be transmitted
to the Lord Justice-Clerk under seal, to be by him communicated to the other judges; and the clerk of Court
was directed to keep the process in a sealed cover, "and
not to exhibit the same except to the agents in person."

---

[1] Allan Maconochie, first Lord Meadowbank, was a very able judge and the
father of Alexander Maconochie, who succeeded him on the Bench with the
same title. The latter once interrupted John Clerk when pleading before him
to ask the distinction between the words " also " and " likewise," which Clerk
was using in his argument, and which the judge deemed synonymous. " Your
Lordship's father," retorted Clerk, " was Lord Meadowbank ; your Lordship is
Lord Meadowbank *also*, but not *likewise* ! "

[2] When, in 1808, Lord Chancellor Eldon's Bill for the reform of the Court
of Session became law (48 Geo. III. c. 151), the old Court, long and honourably
known as " The Fifteen," as all the judges sat together, was divided into two
Divisions. " Instead of the present system of four judges in each, the Act of
1808 provided that there should be eight in the First Division, including the
Lord President, and seven in the Second, including the Lord Justice-Clerk.
Two judges, one for each Division, were to sit each week in the Outer House.
The Court sat as one chamber for the last time on the 11th of July 1808."—
Omond's *Lord Advocates of Scotland*, vol. ii. p. 227. See *Kay's Portraits*, No. cxxx.

Such solicitude for the morals of the macers would have been grateful to my Lord Glenkindie.

On 9th March their Lordships, having considered the condescendence and answers, allowed a proof, and remitted to the Lord Justice-Clerk (Hope) and the Lord Ordinary (Meadowbank) to take the evidence *in camera.* Thereafter both parties moved the Court "to permit the proof to be printed, under the limitations that a person on whose secrecy dependence could be placed be procured to undertake the work; that the number of copies should be limited to twenty; and that the whole of these, at the conclusion of the cause, should be destroyed or otherwise disposed of under the authority of the Court," all which was directed to be done. (So that you and I, reader, in perusing these papers, are guilty of contempt and ought to be punished accordingly; but no doubt the reviewers will see to that.) The hearing of evidence, "with shut doors," began on 15th March and was not concluded till 23rd May.

To those familiar with present-day procedure and accustomed to the employment of common sense in the conduct of legal business, it is surprising to find that the parties to an action were not at that date competent witnesses in their own cause. Here the pursuers, in view of the exceptional circumstances of the case, offered themselves in evidence; but the defender objected to their admission as "unprecedented," so they were not examined. As was pointed out for them at the time, had they elected to proceed against Jane Cumming and her associate in slander, Janet Munro, the mouths of those young ladies, like the doors of the Court, would have been closed; and as no other evidence but theirs was forthcoming, the case would have collapsed. By calling Lady Cumming Gordon as defender, the pursuers made plain the way for the two handmaids of Truth.

The impressions of the judge who sees and hears the witnesses examined must ever afford a valuable commentary

on their evidence as printed. Here, it may be anticipated, both the Lords Commissioners (as they were called)
formed and expressed a very strong opinion that Jane
Cumming's story was, in the historic phrase of later times,
"a frigid and calculated lie," which so far as endorsed by
Munro, was due to the poisoning of that damsel's mind by
her more experienced companion. The defender, who on
account of the various devices whereby for ten years she
contrived to bolster up a bad case and drag her hapless
"pursuers" from Court to Court, might be named Lady
"Cunning" Gordon, with much art made Munro her first
and principal witness, calling "the only begetter" of the
slander merely to corroborate her! But it was established
by the evidence that Janet, a pretty Scots lass, not over-
burdened with brains, thought no evil of her mistresses
until she was contaminated by the foul imaginings of the
Indian. The judges before whom they were examined
comment upon the very different appearances made by
these girls in the box. Munro gave her evidence with
modesty and frankness, without more hesitation than its
indelicate nature required. She freely admitted that but
for the promptings of Cumming she should not have suspected that there was anything improper in the pursuers'
behaviour.

In the case of Miss Munro she had got a glimpse of a theory, which
she applies rashly and decides upon presumptuously, but I am willing to
believe, *bona fide*. Miss Cumming stands in a very different situation.
She is the inventress of the theory, and she alone of all the witnesses
takes the credit of understanding it. The married ladies are in this
respect as unfortunate as the unmarried . . .

Thus Lord Meadowbank; and as to the way in which
Cumming gave her evidence, his Lordship further observes:

My Lord President [1] and I concurred entirely in our opinion on the
manner in which it was delivered, viz. that the long silences in answer-

---

[1] Charles Hope of Granton, Lord Justice-Clerk at the time of the proof, was
promoted Lord President on 12th November 1811, *vice* Robert Blair of Avontoun,
deceased.

ing the questions sometimes indicated long deliberation how an answer might operate, sometimes great puzzle, under which invention was at work to get extricated; and that a daring attempt was betrayed to create impressions not supported by the truth of the fact; and all this accompanied with unaccountable concealment or forgetfulness, wherever there was room to apprehend that true or fair answers must operate in favour of the pursuers.[1]

"If I had sat as a single judge taking this proof," said the Lord Justice-Clerk, "I should have committed Miss Cumming for prevarication . . . and *I fear I was swayed by too much respect for the family of Lady Cumming in not doing so*" (!) His Lordship added that he had "sent a woman to the pillory for less prevarication than Miss Cumming was guilty of." "And I cannot help observing," he continued, "that any hesitation which she shewed in the course of her examination was *never* in the points of *indecency*,[2] but always when she was called on to reconcile her own contradictions. She was *thinking* and *contriving*." The italics are his Lordship's. So inveterate was she against her late mistresses, that when a point of guilt or innocence turned upon a single vowel in a word reported as overheard by her, the Lord Justice-Clerk notes "the teeth and bitterness" with which the witness insisted on the evil reading.

The defence set up for Lady Cumming Gordon was twofold; *bona fides*: that in speaking and writing as she did, she acted in good faith—which was a question of law; and *veritas convicii*: the truth of the charge—which was a question of fact. At the first hearing, it was stated that the pursuers were publicly hooted at the Water of Leith; that Cumming had *seen* impropriety; and that the servant, Charlotte, *repeatedly saw* misconduct, had called them "nasty brutes" to their faces, and had put out her tongue at them in derision before the scholars. At the second

---

[1] *Speeches of the Judges of the Second Division of the Court of Session upon Advising the Cause*, p. 34.

[2] Jane was less nice than Winifred in *The Devil's Law-Case*, who prefaced her evidence thus: "Please your Lordship, question me in Latin, for the cause is very foul."

hearing all these allegations were abandoned, and the proof rested solely upon what Cumming said she *heard*. The main difficulty of the pursuers was to rebut the ambiguous suggestions of the black, which were artfully framed to fit actual occurrences; but in one instance, happily, she so far overreached herself in her zeal as to prove conclusively that she was lying. She swore that Charlotte Whiffin, the maid, looking through the keyhole of the drawing-room door, beheld her mistresses in a compromising situation on the sofa. So important did this point appear to the Court, that on 14th March the judges took the unusual course of driving to Drumsheugh in the Justice-Clerk's carriage in order to inspect the *locus*. They found, and reported to the Division (a) that *there was, in fact, no keyhole in the drawing-room door*, and (b) that even with the door open it was impossible to see the sofa, which was situated, obviously in its wonted position, out of eyeshot! [1]

Charlotte Whiffin, who haled from the county of Kent, deponed that she entered the pursuers' service at Whit-sunday 1810. She denied that she had ever seen—through the non-existent keyhole or otherwise—any impropriety in their conduct, or that she at any time spoke disrespectfully of them to anyone. She mentioned certain festivities held at Drumsheugh in celebration of Miss Woods' birthday, when her fellow-servant, Nancy, "put on men's clothes, by way of diverting the young ladies." This merry maiden, though justly enjoying a right to the adjective, was regrettably found to have no title to the noun; she was accordingly dismissed and the situation filled by Bell Crawford (who deponed, by the way, that Charlotte said it was a very good place and urged her to take it). The day after the involuntary break-up of the school, Charlotte, walking in the square of her name, met Miss Jane Cumming, who asked her how things were going at Drumsheugh, and was told that, as regards the girls, they were already gone.

---

[1] "The horsehair sofa which was never moved from its accustomed place along the wall."—*Can You Forgive Her ?*, chapter iii.

Whereupon that daughter of the Philistines rejoiced. She clapped her hands "and seemed very glad at it," though she informed Charlotte that *she did not know the cause of their withdrawal.* Whiffin said she thought that the pursuers had "failed." She further deponed that it was her duty to make the beds at Drumsheugh, and had noticed that Miss Pirie always lay as far from her bed-fellow as the limits of their couch allowed, for a reason which she (the maid) did not hesitate to specify. The Asiatic atmosphere peculiar to Miss Cumming was not, as appears, exclusively moral.

What then were the facts upon which the fertile and infragrant imagination of the half-caste erected this monstrous fiction? We know that these ladies sometimes held midnight conferences by one another's bedside; further, it is in evidence that Miss Pirie suffered from rheumatism, and that Miss Woods was wont to relieve that ailment by rubbing the afflicted part. Munro, twice awakened on such occasions, was merely annoyed at being untimeously disturbed, until the incidents were imbued for her with Miss Cumming's Eastern colour. That young lady boldly asserted that, some two months after the holidays, viz. in the end of September, on four several nights she was awakened by the coming of Miss Woods to Miss Pirie's bed, and had apprised them by her action at the time that their wickedness was discovered. She admitted that it was then dark and that she could see nothing, but said that she relied upon the evidence of her other senses.[1] It is to be noted that although she could not distinguish the respective voices in these whispered conversations, she was able to report divers improprieties uttered. Munro, conveniently deaf, heard nothing of such indecorous speeches. When the latter, during a week-end at home in Elder Street, told

---

[1] Neither Miss Stirling, whose bed was but two feet distant from the Pirie-Cumming combine, nor old Mrs. Woods, who lay behind a thin partition within a foot of their joint couch, was conscious of these visitations; and none of the other girls in the crowded dormitories was similarly aroused or noticed anything unusual.

the story to the paternal domestic, Mary Brown, that young woman expressed the opinion that "Miss Pirie must be a man." But if Cumming spoke the truth, the observation is equally applicable to Miss Woods. Mary further characterised those ladies as "beasts," who ought to be "burnt." In explaining in the witness-box how she came to believe upon the mere word of a schoolgirl so improbable a tale, Mary stated that "she had read about it in the Bible," but did not give chapter and verse for the reference.

The Lord Ordinary having held that the alleged crime, *as described by Cumming,* was in his judgment physically impossible of commission, the defender raked heaven and earth—not to mention another source—in order to procure proof of its feasibility. The fruits of her research, sedulously garnered in twenty quarto pages, intituled *Authorities with regard to the Practice of Tribadism,* and duly lodged in process for the instruction of the Court, would provide pleasant reading for winter evenings round the fire in Charlotte Square. The extracts, of the type significantly catalogued by booksellers as "curious," range from S. Paul, *Romans,* i. 26, to Massinger's romantic play, *The Bondman,* Act ii. sc. 2—probably the only occasion on which an Elizabethan dramatist has been cited as a legal authority. But none of these specialists was better versed in this recondite subject than the juvenile expert who imported to the banks of the Water of Leith the bane which she had gathered by the Ganges. In this connection the pursuers offered proof of the licentiousness of Indian female manners in general, and of the corruptness of the Calcutta schools in particular; but this was objected to, and was disallowed.

As indicating the shifts to which the defender was reduced in order to establish the truth of her proposition, the incident of Miss Pirie's bible may be mentioned. On 12th October 1810, being the birthday of Miss Woods before referred to, her friend presented her with a copy of the scriptures, accompanied by the following letter:—

Accept, my beloved, of that book which can give consolation in every situation; and dearest *earthly* friend, never open it without thinking of her who would forego all friendships but her God's to possess yours. —Ever your own, JANE PIRIE.[1]

Whether or not this note is susceptible of the disagreeable gloss suggested by the defender, is for the reader to judge. He will bear in mind that it was written, and the gift presented at the very time when "this abandoned iniquity" is said to have been at its height. Jane Cumming, who was early at Miss Woods' bedside that morning to offer her "simple, innocent, veracious" congratulations, admitted that she saw both the bible and the note.

The correct and virtuous deportment of the pursuers, their high moral character and repute, were vouched for in the box by divers respectable witnesses, and instructed by the production of letters written by themselves to their friends and relations during the period in question. I have no space for quotation, but they shew these ladies to have been possessed—unless, indeed, they were the worst of hypocrites—by an anxious sense of duty, coupled with strong religious feelings, and extreme solicitude for the welfare, here and hereafter, of the girls committed to their charge. We are all of us familiar with whited sepulchres and wolves in sheep's clothing; and we know of what frightful inconsistencies human nature, even at its best, is capable; but there is about these private and familiar letters a tone that to me rings truer than the exotic whisperings of Jane Cumming. And one or other must be false as hell.

The proof concluded, counsel for the parties addressed the Court: Clerk and Gillies for the pursuers; Cranstoun and Henry Erskine for the defender. I wish I could print in full, from the MS. before me, the speech of John Clerk, delivered by him on 11th June 1811. It is so strong, so trenchant, so characteristic of the speaker; but, alas,

---

[1] *Productions for Pursuers*, p. 139.

having such a long way yet to go and so much to carry, I
must be satisfied with two or three extracts. Once, like
Silas Wegg, he "drops into poetry," but the example of
his muse is rather too racy for quotation. Neither can I
venture to follow him in his analysis of the evidence or in his
argument on the merits, seeing that he handles his material
with the gloves off, as the phrase goes, which I may not
do. Of Lady Cumming Gordon's conduct he remarks:

> I hope there was no intended barbarity in the method that was
> taken to ruin the pursuers. Certain it is, in point of fact, that the most
> savage cruelty could not have invented any thing more painful to feel-
> ing and virtuous minds. Lady Cunynghame did not see a thousandth
> part of the misery it created, and yet she could not refrain from tears
> in describing what she saw. . . .

Of Jane Cumming and Janet Munro he observes:

> As to Miss Cumming, it is presumed that your Lordships will think her
> totally unworthy of credit. She was received *cum nota*, merely because
> she could not be rejected, but received as a witness of the most suspicious
> nature. I shall not enlarge on those obvious grounds of suspicion to
> which she is exposed. . . . Her eagerness to criminate the pursuers
> will be well recollected by your Lordships, her savage joy and triumph
> when she heard of their ruin. To her the honour is due of having raised
> up the present litigation.

> .   .   .   .

> Miss Munro was evidently a witness of the most limited capacity.
> She had indeed beauty and blushes and tears, for which reason she
> was brought forward as the leading witness, and the copy has always
> ushered in the original. Miss Cumming only confirms Miss Munro,
> although it is evident that Miss Munro derived her impressions from
> her, as she did her first information. Nor is there much candour in
> this witness, unless we suppose that her mind was completely governed
> or poisoned by another.

And of the servant:

> Charlotte Whiffin is said to be perjured. Her word was as good as
> the oath of the defender's other witnesses. . . . Conceive how difficult
> it is to take in or comprehend the nature of the accusation against the
> pursuers. Was an ordinary servant maid to take the hint at once, and
> suppose them guilty of an unknown enormity? *This was a poison
> from the banks of the Ganges with which the Maid of Kent was not familiar.*

Had Miss Cumming alluded to common gallantries, Charlotte would have understood her more easily. . . . Recollect, my Lords, the manner in which Charlotte gave her evidence. *She* did not sit for five or ten minutes at a time, brooding over former falsehoods and inconsistencies, exerting her cunning and not her memory to find the most unsatisfactory answers to the plainest questions. No ; it will be remembered that the answer to every question was ready and given with the utmost promptness, and yet the defender will in vain look for a single inconsistency in the whole deposition. She invariably answered to the fact immediately, before it was possible for her to form the least notion as to the bearing of it upon the cause. Yet she is called a perjured witness ! *The defender's counsel did not chuse to cross-question her*, though that is the common way of detecting perjury. The pursuers, with proper delicacy, totally abstained from communication with Charlotte, and even refused to give her a character, lest it should be supposed by unthinking people that there was any connection between them.

Finally, and in peroration:

The atrocity of the defender's accusation from the first is discoverable in every circumstance of the case. Look at Lady Cunynghame's evidence. That excellent woman, so much disposed to protect the pursuers, renounced them at once upon hearing it, the baleful breath of slander. If Miss Cumming had been the *cobra de capello* of her native Ganges, she could not have killed them more quickly. They fell ; and what was worse, without the pity, but with the hatred, the contempt and execration, of the just. Nothing can be more absurd than to argue that persons who have sustained such an injury are entitled to no redress. They are innocent, and yet they are ruined. Was Lady Cumming entitled to attend to the safety of her grand-daughters and officiously to look after the conduct of those who did not wish for her interference, and at the same time totally to forget the justice that was due to the pursuers ? It is needless to enquire what she might have done. The question is what she did do. She destroyed the reputation of worthy people, upon listening to the false and absurd suggestions of a person who ought to have had no more credit with her than she will have with your Lordships.[1]

But there Clerk was wrong. At the advising of the case by the Second Division on 25th June 1811, although three of the seven judges were in favour of the pursuers,[2]

---

[1] Original MS.

[2] Lord Justice-Clerk Hope ; Lords Meadowbank and Boyle.

four, presumably swayed by the brilliant sophistries of
Harry Erskine, found for the defender.[1] "Sustain the
defences and assoilzie" was accordingly the judgment of
the Court. Nowadays the only remedy open to the
pursuers would lie in an appeal to the House of Lords, but
in those times it was competent for them, on cause shewn,
to present to the Division a petition for review.

On 10th October 1811 such a petition was presented,
setting forth that the decision complained of had been
"pronounced by the narrowest possible majority of the
Court"; and that "considering the strong doubts and
hesitation expressed by those of your Lordships who concurred in the judgment, and the awful importance of the
question at issue to the petitioners, they humbly submit
the interlocutor to review."

On advising the cause, your Lordships were much divided in opinion.
The Head of the Court [Hope] and the Lord Ordinary [Meadowbank]
were quite clear of the perfect innocence of the petitioners; and one
more of your Lordships [Boyle] concurred in that opinion. But even
those of your Lordships who were against the petitioners expressed your
opinions as formed with great doubt and hesitation; so much so that
one most eminent Judge (whom the petitioners can no more address) [2]
said that if the petitioners were upon trial, his verdict as a juryman
would be Not Proven.[3]

The petition, which is signed by Clerk and Moncrieff,[4]
is a masterly piece of pleading, and covers the whole
history of the cause. The defender's repeated changes of

---

[1] Lords Robertson, Glenlee, Newton, and Polkemmet. It fell to the last-
named to give the casting vote. "Lord Justice-Clerk, turning to Lord Polkemmet: 'This case now comes to your Lordship's vote. Is your Lordship
prepared to give your opinion now, or had you not better take some time to
consider of the case?' Lord Polkemmet: 'My Lord, I have formed an opinion
in this cause, and I am ready to deliver it. My opinion is to sustain the defences.'"
—Notes of the Speeches of Lords Robertson, Glenlee, Newton, and Polkemmet at
Advising the Case, p. 16.

[2] Charles Hay, Lord Newton, who died that month, and was succeeded by
Adam (Lord) Gillies, one of the counsel for the pursuers.

[3] Additional Petition for Pursuers, p. 17.

[4] The copy in the Moncrieff Collection bears the holograph note: "All
written by me. Jas. M."

front are exposed, and the fact noted that all the grosser charges were now dropped and only the alleged conversations founded . on. .The imputation of Lady Cumming Gordon is described as "one of the most atrocious calumnies that ever was discussed in a court of justice." The sting of the charge was in its shocking nature, proceeding from such a quarter, the mere mention of which, whether true or false, by one of her quality meant ruin. The pursuers were stabbed in the dark, with no chance of vindication. The slander was whispered, under seal of secrecy, to those with whom their fate rested. They lost their all—fortune, character, their very existence in society. And the defence to their just claim for reparation is—the truth of the charge! "Should we fail in establishing a complete proof," wrote Lady Cumming Gordon to Mrs. Stirling, in attempting to suborn her daughter, "it lands all who are concerned in the charge of being *the inventors of this most horrible story.*"

Your Lordships will judge how far Miss Cumming did not see that she, proved to be the original source of the whole, could never have lifted up her head in the world if, when she came before your Lordships, she had not made every effort to support the story. She comes therefore, as a witness, with almost every possible objection to her credit—relationship, dependence, the most dreadful interest that ever a witness had. *If she had been a lawful grand-daughter she could not have been admitted at all.*[1]

Answers for the defender were lodged on 22nd February, in which the truth of the charge, as instructed by the oaths of Cumming and Munro, is insisted in; but it is argued that, even if the petitioners were innocent, the respondent had reasonable and probable grounds for her belief to the contrary, and was warranted in acting as she did.[2] "If she had examined into the facts as patiently and ably as your Lordships have done, is it credible that she would have formed an opinion different from yours,

---

[1] *Additional Petition*, p. 60. Thus had the black girl profit of her bastardy.

[2] " It is always a silly thing to give advice, but to give good advice is fatal."
—OSCAR WILDE.

who were neither in *mala fide*, nor precipitate, nor culpably negligent?" The Court, however, granted the prayer of the petition, and the whole business was debated afresh. On the 26th, their Lordships, by a majority of one judge— four for the pursuers and three for the defender—recalled the interlocutor reclaimed against, repelled the defences, and found the defender liable in damages and expenses.

The personnel of the Court had suffered some change between the dates of the two advisings. Charles Hope, promoted Lord President, was translated to the First Division, and his place as Lord Justice-Clerk occupied by Boyle. Polkemmet had resigned, and was succeeded by Craigie; Newton was dead, and Gillies sat in the seat of "The Mighty." Lacking on this occasion the countenance of Hope, the pursuers lost their strongest and staunchest supporter, who had begun his former judgment in their favour with the forcible words: "I have no more suspicion of the guilt of the pursuers than I have of my own wife." Meadowbank and Boyle repeated their elaborate and closely reasoned arguments to the same effect: the former had "no shade of doubt that the criminal imputation against the pursuers is false and groundless"; the latter, that Cumming's evidence "is entitled to no sort of regard." Gillies and Woodhouselee gave powerful new speeches for the pursuers. The opinions of the minority of the Court are interesting. Glenlee is for sustaining *both* defences, conceiving the pursuers' guilt more probable than the capacity of Cumming to invent it. Robertson sustains the *first*, but not the second defence; Craigie the *second*, but not the first. And Solomon tells us that "in the multitude of counsellors there is safety"! Thus each of the contestant parties held a judgment by a majority of one in seven.

But Lady Cumming Gordon, having fought so far, was not going to accept defeat. Her ladyship was minded to appeal unto Cæsar; and on 17th March 1812 she formally confided her patrician fortunes to the arbitrament of the

House of Peers. Before that august tribunal, in addition
to her old counsel, the appellant strengthened her forces
by retaining Sir Samuel Romilly, John Greenshields, and
Francis Horner. The respondents' team comprised John
Leach, John Clerk, Francis Jeffrey, and James Moncrieff.
From motives of secrecy no *viva voce* pleadings took place
in the Lords, and the cause was decided on the printed
appeal cases, which are surely vast and voluminous enough
to serve the purpose. The decision of their Lordships' House
was as follows:—

Die Lunæ, 12° Julii 1819. Upon consideration of the petition and
appeal of Dame Helen Cumming Gordon, relict of Sir Alexander Cumming Gordon of Altyre and Gordonstoun, Baronet . . . It is ordained
and adjudged by the Lords Spiritual and Temporal in Parliament
assembled, That the said petition and appeal be, and is hereby dismissed this House, and that the said interlocutors therein complained
of be, and the same are hereby affirmed.

HENRY COUPER, *Dep. Cler. Parliamentor.*[1]

The case came back to the Court of Session; and their
Lordships, having considered a petition to apply the
judgment of the House of Lords, on 1st December 1819
ordered the pursuers to put in a condescendence of the
damages claimed by them, which was duly lodged on 28th
January 1820. Had their establishment continued, the
ladies estimated their profits thus:

Twelve night-boarders for £40 per annum, . . .			£480 0 0
Branches of education taught to these boarders by Misses			
Woods and Pirie, ...			448 16 0
Twelve day-boarders at £25 per annum, .	£300 0 0		
Branches of education taught to these, .	. 448 16 0		
			748 16 0
			£1677 12 0
The household expenses, . . .	£600 0 0		
House-rent, taxes, wages, . . .	. 95 0 0		
			695 0 0
			£982 12 0

[1] *Petition to Apply Judgment of House of Lords,* 30th November 1819.

According to these data, the claim of damages stood thus:

Loss on furniture, rent, wages, &c., ...	£450	0	0
Loss on profits to Martinmas 1819, ...	3240	0	0
Loss on profits after that date, ...	3000	0	0
Extra expenses by account to be proved, . . .	783	16	5
	£7473	16	5
Solatium, ...	2000	0	0
	£9473	16	5 [1]

For a whole year the defender fought this claim foot by foot and inch by inch, availing herself of all the cumbrous machinery—Notes, Petitions, Answers, Replies, Duplies, etc.—whereby the litigants of those spacious days were enabled to baffle justice and keep their opponents at bay. Miss Woods, we learn, was after a time, through the kindness and sympathy of friends, enabled to win a bare subsistence for herself and a near relation, "an aged lady who depended upon her exertions"—from which it appears she had taken up again her old-time burden, Leonora. Miss Pirie's case was even harder. "In consequence of the affliction produced by the defender's calumny, she has suffered so severely in her health and constitution as certainly to embitter the remainder of her days, and in all probability greatly to shorten her life." Unable to earn a living, she had contracted "very considerable debts." So that to both ladies the matter was one of vital importance. They suggested that the Division, if their Lordships could not themselves dispose of it, should send the case for trial to the Jury Court,[2] but to this the defender would by no means agree. Finally, outworn by the dowager's tactics and in mere despair, the pursuers offered to compromise for £5000. This offer was refused. They then reduced their terms to 4000

---

[1] *Condescendence of Damages*, p. 5.

[2] Trial by jury in civil causes was introduced into Scotland in 1816 by the institution of the Jury Court, which ceased to exist as a separate Court in 1830. It was not found to be a success and passed away unmourned.

guineas, intimating that as their last word. The dowager
tendered £3500. On 1st February 1821 the pursuers gave
in a Note, stating to the Division how the matter stood.
Miss Pirie dissented from the proposed terms of settlement.

The defender offers, ...	£3500	0	0
Deduct expenses of Appeal, ...	783	16	5

	2)2716	3	7
Divide this between Miss Woods and Miss Pirie, it			
leaves to each, ...	£1358	1	9½ [1]

Although Mr. Mantalini would have deprecated the halfpenny, poor Miss Pirie needed all that she could get:
she estimates at £1400 her total losses in this uncivil war.
After all, it was not so very much to ask for a ruined life.
What the pursuers ultimately got—if indeed the defender
did not resist to the death—I cannot tell, my authorities
subserving no farther.

.   .   .   .

My claim—I trust not so implacably contested—is to
have recovered a lost chapter in the social and legal history
of Edinburgh, and to have added to Lord Cockburn's
chronicle a curious footnote.

In 1811 our Edinburgh society still continued unchanged in its
general character. Napoleon's continental padlock still sent us good
English youths and families : society and literature adorned each other :
the war sparkled us with military gaiety and parade : London had not
absorbed the whole of our aristocracy either of wealth or of rank ; and,
notwithstanding several important emigrations, we still retained far
more native talent and reputation than could be found in any other
town in the empire, except London.[2]

Little wonder, then, that his Lordship's complacent retro-
spect makes no mention of Miss Cumming's "native
talent," of the dowager's "reputation," or of the portentous
scandal of Drumsheugh.

---

[1] *Note for Pursuers*, p. 2.
[2] *Memorials of His Time*, by Henry Cockburn, p. 264. Edinburgh : 1856.

Note I.—THE CUMMING-GORDONS

The following particulars regarding the husband and children of Lady Cumming-Gordon are taken from Burke's *Peerage and Baronetage*, 1840.

Sir Alexander Penrose Cumming, being heir and representative of the last Sir William Gordon, Baronet, of Gordonstoun, assumed the name and arms of Gordon, and was created a Baronet 21st May 1804. He was M.P. for the Inverness district of burghs. Died 10th February 1806. Sir Alexander married in 1773 Helen, daughter of Sir Ludovick Grant of Grant [born May 1754 ; died January 1832—see *The Scots Peerage*, vol. vii. p. 485], and left issue :—

1. Sir William.
2. Charles Lennox Cumming-Bruce, M.P., of Roseisle and Kinnaird, born 20th February 1780, married Miss Mary Bruce of Kinnaird, granddaughter of James Bruce, the Abyssinian traveller [his daughter married the eighth Earl of Elgin].
3. Margaret, married Major Madden, of the 15th regiment of foot.
4. Helen, married Sir Archibald Dunbar, Baronet, of Northfield.
5. Louisa, married John Hay Forbes of Medwyn, Lord of Session.
6. Edwina, married Thomas Miller of Glenlee.
7. Jane Marianne.
8. Mary.
9. Emilia.
10. Sophia.

Note II.—JANE CUMMING'S PURPOSE

The ruin wrought by the abominable libel of the half-caste greatly exceeded in magnitude of result her original intention. Being determined to escape from the school, she hit upon a tale which, by reason of its unmentionable nature, need only be whispered to attain her end: a word to her grandmother would suffice. She could not have foreseen that the dowager would broadcast the scandal, and that she herself must swear to her story in the witness-box. But having thus wantonly sown the wind, she had to abide the reaping of the whirlwind.

PRETTY FANNY'S WAY;

OR, THE IMPORTANCE OF BEING ERNEST

PRETTY FANNY'S WAY;

or, The Importance of being Ernest

Those who find ugly meanings in beautiful things are corrupt without being charming. This is a fault. —The Preface to *Dorian Gray*.

"THE door, which was equipped with neither bell nor knocker, was blistered and distained. Tramps slouched into the recess and struck matches on the panels; children kept shop upon the steps; the schoolboy had tried his knife on the mouldings; and for close on a generation no one had appeared to drive away these random visitors or to repair their ravages." Thus, as the reader will recall, does Stevenson represent the sinister portal of Dr. Jekyll's laboratory; and just such another door, similarly neglected and disused, likewise associated with a strange case, was till lately to be seen in Edinburgh, at the west end of George Street, on the south side of that dignified and stately thoroughfare. In the course of my pilgrimage, social and professional, I had passed that door innumerable times without remarking its woebegone condition or speculating upon the causes of its desuetude. Only when the facts of the case we are about to consider came to my knowledge had I the curiosity to look for No. 136. I found it such as I have described; but alas, nowadays nothing is suffered to remain as it was: no sooner had I begun to be interested in it than the mysterious entry, which all my lifetime had stood faded and forgotten, was of course suddenly and wantonly refurbished!

The street distinguished by the name and effigy of George the Magnificent and the Good, though now like Princes Street wholly abandoned to business pursuits,

149

was at first intended for residential purposes and consisted of opposing rows of "self-contained" private houses, three storeys high, with attics above and areas beneath, diversified by flats for less ambitious indwellers. Our door formerly gave access to the common stair by which one of these comprehensive tenements was approached; but the upper floors to which it led being in later years absorbed by an hotel round the corner in the adjacent square, the occasion for its employment ceased, and it survived, a useless and unsightly object, until the other day, when the building of which it forms part having been acquired by an insurance company, it once again became as spruce and bright a door as one could wish to enter—though whether or not it even now leads anywhere I have my doubts.

It is curious, by the way, to note how regrettably Hanoverian is the nomenclature of the New Town of Edinburgh. We have Regent, Carlton, and Royal Terraces; George, Frederick, and Hanover Streets; Charlotte Square and Saxe-Coburg Place. Even the incomparable Princes Street was originally dubbed "Prince's Street," in compliment to some scion of the House of Brunswick. The most important improvement in the Old Town was named George Square; and George IV. Bridge commemorates the visit of that gorgeous monarch to his humble Scottish capital. Surely our own rich history could furnish designations more congenial to national feeling; and when after the War the Royal Family discarded its German patronymic, we also might have taken the opportunity to get rid of these incongruous and Hunnish appellations.

In life there are many closed doors, long since sealed up by time and circumstance, which lead nowhere and of which the keys are lost, while the dust of old years lies thick upon the threshold. Perhaps it were wiser to pass them by. Let us, however, venture to open this one—not wide, but merely a discreet chink—and see what secret of yore lay ambushed behind its dingy and disregarded panels.

I.

In the year of grace 1871—when the present historian, then viewing the world from his bassinet, had no personal acquaintance with the fact—there lived in comfortable lodgings at No. 136 George Street, Edinburgh, a gentleman named John Safford Fiske. He had done so for two and a half years, his landlady gave him an excellent character for sobriety of conduct, and in the Edinburgh society of the day he was an acceptable and welcome figure. An American citizen, he represented the United States as consul at Leith. The most intimate of his associates was a young man named Louis Charles Hurt, who lived in lodgings near him at No. 118 Princes Street, at the south-west corner of Castle Street, and was employed in the surveyor's department of the General Post Office. Readers of Anthony Trollope's *Autobiography* will recall the account he gives of the duties performed by that peripatetic staff, of which he himself was so long a member. Hurt had been three years in Edinburgh; No. 118 was his base, but he was often absent on periodic tours of inspection throughout the country. From October 1868 to April 1869 Mr. Hurt's celibate seclusion was brightened by a visit from a young friend of his, whom he had known from boyhood.

Ernest Boulton, the son of a London stockbroker, was twenty-two years of age, extremely good-looking in an effeminate way, musical, and the possessor of a wonderful soprano voice. His inseparable companion was a youth of his own age, tastes, and accomplishments, named Frederick William Park, son of one of the Masters of the Superior Courts. To these engaging lads was Fiske introduced by Hurt, and the cultured American conceived for Ernest an enthusiastic, but ill-fated admiration. In compliment to their pseudo-feminine charms the young Londoners were known familiarly in their set as Stella and Fanny. Their favourite diversion was the playing of female parts in amateur theatricals, and of the realism with which they sustained such rôles there will be much to say. Unhappily, as it turned out, the success they enjoyed in this regard led to their carrying their art beyond the footlights and continuing in the cold publicity of day their remarkable impersonations. Of these irregular performances neither Mr. Hurt nor Mr. Fiske approved; but with the giddy carelessness of youth Stella and Fanny continued to indulge their fancy. Their appearance, even in male attire, was sufficiently conspicuous to create remark and speculation in the decorous Edinburgh of the Seventies, and bets were made by sporting persons on the question of their sex. When in the springtime the captivating Stella, refreshed by her sojourn in the North, returned to the scene of her metropolitan triumphs, poor Mr. Fiske, having nothing to console his loneliness but some agreeable memories and an extensive collection of photographs, continued to write to his young friend, in a strain exaggeratedly romantic, letters which his irresponsible correspondent imprudently preserved.

So matters rested until the night of 28th April 1870, when Stella, under the style and title of Mrs. Graham, and her friend Miss Fanny Winifred Park, having attended in most becoming frocks a performance at the Strand Theatre, were being escorted to Mrs. Graham's private brougham by a couple of cavaliers, the party was rudely held up by a detective officer, who desired them to accompany him to Bow Street police station. In the confusion following upon this unlooked-for invitation one of the gentlemen ungallantly decamped. The other, with his fair charges, acceded to the official request. Subsequently their apartments were visited by the police, and among other interesting items was found the Fiske correspondence.

Seeing the amount of trouble gratuitously brought upon themselves every day by people who write unnecessary letters to other people stupid enough to keep them, it is surprising that anybody has the hardihood to put pen to paper except on matters of business. It has been well observed that if only private letters were written in ink which after a reasonable interval became invisible, what a blessing it would be for all concerned! But if folks will write foolishly and without a view to publication, they must abide the consequences. Verily, this form of *cacoëthes scribendi* carries with it its own Nemesis.

So on 9th June 1870, to Mr. John Safford Fiske, taking his ease in his bachelor rooms in George Street, there entered by the ominous door to which I have referred the messenger of Fate in the guise of a police inspector, charged with the duty of searching the premises for compromising matter. The American consul was not unprepared for such a visitation. He had been apprised of the untoward happenings at the theatre and of the command performance at Bow Street. Mr. Hurt, who had gone up to London at the time of the occurrence, wrote to him on 18th May 1870 as follows:—

I am heartily glad that I came here. There is no warrant against me. It is believed that the worst letter the prosecution have has been put in, and that is yours. They are anxious for you to come up, and I really believe it would be your best course. It would be better than staying away. I think your name must appear. E[rnest] begs you will destroy any letters from him you may have in your possession. I hope you will, if you have not already done so.

And in a later letter he writes:—

I have seen a copy of the suppressed letter which, as I have telegraphed to you, contains your full name and address. There is nothing indecent in it, of course, but it is the most high-flown language. After this letter I cannot understand why your rooms have not been searched, perhaps because you have been Consul.

Mr. Fiske's diplomatic rank, as we have seen, did not render him immune from such a visitation. In a third letter Hurt says:—

We have just seen copies of the letters. We think no more names or letters will be published. I am rather afraid of some letters of mine

which arrived for me in Edinburgh after my departure. My letter to
Park was destroyed.

And finally, on 3rd June, after the committal of the
prisoners for trial:—

> It is possible I shall be called upon as a witness for the defence, and I
> advise you to go to London at once in case you should be required. I
> really think that for your own sake, as well as for Ernest's, you should
> go and explain, if called as a witness, what utter nonsense your letters
> were. At any rate send an explanation of your letters and a full state-
> ment of your acquaintance with him.[1]

Such were the epistolary gleanings of Mr. Fiske's
cabinet. That gentleman, however, was not called upon
to explain in the witness-box the perfervid quality of his
literary style, for when, acting upon his friend's advice,
he went to London, both he and Hurt were arrested and
their lips consequently sealed. In addition to these letters,
Mr. Fiske, being pressed to disclose every article of his
collection, produced from behind the grate in his bedroom
—not, one should think, the most convenient receptacle
for ready reference—an album, described as containing
"a number of photographs, beautifully executed, of
Boulton in female attire," in one of which the fair Stella
was represented "in an attitude of prayer." The concealment of this album Fiske characterised as "weakness."
He admitted having destroyed all his friend's letters, but
evidently could not find it in his heart to sacrifice the
photographs. A victim of the artistic temperament, in
thrall to his mid-Victorian environment—grisly wax
flowers, ghastly chandeliers, gruesome antimacassars, grim
horsehair-cum-mahogany furniture—small wonder that he
cherished things which he deemed elegant and pleasant to
the sight as an antidote to such atrocities.

The original offence for which the prisoners were

---

[1] *The Trial of Boulton and Park, with Hurt and Fiske. A Complete and
Accurate Report of the Proceedings extending over Six Days, from Tuesday, May 9th,
to Monday, May 15th*, 1871. Manchester : John Heywood, 1871, p. 26.

arrested was of appearing in public in women's clothes, which of itself amounted only to a misdemeanour. But on the report of the police surgeon, who had taken upon himself, without a warrant from a magistrate, to examine the accused, a graver charge was preferred against them. In the end the authorities, finding the evidence insufficient to support that charge, indicted the two accused, together with six of their associates, for conspiracy to commit a felony. Among the friends thus signalised by official notice were Messrs. Hurt and Fiske, who having gone South to swear, remained to plead. The case aroused an immense amount of interest—there is nothing that so appeals to really respectable people as a good rousing scandal; and the Tichborne claimant, who till then had been the public's favourite and whose name was familiar in its mouth, must have resented this temporary infringement of his popularity.

II.

At Bow Street [on 29th April 1870], Ernest Boulton, 22, residing at 23 Shirland Road [Paddington], Frederick William Park, 23, of 13 Bruton Street, Berkeley Square, law student, both of whom were in female costume, and Hugh Alexander Mundell, 23, of 158 Buckingham Palace Road, were brought before Mr. Thomas, charged with frequenting the Strand Theatre with intent to commit felony. The prisoners Boulton and Park were defended by Mr. Abrams. When placed in the dock Boulton wore a cherry-coloured silk evening dress, trimmed with white lace; his arms were bare and he had on bracelets. He wore a wig and plaited chignon. Park's costume consisted of a dark green satin dress, low necked, trimmed with black lace, of which material he also had a shawl round his shoulders. His hair was flaxen and in curls. He had on a pair of white kid gloves.[1]

The unusual circumstances of the case, when known, drew an enormous crowd, and the court-house was literally besieged. From day to day the evidence given at the successive remands was very fully reported by the *Times*, which devoted as much space to the preliminary proceed-

---

[1] *Times*, 30th April 1870.

ings, under the arresting caption: "The Men in Women's
Clothes," as to the subsequent trial. The hearing was
resumed on 6th, 15th, 20th, 22nd, 28th, and 30th May,
upon which date Boulton and Park were committed for
trial, bail being refused. At the later hearings Mr. (afterwards Sir Harry) Poland conducted the prosecution;
Mr. Besley and Mr. (afterwards Sir Douglas) Straight
respectively appeared for the prisoners. On the conclusion
of the first hearing Mundell was discharged, and became
one of the witnesses for the prosecution.

Among the several names associated with the case was
that of Lord Arthur Pelham Clinton,[1] who was included
in the indictment upon which the prisoners were brought
to trial. But Lord Arthur did not live to face the music;
he died on 18th June 1870 at the King's Arms Hotel,
Christchurch, Hampshire, "from exhaustion resulting from
scarlet fever," aggravated by anxiety caused by the charge.
His solicitor, W. H. Roberts, on that date forwarded to
the *Times* a letter which Lord Arthur had intended sending
to that journal, in which he wrote:—

> I pledge myself to surrender at the trial at the Central Criminal Court
> on the day appointed, as I am desirous of courting the fullest public
> inquiry, being conscious that the greater the light which can be thrown
> on this unfortunate case, the clearer will be my exculpation.[2]

There was later published a paragraph, reprinted from
the *Lancet*, giving a medical account of his illness, during
which, as appears, the patient was professionally attended
by Mr. Wade of Christchurch and Dr. Roberts Thompson
of Bournemouth.[3]

III.

On Tuesday, 9th May 1871, in the Court of Queen's
Bench, before the Lord Chief Justice of England (Sir

---

[1] Third son of Henry Pelham, fifth Duke of Newcastle. Lieutenant R.N.;
M.P. for Newark. Born 23rd June 1840; died 18th June 1870.—Burke's
Peerage.

[2] *Times*, 20th June 1870.   [3] *Ibid.*, 24th June 1870.

Alexander Cockburn) and a special jury, Ernest Boulton,
Frederick William Park, Louis Charles Hurt, and John
Safford Fiske were placed at the bar, charged with con-
spiracy to commit a felony. For the Crown, the prose-
cutor, were the Attorney-General (Sir Robert Collier), the
Solicitor-General (Sir John Duke Coleridge), Mr. Hardinge
Giffard, Q.C. (afterwards Lord Halsbury), Mr. Henry
James, Q.C. (afterwards Lord James of Hereford), Mr.
(afterwards Sir Harry) Poland, and Mr. Archbold. There
appeared for Boulton, Mr. Digby Seymour, Q.C., Mr. Ser-
jeant Ballantine, and Mr. Besley; for Park, Mr. Serjeant
Parry and Mr. (afterwards Sir Douglas) Straight; for Hurt,
Sir John Karslake, Q.C., Mr. F. H. Lewis, and Mr.
W. Ballantyne; for Fiske, Mr. Henry Matthews, Q.C.
(afterwards Viscount Llandaff), Mr. Serjeant Sleigh, and
Mr. Purcell. Not even the mighty Tichborne case itself,
that gigantic litigation, could boast a more brilliant Bar.[1]
Included in the indictment were the names of Lord Arthur
Pelham Clinton, William Somerville, Martin Luther Cumming, and C. F. Thomas, who were charged with the same
offence. Lord Arthur, as we know, had been cited to
attend a higher tribunal; the others had successfully
eluded the perquisitions of the police. "The defendants
had a very youthful appearance, but Park had lost somewhat of his feminine looks by reason of his whiskers.
Boulton had a slight moustache." [2] During its relatively
short run of six days the piece proved a greater draw
than the more legitimate drama at Westminster Hall.[3]

The case for the Crown was opened by the Attorney-
General with confidence and vigour; but as he promised
to prove rather more than, in the event, he was able to
perform, and as the case produced no less than ten speeches

[1] It is interesting to note that the great civil suit, *Tichborne* v. *Lushington*,
began the following day : Wednesday, 10th May 1871 : in the Court of Common
Pleas, Westminster, before Sir William Bovill, Chief Justice, and a special jury.

[2] *Trial*, p. 3

[3] For a competent account of the case *cf.* "The Boulton and Park Trial,"
The Annual Register for the Year 1871, pp. 220–224. London : 1872.

of counsel, as well as the judicial charge, there is no use
going over the same facts so often: I shall let the witnesses
tell their own tales.   Of these the first was Mundell, who
had been taken into custody with the two "ladies" and
was afterwards released.   Examined by the Solicitor-
General, he said he first saw the accused at the Surrey
Theatre on 22nd April 1870.   He was told that "there
were two ladies in men's attire in the dress circle," and said
he should like to see them.   At the interval they adjourned
to a neighbouring place of refreshment.   He followed, and
entered into conversation.   He believed them to be women
from their manner and appearance.   When the piece was
over, he walked with them across Waterloo Bridge and
left them in the Strand.   An appointment was made to
meet at the theatre on Tuesday, the 26th.   On that occasion they had a private box and were dressed as women.
"I bought two roses—one for each."   Boulton gave him
a letter, since destroyed, in which it was stated that they
were men dressed in women's clothes.   He did not believe
it and thought they were joking.   Boulton was called
Stella; Park, Fanny.   They told witness to call for Mrs.
Graham's brougham.   Another gentleman, who was of
the party, accompanied them to the Gobe in Tichborne
Street, where they had supper, for which the gentlemen
paid.   He had treated Boulton as a gay woman, but "she
kept him at arm's length."   They parted after the meal,
Park giving witness his address: 13 Bruton Street.   He
arranged to call on Thursday, the 28th, and take them out
to lunch.   They were then dressed as men, but he talked
to them as if they were women.   They asked for the letter
they had given him, and when he produced it, tore it up.
Two other gentlemen called; the conversation was about
theatrical matters, and they all went out for lunch, after
which the "ladies" departed in a cab.   He met them
again that evening at the Strand Theatre, in Mrs. Graham's
box.   One of the gentlemen was with them.   They were
dressed as women.   On leaving the theatre the party was

arrested, except the other gentleman, who ran away.
"I believed they were women, although they told me
several times they were men." Cross-examined by Mr.
Seymour, the gentleman told him in the box "that they
did it for a bit of fun, and that it was the finest get-up in
London." Witness treated them as ladies—"of that sort."
There was no impropriety, and such advances as he made
were turned down. Their conversation, which was entirely about theatricals, was lively and agreeable. Re-
examined, he thought they were gay women from their
looks and dress.

William Chamberlain, detective officer, said that he
had been watching Boulton and Park since 1869. Sometimes they were dressed as women, sometimes as men.
He had seen them with the absent defendants Cumming
and Thomas. On 28th April he saw the defendants come
out of a house at 13 Wakefield Street, Regent Square,
between 7 and 8 p.m. and go in a cab to the Strand Theatre.
They were dressed as women. Witness followed. They
were met by Mundell and entered a private box. They
afterwards visited the bar. "From there Park went to the
ladies' retiring-room." When they returned to their box
another gentleman joined them. Witness then described
the arrest and the escape of the second man, whom he
knew to be Thomas, one of the missing defendants.

When we got to the station I saw that Boulton had on a scarlet dress
and a muslin shawl over it. It was partly satin, and I believe the rest
was white moire antique. Boulton had false hair and chignon of a fair
colour, like the ordinary hair I have seen females wearing. He had
ornaments—bracelets, rings, and lockets. It was a very low dress,
and the arms were bare. He wore white kid gloves. I found afterwards
that he wore petticoats and stays, and a white skirt. He wore ladies'
white boots. The bosom was padded to make it appear very full. Park
wore blue silk and complete female dress. He wore earrings.[1]

Next morning witness went to the rooms in Wakefield
Street and saw there female jewellery and dresses. He

[1] *Trial*, p. 11.—For the curiously hideous headgear worn by the women of
that day see the drawings by Du Maurier in the contemporary pages of *Punch*.

locked the door of the room and took away the key.
Returning at noon with Inspector Shenton to complete
his search, he found that the door had been broken
open, and certain articles removed. The people of the
house informed him that this had been done by Cumming,
Thomas, and Gibbins, who claimed the things as their
property.

Other police officers having given evidence regarding
the habitual public appearances of the prisoners in women's
dress, Sergeant Kerley stated that he accompanied the
accused to the police station in a cab on the night in
question. On the way Park said, "It will do you no good,
old fellow, to take us to the station. Anything you like
you can have to let us go." Boulton said, "Any amount
you like you can have; only let us go." Witness declined
these overtures.

John Reeves, manager of the Alhambra, Leicester
Square, said he had known Boulton and Park for some
three years. His attention was called to them, as being
in women's dress. "They walked about the house in an
unbecoming manner. The faces of the defendants were
painted. Their dresses were very low, and they were
powdered on the neck and shoulders. A lot of men got
round them. I ordered them out at once." On another
occasion he saw them in a box, dressed as men.

They were hanging over, lighting cigarettes from the gas jets below the
box. All the people in the auditorium below were looking up at them ;
they were making stupid noises, chirruping to each other with their lips ;
they were chucking each other under the chin, and playing at frivolous
games. A third person was with them ; he was Gibbins. They were
turned out, and the price of the box returned to them.[1]

Cross-examined, this incident occurred in the first week
of March 1870. While in the house they spoke only to
their own friends or to those who appeared to be such.
Re-examined, they had no moustaches or whiskers, and

---

[1] *Trial*, p. 14.

"their appearance was very different from what it is to-day." [1]

George Smith, sometime beadle at the Burlington Arcade,[2] said he had seen Boulton and Park there several times. One day he saw Boulton when walking with Cumming "turn his head and wink, and make a chirrup with his lips same as ladies might do—ladies of Burlington Arcade." He told them they were unfit persons to be in the Arcade, and forcibly ejected them. On subsequent occasions he prevented them from entering the Arcade. They were always dressed as men and were always painted. He had seen them there. a dozen times in all. Cross-examined, all this occurred two years ago, before he resigned his post. His resignation was compulsory: "because I received money from the women who are the best supporters of the Arcade." He could not tell "within a thousand" how many times he had accepted money from these ladies. His orders were to keep such women out of the Arcade, but he had to use discretion; sometimes a tradesman would say, "That lady you turned out is one of my customers." What was a man to do under these circumstances? Since demitting office he had been in turn a ticket-collector, a policeman, and a bus conductor. He only got 14s. from the Treasury for bearing witness in this case, and in the old days he had often got from gentlemen a sovereign for opening a lady's carriage door.

THE LORD CHIEF JUSTICE : Brother Parry, do you think that you can possibly prove this witness to be less credible than you have already shewn him to be ?

SERGEANT PARRY : No, my Lord.

So the witness was ordered to stand down, and the Court adjourned.

---

[1] The absence of whiskers was, for the bearded virtuous of the Seventies, in itself suspicious, being regarded as presumptive evidence of naughtiness.

[2] The " Beadle of Burlington " was sufficiently a British institution to be included by Gilbert in his catalogue of " all the remarkable people in history."— *Cf.* the Colonel's song in *Patience*, Act I.

IV

Next morning the scene was changed to the Oxford and Cambridge boat race of 6th April 1870. A livery stable-keeper of Torrington Mews deposed that on that date he was ordered to 13 Wakefield Street with a brougham. The defendant Park, dressed as a woman, came out and said, "My sister is not ready." Afterwards Boulton, in similar guise, appeared. He drove them to the boat race and then back to an hotel in the Strand. No one joined them at the boat race. He drove the same parties in "Mrs. Graham's brougham" to the Surrey Theatre on 26th April. He had no idea they were not women. Cross-examined, no one spoke to them at the race nor did they speak to anyone. Martha Stacey said that Boulton and Park had lodged in her house in Wakefield Street for the last year. They never lived there for more than a day or two at a time. They occupied a bedroom and sitting-room on the first floor; Gibbins and Thomas had rooms on the ground floor. All four went about dressed as women and had latchkeys. She saw Thomas break open the door and take away dresses, etc. Cross-examined, Gibbins told her they belonged to him and were used for amateur theatricals. There was neither impropriety nor concealment about their behaviour. She understood they were dressing for theatricals. Sometimes they were not there for months. Re-examined, Thomas was introduced by Boulton. The dresses they wore were, she admitted, "very extreme." Inspector Shenton described his domiciliary visit to Wakefield Street with Detective Chamberlain in April 1870, and identified certain articles produced as found by him.

There were sixteen dresses, satin, rep, and glace ; green cord silk (estimated at £9, 9s) ; violet glace silk, trimmed with white lace (estimated price £10, 10s.) ; black satin, trimmed with mauve satin (estimated at £6) ; blue and white satin, piped with white satin (put at £7) ; a mauve rep silk (put at £8) ; a gray moire antique (put at £10, 10s.) ; a white glace, trimmed with blue satin and lace (£8, 8s.), and a white corded silk (£6, 6s.). Then there were a dozen petticoats, ten cloaks and jackets, half-a-dozen bodices, several bonnets and hats, twenty chignons, and a host of miscellaneous articles—stays, drawers, stockings, boots, curling-irons, gloves, boxes of violet powder and bloom of roses, etc. The estimated value was about £170.[1]

Eleanor Coulton, attendant in the saloon of the Lyceum Theatre, said that Boulton, Park, and Gibbins (whom she had recognised at Bow Street) came into the grand saloon on 27th April and ordered brandies and sodas. They were dressed as women. "They then asked, had we a ladies' room? I said, 'Yes, madame, follow me.' Boulton went into the retiring room, Park remaining outside. Witness next shewed them to their private box, "facing the Prince of Wales's." She took them to be fast women.

The next branch of the evidence involved Lord Arthur Pelham Clinton's relations with the accused. Maria George, née Duffin, said she was servant to Mrs. Peck, at 36 Southampton Street, Strand, from July to November 1868. Lord Arthur lodged in the house all the time she was there, as sometimes did Boulton and Park. She twice saw Boulton dressed as a man ; he usually dressed as a woman. Although she thought him such, she once accused him of being a man. "He said, 'I am Lady Clinton, Lord Arthur's wife.' He shewed me a wedding ring and a keeper on his wedding finger." Park always came there dressed as a gentleman and left dressed as a lady. A hairdresser came every morning to do "Lady Clinton's" hair. Cross-examined, she swore she was in Mrs. Peck's service from July till November. She admitted that Lord Arthur and Boulton went once to Scarborough. Boulton took ladies' clothes with him, but she would not swear he was then dressed as a woman. "He was always dressed as a woman, and always passed as a woman." During the day he wore a woman's dressing-gown. Re-examined, he had a new white muslin dress made for the trip to Scarborough. She mentioned the situation to her mother, who advised her to

---

[1] *Trial*, p. 20.—These articles are other than those abstracted by Gibbins and Thomas.

leave, which she did. Mrs. Susan Duffin, mother of Maria, corroborated. William Dorrell, stationer, Charing Cross, said that he knew Lord Arthur Clinton as a customer. In July 1868 his lordship ordered a seal, to be engraved "Stella"; also a number of visiting cards with the name "Lady Arthur Clinton." The deposition of Francis Egan Cox, who had since died, was then proved and read. He was introduced by a friend to Lord Arthur and Boulton in the Guildhall Tavern in the City. Boulton was dressed as a man but looked like a woman, as deponent believed him to be. He stood them a champagne lunch. "I kissed him, she, or it, believing at the time it was a woman." Lord Arthur appeared to be jealous and left the room. Boulton presented deponent with his photograph, "secretly, so far as Lord Arthur was concerned." He later learned the sex of Boulton, and meeting the pair again at Evans's said, "You damned set of infernal scoundrels, you ought to be kicked out of this place!" [1] Cross-examined, he admitted that Boulton never said he was a woman. "I flirted with him, believing him to be a woman." Ann Empson, 46 Davies Street, Berkeley Square, said that in December 1868 Lord Arthur went to lodge with her. Boulton came on a visit to him; he said he was his cousin. He was dressed as a man. She subsequently gave them notice, and Lord Arthur said "he must go and live in the country with Boulton, and that I had ruined him by turning him out." She detained his lordship's luggage for a debt of £20, 10s. due by him to her, which was still unpaid.

Passing next to the cases of Hurt and Fiske, the Attorney-General called Agnes Dixon, 118 Princes Street, Edinburgh, who stated that Hurt lodged in her rooms for three years. Boulton stayed with him there from October to April 1868–69, occupying sometimes a spare

---

[1] The famous Coffee-House in Covent Garden, the prototype of the " Cave of Harmony " in *The Newcomes*. Serjeant Ballantine devotes a chapter to the house and its frequenters.—*Some Experiences of a Barrister's Life*, vol. i. p. 278. London : 1882.

room, sometimes a sofa bed.   Boulton played the piano a
great deal; but the people in the flat above objected to
his playing on Sunday.[1]   Otherwise his conduct throughout was irreproachable.   He used to be out visiting his
friends by day, and was always home in good time at night.
She never heard that he took part in private theatricals.
Hurt paid all expenses.   Park called from time to time,
as did Fiske.   Detective Holland, of the Edinburgh police,
told how on 9th June 1870 he visited Fiske's rooms as
before related, and described the finding of the album,
also the letters from Hurt to Fiske already quoted.

The sitting closed with the medical evidence for the
Crown, which is not reported but is described as "rather
favourable to, than against, the prisoners Boulton and
Park, to whom it alone applied."   Of the eight "medical
gentlemen" who examined the prisoners in Newgate, the
prosecution called four.   Dr. Paul, the police surgeon,
admitted that he did so without an order from a magistrate.
He was reprimanded by the Lord Chief Justice, who warned
him that if he acted in such a manner again he might find
himself involved "in very unpleasant consequences."   The
other experts were Mr. Gibson, surgeon to Newgate Prison;
Dr. A. S. Taylor, the eminent authority on Forensic
Medicine, who had lately made so conspicuous an appearance in the Palmer case; and Mr. Barwell, of Charing
Cross Hospital.

V

The third day was occupied in the proving and reading
of the voluminous correspondence in which the parties
concerned had all too exuberantly indulged.[2]   Interesting
as the letters are, they are so long and many that I have
space but for such samples as are required to carry on the

[1] To " make a joyful noise " upon the Sabbath Day was then, and still is, an
offence to the godly of Edinburgh.

[2] "About 2000 letters and documents were sent to the Treasury.   The
letters produced were selected from the mass."—Evidence of Mr. Pollard.

tale.   They are divisible into six groups: Hurt to Boulton,
Hurt to Fiske, Hurt to Lord Arthur, Fiske to Boulton,
"Willie" to Boulton, and Park to Lord Arthur.   "Willie"
was a young gentleman named Somerville, a City clerk,
who figured in the indictment, but had not surrendered.

Hurt wrote to Boulton from Lochalsh, Inverness, and
Wick, whither his official duties had taken him in April
1870.   He invited his friend to visit him and his mother
in France later in the month.   "I have told my mother
that you are coming, but have not yet had time to receive
her answer.   I thought it well to tell her that you were
very effeminate, but I hope you will do your best to appear
as manly as you can—at any rate in the face.   I therefore
beg of you to let your moustache grow at once."   He
disapproves of his friend's public impersonations: "even
if in town, I would not go to it [the Derby] with you in
drag"—"drag" being, as appears, the slang term for
women's dress.   And later: "I am sorry to hear of your
going about in drag so much.   I know the moustache has
no chance while this sort of thing goes on.   You have now
less than a month to grow"—before joining Mrs. Hurt at
Bayonne.   "Of course I won't pay any drag bills, except
the one in Edinburgh"; and he concludes with the good
advice: "I should like you to have a little more principle
than I fear you have as to paying debts."

From Hurt's letters to Fiske after the Bow Street
business I have already quoted; but the two consular
communications upon which the Crown mainly relied must,
regrettably, be given in full.

(1)

EDINBURGH, 136 GEORGE STREET, 18th April 1870.

MY DARLING ERNIE,—I am looking for Louis [Hurt] tonight, and
wishing as I do a hundred times each day that you were to be here.   I
have eleven photographs of you (and expecting more tomorrow) which I
look at over and over again.   I have four little notes which I have sealed
up in a packet.   I have a heart full of love and longing ; and my photographs, my four little notes, and my memory are all that I have of you.

When are you going to give me more ? When are you going to write a dozen lines of four words each to say that all the world is over head and ears in love with you, and that you are so tired of adoration and compliments that you turn to your humdrum friend as a relief ? Will it be tomorrow or will it be next week ? Believe me, darling, a word of remembrance from you can never come amiss, only the sooner it comes the better. " Hope deferred "—you know the saying. Adventures do turn up, even in Edinburgh. Perhaps you would envy me for five whole minutes if I were to tell you of one that I've had since you left ; but I will keep it for your own ear when very likely you try after the same happiness. I shall not write you a long note, darling, at least not tonight, perhaps never again, if you don't write to say that I may. I hear Robbie Sinclair is coming here ; his smiling face with the clear grey eyes and vivid roses. I wonder if Louis will like him. I hope not— at least not too much. I am getting very fond of Louis, and as I am fond of Robbie too, I don't want them to take too violently to each other. But what are these fancies and likings to the devotion with which I am yours always, *jusqu' á la mort,*   JOHN S. FISKE.

À un ange qu'on nommé Ernie Boulton, Londres.

(2)

OFFICE, EDINBURGH, *April* 20.

MY DARLING ERNIE,—I had a letter last night from Louis which was charming in every respect except the information it bore that he is to be kept a week or so longer in the North. He tells me you are living in drag. What a wonderful child it is ! I have three minds to come to London and see your magnificence with my own eyes. Would you welcome me ? Probably it is better I should stay at home and dream of you. But the thought of you—Lais and Antinous in one—is ravishing. Let me ask your advice. A young lady, whose family are friends of mine, is coming here. She is a charmingly-dressed beautiful fool with £30,000 a year. I have reason to believe that if I go in for her I can marry her. You know I never should care for her ; but is the bait tempting enough for me to make this further sacrifice to respectability ? Of course, after we were married I could do pretty much as I pleased. People don't mind what one does on £30,000 a year, and the lady wouldn't much mind, as she hasn't brains enough to trouble herself about much beyond her dresses, her carriage, etc. What shall L do ? You see I keep on writing to you, and expect some day an answer to some of my letters. In any case, with all the love in my heart, I am yours,

JOHN S. FISKE.[1]

---

[1] *Trial,* pp. 27–28.

Probably even the limited intelligence attributed to the proposed bride would, after the publication of this letter, be sufficient to apprise her that Mr. Fiske was hardly like to prove an ideal husband. The Attorney-General founded strongly on the classical allusion.[1] For the rest, the letters are strangely anticipative of those produced twenty-four years later upon another and more notorious trial.

Of the Boulton-Clinton series, the first is dated 4th December 1868: "My dear Arthur,—I am just off to Chelmsford with Fanny [Park]. We stay until Monday. Not sent me any money, wretch!—STELLA CLINTON." In another: "I shall be unable to come down on the 18th. Write at once; and if you have any coin, I could do with a little." Again: "My dear Arthur,—We were very drunk last night, and consequently I forgot to write. . . . And now, dear, I must shut up, and remain affectionately yours, —STELLA." "My dear Arthur,—I have waited for two hours for you, and do not like to be treated with such rudeness . . . I shall not return to-night—not at all, if I am to be treated with such rudeness." Finally, and in milder mood: "I am consoling myself in your absence by getting screwed. . . . Mamma sends her kind regards, and will be glad to see you on Sunday."

To make an end of a long story, the following examples of the sprightly Fanny's epistolary manner may be cited:—

(1)

DUKE STREET, *Nov.* 21.

MY DEAREST ARTHUR,—How very kind of you to think of me on my birthday! I had no idea that you would do so. It was very good of you to write, and I am really very grateful for it. I require no remembrances of my sister's husband, as the many kindnesses he has bestowed upon me will make me remember him for many a year, and the birthday present he is so kind as to promise me will only be one addition to the heap of little favours I already treasure up. So many thanks for it,

---

[1] Classical allusions are perilous for the profane ; none but the initiate may employ them with impunity.

dear old man. I cannot echo your wish that I should live to be a hundred, though I should like to live to a green old age. Green, did I say ?
Oh, *ciel !* the amount of paint that will be required to hide the very
unbecoming tint. My " caw fish undertakings " are not at present
meeting with the success which they deserve. Whatever I do seems to
get me into hot water somewhere. But, *n'importe.* What's the odds
as long as you're happy ? Believe me, your affectionate sister-in-law,

FANNY WINIFRED PARK.

(2)

MY DEAREST ARTHUR,—You really must excuse me from interfering
in matrimonial squabbles (for I am sure the present is no more than that) ;
and though I am as you say Stella's *confidante* in most things, that which
you wish to know she keeps locked up in her own breast. My own opinion
on the subject varies fifty times a day when I see you together. She may
sometimes treat you brusquely ; but on the other hand see how she
stands up for your dignity of position (in the matter of Ellis's parts, for
instance), so that I really cannot form an opinion on the subject. As to
all the things she said to you the other night, she may have been tight
and did not know all she was saying ; so that by the time you get my
answer you will both be laughing over the whole affair, as Stella and I
did when we quarrelled and fought down here—don't you remember
when I slapped her face ? My address is the same, as I do not move
out of this street. I have enclosed a note to you in the one I wrote
Stella last night. Good-bye, dear.—Ever yours,   FAN.

(3)

DUKE STREET, *Friday.*

MY DEAREST ARTHUR,—I think I would rather you came in the
middle of the week, as I fancy I am engaged on the Saturday (15th) in
London, though I am not certain yet. If you came on Wednesday and
stayed until Saturday morning (if you could endure me so long), we could
all go up together—that is if I go. But please yourselves. I am always
at home and a fixture. I shall be glad to see you both at any time.
Is the handle of my umbrella mended yet ? If so, I wish you would
kindly send it me, as the weather has turned so showery that I can't go
out without a dread of my back hair coming out of curl. Let me hear
from you at any time ; I am always glad to do so. Ever your affectionate,

FANNY.[1]

When with the reading of the letters the Crown case
closed, Sir John Karslake for Hurt and Henry Matthews

---

[1] *Trial*, p. 29.

for Fiske, maintained that there was no evidence regarding their clients to go to a jury, and protested against their being mixed up with acts and persons of which they knew nothing. The Lord Chief Justice, while sympathising with their position, refused to withdraw the case as against them from the jury.

VI

The fourth day was mainly devoted to the opening speeches of the four leading counsel for the defence. As we must hear these gentlemen again at the end of the trial I shall go on with the witnesses called for the defendants. Of these the first was Mrs. Boulton, the wife of a stockbroker and the mother of Ernest. She stated that he was twenty-two years old, and had dressed up as a girl from the age of six. As a child his favourite rôle was that of a parlourmaid, in which he deceived even his own relations. He was constantly occupied with private theatricals either at home or with friends, and always played female parts. She knew Lord Arthur Clinton as a friend of her son; they used to act together. Ernest stayed with him with her consent, and she and her husband visited them at Lord Arthur's rooms in Southampton Street. They had performed together at the Egyptian Hall, at Chelmsford, Brentwood, Scarborough, and Southend. Ernest used to send her his press notices and all his photographs in character. "His success was something wonderful; bouquets were thrown on the stage." She had known Mr. Park for three years. He often visited her son, who in turn stayed with Park's people at Isleworth. She had known Mr. Hurt intimately. Her son travelled with him and stayed with him in Scotland. She supplied Ernest with money as he required it. He had been in a bank but had to leave, his health being very delicate; he was threatened with consumption. He told her he was called Stella as a nickname. He was always a dutiful and affectionate son, and his only fault was love of admiration.

Cross-examined, she knew nothing of the rooms in Wakefield Street, nor was she aware that her son was going about London in women's dress.

A Scarborough photographer spoke to Boulton and Lord Arthur performing at the Spa Rooms, and to his taking thirty-two photographs of them in character. George Reeves Smith, manager of the Spa Rooms, produced a poster of their performances in 1868. The plays were *A Morning Call*: "Sir Edward Arnold—Lord Arthur Pelham Clinton, M.P.; Mrs. Chillington—Ernest Boulton, Esq."; and *Love and Rain*: "Lady Jane Desmond, a Young Widow—Ernest Boulton, Esq.; Captain Charles Lumley—Lord Arthur Pelham Clinton, M.P." etc. Lord Arthur was also billed for Serjeant Buzfuz's speech from *Pickwick*. The plays were very successful; the speech not so much so. "It needed a serjeant to make it," observed the Lord Chief Justice. The performers cleared £30 by the show.

C. J. Pavitt, actor and musician, said he had known Park, who was articled to a solicitor, since 1867. Park was passionately fond of acting. Witness arranged with Boulton's parents that he should act with Park. They toured Essex with much success. Witness produced a bill: "Mr. Boulton will appear in his wonderful impersonations of female character, which have gained for him a great reputation in London and the provinces," and extracts from laudatory notices in local papers. Sometimes Boulton had as many as fourteen bouquets at one performance. They were often asked out to country houses after the show. Cross-examined, they sometimes went in their professional costumes, when invited to do so. They made profits by their performances, "but they spent them."

Mr. Park, senior, said he was a Master in the Court of Common Pleas and the father of the defendant. He deposed to his son's theatrical proclivities, which were manifested at an early age, and gave evidence as to the dramatic entertainments in which his son took part. He allowed his son a liberal income; since 1866 he had given him about £2500. Boulton had visited at witness's house.

A. E. Gladwell, art dealer, 106 Strand, and Sarah his wife, deposed that they lived in Mrs. Peck's house all the time that Lord Arthur Clinton and Boulton were there. They saw the latter every day, and always dressed as a man. They only once saw him made up as a woman for a private show. They never observed the least impropriety in their conduct. Mrs. Peck, the landlady, gave similar evidence. She had no reason to doubt that Boulton was a man, "except that he was very nice looking." From the evidence of these three witnesses it appeared that, in addition to Maria Duffin, there had been employed in the house at the time another servant, named Eliza Clark, who had not been called by the Crown.

Next day the evidence for the defence was concluded and the hearing of counsel begun. A Chelmsford photographer spoke to having "taken" Park and Lord Arthur in a group. It sold by hundreds after the performance. H. W. Hughes, surgeon, said he had professionally attended Boulton since 1868. He often saw and examined him, both in his father's house and when staying with Lord Arthur. He suffered from extreme constitutional weakness, resulting in an abscess, for which witness operated. Dr. Le Gros Clarke, Mr. H. J. Johnson, and Mr. Harvey, who had examined Boulton and Park, gave medical evidence, of which it is sufficient to state that it was "highly favourable to the defendants," and subversive of that given by the Crown experts.

Evidence was then led in behalf of Hurt. Three officials of the General Post Office, Edinburgh, deposed that they had known the defendant since he entered the service in 1868. They had repeatedly seen Boulton when staying with Hurt; he was never dressed as a woman. Hurt and Boulton had dined at their respective houses. Mrs. Brown, designed as "a Scotchwoman," landlady of the Galloway Inn, Markinch, said that Hurt used to put

up at her house on his official visits to the district. He
was twice accompanied by Boulton, who spent his time
playing and singing at the piano. "He was a vera pleasant
sort of young man—he did not amuse me, he amused
himself." Their behaviour was perfectly proper.

The evidence given for Fiske was as follows: Donald
Sinclair, clerk in the Register Office, Edinburgh, said he
had known defendant since 1868. Fiske mixed much in
Edinburgh society—"he sought the society of ladies a
great deal"—was a man of taste and culture, and a good
musician. Witness often dined with him in his rooms in
George Street. On one occasion when Mr. Bowman, an
American; Professor Van Hoe; his brother, the "Robbie"
of the letters; and himself were guests, witness "expressed
a wish to see young Boulton," of whom he had favourably
heard. Whereupon their host wrote and shewed him the
following note: "Darling Ernie,—do come up tonight.
Everybody is too drunk to mind. Donald is here and
wants to see you. So come, love." There was a post-
script: "Bring Mr. P.", which referred to Park. Boulton
came in morning dress. There was not the slightest impropriety that evening on the part of anyone. Cross-
examined, the dinner was on Boat Race night, 1870.
Despite the written testimony of the host, nobody was
drunk. He understood the phrase: "everybody is too
drunk to mind": to refer to morning dress. Eliza Corner,
of 136 George Street, Edinburgh, said Fiske had occupied
her rooms for two and a half years, and had never been
absent one night. He used to give dinner parties. Boulton
dined there once. He called several times in the spring
of 1870, but all his visits were within a fortnight. Charles
Doeg, one of the clerks of the Court of Session, said he
had known Fiske intimately. He was well bred, well
educated, and delighted in musical and literary society.
His expressions were sometimes romantic and exaggerated.
Witness regarded him as a man of high moral character,
"remarkably sensitive to the feelings of others." The

evidence for the defence was then closed, with the exception of that of the missing witness, Eliza Clark, who had now been traced and would be adduced when procurable.

VII

Four long and eloquent addresses were made by counsel for the defence. Digby Seymour, for Boulton, urged the jury not to be carried away by any prejudice excited by the fóolish conduct of these young men in wearing women's dresses, nor from such folly rashly to assume criminality. There was not an atom of evidence of any incitement to immorality by the defendants, either as to themselves or others. The dresses were procured for theatrical purposes; the photographs were taken to supply the public demand created by Mr. Boulton's performances. They were none of them immodest. What was there beyond these dresses and photographs? Nothing but a few ambiguous passages in boyish and foolish letters. How, in view of the mother's evidence, could the cruel inferences of the, prosecution be upheld? The Attorney-General would probably say that there was mischief in these dramatic performances.

THE LORD CHIEF JUSTICE : I am quite sure he will not.

THE ATTORNEY-GENERAL : Certainly not, my Lord. I expressly stated that the theatricals were perfectly innocent.

THE LORD CHIEF JUSTICE : It is not worth while to raise up giants simply in order to slay them.

Mr. Seymour said he was only too glad that any giants had been slain in that wretched case. If all these tours were innocent, what remained that was indicative of guilt? —that these foolish youths, with their wardrobe of theatrical dresses, went on to use them in their idle and culpable frolics in London. Counsel was hard upon the "Beadle of Burlington," whom he unkindly described as a blackmailer of prostitutes; and he pointed out that the Alhambra incident was plainly a case of mistaken identity, for in

March 1870 Boulton was proved to have been in Edinburgh. As to the Southampton Street episode, the Crown relied on a single witness, contradicted expressly and entirely by four respectable witnesses. It was most important that Mr. and Mrs. Boulton were aware that their son was staying with Lord Arthur Clinton, and themselves visited at the house. The Treasury knew that Clark, the other servant, would not confirm Duffin, and therefore they had shewn no anxiety to obtain her attendance, but that would now be done by the defence. Having reviewed the medical evidence, he said it was proved that this unhappy young man had been labouring under painful disease during the very period covered by this alleged conspiracy, and was actually under medical attendance during his visit to Lord Arthur Clinton. Yet the whole case for the prosecution was based upon the assumption of Boulton's guilt. The jury would not fail to bear in mind that in this matter it was not Boulton alone who was concerned, but the character of Lord Arthur Clinton, who was dead and beyond the reach of human judgment, but whose memory was dear to his relatives and friends, and ought not, without evidence, to be branded with shame.

The two addresses of Serjeant Parry for Park are more readable and racy than the speeches of his learned friends, either because they are better reported or because he was more eloquent than they. The essence of the indictment, he pointed out in his opening, was agreement to commit a crime. No man could be indicted for mere intention to commit a crime, and the agreement must be shewn by overt acts. The Crown was trying to get a conviction for conspiracy to commit crime, without any evidence but such as was insufficient to prove the crime itself.

But what evidence was there of the supposed conspiracy beyond the mere going about as women ? And this had arisen naturally from their assumption of female characters. Park, no doubt, had imbibed from Boulton this wretched taste for performing female characters. In former times these characters were always performed by boys ; yet

it was a remarkable fact that in the immoral reign of Charles II., when
this was frequent, no immorality appeared to have attached to the
practice.   These young men had performed female characters in many
towns, openly and publicly, for charities, to the knowledge of the whole
community ;   and they were actually invited to parties after the performance and desired to retain their female costume.   The practice of
men performing female characters prevailed at that moment upon the
stage, even with the sanction of the Lord Chamberlain.   These things
were done ;   and if so, why should guilt be inferred against these young
men because they did it ? [1]

A greater degree of familiarity necessarily prevailed among
actors than among graver classes of society, and it was
most unfair to judge these young men by the harsher
standard of life and manners prescribed by those who had
no sympathy with theatrical amusements.   This did not
excuse their going about the streets as women, but it led
to it.   It did not excuse the various acts of impropriety
which they seemed to have committed, "and which would
have well warranted their being kicked out of the places
where they appeared."   But there was a great gulf between
culpable, idiotic folly and criminality.   Their theatrical
dresses had been paraded by the police in court at Bow
Street, and he (counsel) was told by a friend that a thrill of
horror ran through the jury-box!   Photographs and letters
had also been produced; but after all that had been
rumoured it must be a relief to the jury to find that not
one indecent photograph, not one indecent word, had been
discovered in any of these.

The letters of Park to Lord Arthur Clinton had been commented
on ;   but what, after all, did they contain that was not chaff, or that
was not fully accounted for by their manner of life—even to the name
Fanny Winifred Park—a name coined' from his initials after he had
acted female parts !   There could be no doubt whatever that off the
stage they treated each other as females, going by female names ;   and
if the jury had seen these letters unexplained, and knew nothing of the
characters of those who wrote them, they might have put a worse

---

[1] *Trial*, p. 36.—This savours somewhat of that giant-slaying deprecated by
the Lord Chief Justice.

construction on them. But what construction could even the learned Attorney-General put upon such an expression as " Is the handle of my umbrella mended ? " Was it inconsistent with innocence to write, " I cannot go out, it is so rainy, and my back hair will get out of curl " ? And could they upon such expressions find that these young men were guilty of the crime imputed to them ? [1]

Sir John Karslake, for Hurt, complained of the injustice done to his client in mixing him up with the other defendants. The case against him lay in such small compass that it could not have lasted half a day. It consisted of a few letters and a visit of Boulton to Edinburgh. Their acquaintance had been fully explained by Mrs. Boulton: they were old family friends: yet such were the materials out of which the Crown constructed this odious charge. Mr. Hurt was placed in the most cruel position which any innocent man could occupy; however clearly it might be proved that he was unjustly accused, the finger of suspicion would be pointed at him throughout his whole life. He went at once to London and attended the police court, hoping to be called as a witness, when suddenly and without notice he was himself arrested. He was not taken before a magistrate in the ordinary course; he was not sent back to Scotland for trial, where his character and manner of life were known; but the unfair course was adopted of joining his name in an indictment in respect of proceedings in which the Crown well knew he had no possible concern.

Henry Matthews made the same point in behalf of Fiske, against whom he held there was no evidence, beyond a casual acquaintance with Boulton and one or two letters. Had Fiske not been conscious of innocence he could have fled to America; but though for two months the press was ringing with the case and he was warned by Hurt that his name had come out, he not only remained in Edinburgh,

---

[1] *Trial*, p. 37.—One recalls what the Serjeant's learned brother Buzfuz made out of the famous warming-pan passage in *Bardell* v. *Pickwick*.

but volunteered to give evidence, and when he did so was
accused and arrested.

He [counsel] was not going to attempt to justify the execrable taste,
the indelicacy of penning such letters, but he asked them [the jury] to
view them in the light of notes addressed to an effeminate lad ; a dainty
and pleasing boy, who was generally treated as a young girl, and who
was so addressed by Fiske. They would not be able to convict Fiske
on the letters alone ; and consequently it was sought to shew some
opportunity for the commission of the offence. The dinner party was
the occasion that had been fixed upon by the prosecution for that
purpose ; but he urged that the evidence of Mr. Sinclair had demonstrated that nothing of that nature took place there.[1]

VIII

The sixth and last day of the trial opened with the
examination of Eliza Clark, whose attendance, we read,
"had been secured by the earnest exertions of Mr. Lewis,
the attorney for the defendants." This damsel stated
that she was housemaid to Mrs. Peck, Southampton Street,
during the whole period of Lord Arthur's tenancy. Duffin,
her fellow-servant, was only there one month. Boulton
always dressed as a man. She once saw him and Park
dressed as women, when they were going to some private
theatricals. Mr. and Mrs. Boulton used to call to see their
son. Lord Arthur and Mr. Boulton always conducted
themselves as gentlemen. Cross-examined, she admitted
that she had told the Treasury: "We all thought for the
first month that Boulton was a woman dressed in men's
clothes." Mrs. Peck had maintained that as his parents
came to see him, he must be a man; but she and her
fellow-servant still believed he was a woman. Re-
examined, she took Boulton to be a woman only on
account of his voice when singing: he sang like a woman.
Duffin left because she was going to be married.

Mr. Seymour having said he had no observations to
make upon this evidence, the Attorney-General rose to

[1] *Trial*, p. 50.

reply for the Crown. Referring to the complaints of the
defendants' counsel as to the accused not being tried
separately, he said that if ever there was a case in which
it was desirable that there should be only one trial, it was
that case. He held that the case for the prosecution had
been proved, and that it had received no answer.

And it is my duty to submit to you that, considering the conduct and
demeanour of these persons, the manner in which they were associated,
the terms upon which they lived, and the way in which they wrote to
each other—for to the letters I attach great importance—it is for you
to say whether all these appearances are to be referred to innocent
friendship and idle frolic, or to a guilty and immoral confederacy.[1]

The lodgings in Wakefield Street, where the dresses were
kept, were secret and clandestine, and could not have
been taken for theatrical purposes, as there were only two
or three performances in London. The dresses were used for
walking the streets and going to public places of amusement at all hours of the night, with a persistency which
precluded the idea that it was all a mere frolic. The
"frolic" was continued after the most painful humiliations:
after they had been thrust out from the Alhambra and the
Arcade. As to the Southampton Street *ménage*, he argued
that Duffin's evidence was to be preferred to that of those
who contradicted her. It was for the jury to judge from
the letters and all the circumstances what were the real
relations between Lord Arthur Clinton and Ernest Boulton.
He admitted that as against Hurt and Fiske there was no
evidence beyond their letters, but from these he suggested
certain inferences. Having thrown over the police surgeon
and admitted that the medical evidence for the defence
"had gone further than he anticipated," he still maintained
that at least there was evidence of instigation and incitement to immorality, and he accordingly asked for a conviction.

---

[1] *Trial*, p. 53.

The Lord Chief Justice then charged the jury.[1] He expressèd at the outset his disapprobation of the form in which the case had been presented to the Court.

We are trying the defendants for conspiracy to commit a felonious crime, and the proof of it, if it amounts to anything, amounts to proof of the actual commission of crime. . . . I am clearly of opinion that where the proof intended to be submitted to a jury is proof of the actual commission of crime, it is not the proper course to charge the parties with conspiring to commit it, for that course manifestly operates unfairly and unjustly and oppressively against the parties concerned. The prosecution are thus enabled to combine in one indictment a variety of offences which if treated individually, as they ought to be, would exclude the possibility of giving evidence in one case to the prejudice of defendants in others ; and they are thus deprived of the incalculable advantage of being able in one case to avail themselves of the evidence of defendants in others.[2]

This view, his lordship observed, was held also by Lord Cranworth. With regard to the actual facts of the case, what had been proved against the defendants Boulton and Park was sufficient to stamp them with the deepest disgrace, although they might not have had any felonious intention. Their going, for example, to the ladies' rooms at theatres and other public places was an offence which the legislature might justly visit with corporal punishment. But the jury must not allow their indignation at such indecent proceedings to warp their judgment in trying the far more serious accusation; and the question was whether, from this species of conduct, with reference to all the other facts in the case, they could draw the conclusion that the defendants in so acting had the intention and design imputed to them. Now, the explanation offered was that

---

[1] Of Sir Alexander Cockburn it has been well observed : " Equally distinguished at the bar, in the House of Commons, and on the Bench, he is one of the two or three most striking personalities in the legal history of the century."— *Famous Trials of the Century.* By J. B. Atlay, p. 355. London : 1899. Fortunately for the reader, his lordship's summing-up was brief in comparison with his charge in the Tichborne trial three years later, which occupied twenty days and established a judicial record that is unlikely to be broken.

[2] *Trial*, p. 55.

these dresses were purchased for theatrical performances;
and it was proved beyond doubt that such performances
had been going on since 1867. In 1868 they were given
at Scarborough with Lord Arthur Clinton; and in 1869
Boulton and Park were associated in a series of them in
Essex. There was therefore a lawful occasion for the
possession of the dresses. No doubt the last-named defendants afterwards got into the habit of wearing these
dresses in public places; but the jury must say whether
they were satisfied that in doing so the defendants had the
intention imputed to them. There was no proof of any
incitement to immorality. On the contrary it appeared
that they were always with their own party, that no one
except Mr. Mundell ever joined them, and that in this
instance there was no impropriety. As regards the relations of Boulton and Lord Arthur, the evidence of the
servant girl called for the prosecution was contradicted by
that of three other witnesses—the landlady, her sister, and
her sister's husband, and also by the other servant called
that day, who gave her evidence in the most apparently
truthful manner. It was a striking fact that whereas,
according to the evidence for the prosecution, Boulton
always dressed as a woman, the other girl fancied him a
woman, dressed as a man. Having read to the jury the
letters of the defendants Boulton and Park to Lord
Arthur, his lordship observed:—

These expressions were strongly relied upon for the prosecution;
but was there not a solution consistent with innocence? These parties
had been mixed up together in performances in which Lord Arthur
continually acted with Boulton as his lover or husband, and it may have
been that, half in fun at first and then habitually, they spoke of each
other in that kind of way.[1]

The lodgings in Wakefield Street appeared to have been
used for the deposit of theatrical costumes and for the
occasional assumption of female dress in these foolish
masqueradings; but nothing improper was ever observed

[1] *Trial*, p. 57.

there.   With regard to the defendants Hurt and Fiske his
lordship observed:—

I must emphatically say that I am of opinion that Mr. Hurt and Mr.
Fiske ought never to have been put upon their trial in this country at all.
In the first place gross injustice is done them, as they are mixed up with
matters with which they had nothing at all to do, but which are calculated to excite great prejudice ; and the administration of justice is
most seriously embarrassed by the proceeding. . . . Hurt and Fiske
had nothing to do with the conduct of Boulton and Park in going about
in women's dresses ; and Hurt in one of his letters actually remonstrated against it.   In my opinion the offence, if any, was committed in
Scotland, and it is there that these parties ought to have been tried. . . .
    It is easy to see how all this happened.   The police had taken up
the case ; and the whole course and conduct of it confirm the opinion I
have always entertained as to the necessity for a public prosecutor to
control and to conduct criminal prosecutions.   The police seized the
prisoners' letters, and found those of Hurt and Fiske ; they went to
Edinburgh, and without any authority searched their lodgings ; then
they arrested them, and put them on their trial here along with Park
and Boulton, without taking them before a magistrate at all.   Thus
they are tried with the two other defendants for an alleged offence
having no connection whatever with their conduct.[1]

The only thing proved against them was their own letters;
and whatever may have been the meaning of those letters,
the prosecution had to shew that they were received and
responded to in the same sense.   But of that there was
no proof; and it was suggested that they meant no more
than the romantic expression of personal admiration and
affection.   No doubt such feelings and attachments had
existed and might exist without any evil.   It was for the
jury to judge whether there was anything immoral in
these letters, and whether, even if so, there was a concur-
rence in them, such as was essential to support the charge
of conspiracy.

    The jury then retired to consider their verdict, and
when fifty-three minutes later they returned to Court,
they found the four defendants Not Guilty on all counts.
The verdict was received with applause—"Loud cheers,

---

[1] *Trial*, p. 58.

and cries of 'Bravo!'" Ernest, to the shame of his moustache, fainted in the dock and had to be revived with water; it was a last tribute to the shade of Stella. Fanny, fortified by whiskers, never turned a hair.

IX

The epitaph upon this extraordinary trial was pronounced by the *Times* in a sensible and judicious leading article, from which, by way of finale, I take the following excerpts:—

It is not without a certain sense of relief that we record this morning the failure of a prosecution which nothing but a strong conviction of public duty would have justified the Government in instituting. THE QUEEN *v.* BOULTON AND OTHERS is a case in which a verdict for the Crown would have been felt at home, and received abroad, as a reflection on our national morals, yet which, for that very reason, could not be hushed up after popular rumour had once invested it with so grave a complexion. Viewing it as it now appears by the light thrown on it in the Court of Queen's Bench, we may wonder that it was not disposed of before the magistrates in April last, instead of being exalted to the dignity of a State trial. . . . The discoveries which the police were believed to have made, the disappearance of several persons inculpated, and the sudden death of the one whose rank made him the most conspicuous, aggravated these suspicions to the highest degree. . . . Now that justice has been satisfied and the whole story thoroughly sifted, the verdict of the jury should be accepted as clearing all the defendants of the odious guilt imputed to them.[1]

Although the "'orrible tale" told by the police turned out after all to be a mare's-nest, one feels none the less that the defendants deserved a lesson, by which it is to be hoped they profited. And if, for the future, Stella and Fanny confined their realistic impersonations to the boards; if Mr. Hurt chose his acquaintances with greater discretion; and if Mr. Fiske learned to frame his correspondence in better harmony with the precepts of *The Complete Letter-Writer*, it would doubtless be more comfortable for all concerned.

---

[1] *Times*, 16th May 1870.

MRS. JEFFRAY'S RATS:

A VILLAGE TALE

MRS. JEFFRAY'S RATS:

A Village Tale

The possession of poisonous matter by the person charged with the administration of it is always an important fact, and when death has been caused by poison of the same kind, and no satisfactory explanation of that fact is given by the accused or suggested by the surrounding circumstances, a strong inference of guilt may be created against the accused ; especially if he has attempted to account for such possession by false statements.

—WILLS *On Circumstantial Evidence.*

IT is long since I "did" a murder; and some of my less gentle readers, accustomed to taste the blood of my providing, may have found the relatively mild misconduct of my late protagonists rather insipid. So to make up for lost time and to give them, the ungentle ones, full value for their money, I have chosen a case of notable depravity, embracing in its sanguineous scope no fewer than two homicides equally atrocious, and concluding—I trust as well to their satisfaction as to that of justice—with the judicial extirpation of the culprit.

I hope, too, that they may share the relief I personally experience in returning once again to my native land. No mere English malefactor is, to my mind at least, a patch upon the kindly Scot, whose crimes, in common with the national products, whisky and haggis, have about them a distinctive flavour not to be found in the concoctions of the sister realm. The Sassenach may on occasion be as bloody-minded and abandoned, but he wears his rue with a difference. Further, our forms of trial, no less than of our crimes, have for me as a Scot the stronger appeal; and indeed (to let you into a secret) it is both easier and more congenial to work with authorities local and familiar

187

than to go a-whoring—if I may so biblically phrase it—
into strange lands upon an alien quest.— But unhappily,
as I have elsewhere deplored, the supply of purely Scottish
crime adapted to my purpose waxes low. In my own day
—now, alas, a fairly long one—I have been privileged to
attend in Edinburgh but half-a-dozen murder trials; in
quantity a ·poor crop, but the quality was of the best.
Some incidents of these recur to me·as I write: the wailing
of Jessie King, the baby-farmer of Stockbridge, as she was
carried from the dock to the cells below—my first experience, and a gruesome one; Laurie, the Arran murderer,
receiving unmoved his death sentence late on a November
night, in the gloomy courtroom with candles gleaming on
the bench, and turning round to face the crowded audience,
declaiming: "Ladies and gentlemen, I am innocent of this
charge"; the moment when imperturbable Mr. Monson,
of Ardlamont, as the Solicitor-General closed his thrilling
reconstruction of the alleged attempt to drown young
Hambrough, asked for a brief adjournment; Oscar Slater's
heart-rending outbreak upon the pronouncement of his
doom; and last but not least, the brilliancy of Mr. Craigie
Aitchison's defence of the lad Merrett upon the fearful
charge of matricide.

With some of these famous cases it has been my lot,
whether as editor or essayist, to deal; and I have also for
many years assiduously searched, not without result, our
criminal records. Yet what are these my inconsiderable
gleanings to the glorious harvests of the South? English
Sunday papers have a brand new murder in well nigh
every column! As a sober Scot I stand aghast at what
must be going on beyond the Border. It would seem that
the Englishman's house, no longer his castle, is become
for him a slaughterhouse; and if I may believe the Sab-
batical newsmongers aforesaid, there will soon be more
murderers in England than jurymen to send them to the
scaffold—a sad reflection upon the boasted progress of
civilisation.

While of course I should deprecate such a shocking state of things in Scotland, I cannot but feel that loyal Scots might do more to keep me supplied with suitable material. Like Mr. Jingle, I do "not presume to dictate"; I merely throw out this hint to my contemporaries, trusting that their natural good feeling and sense of patriotic duty may move them to redress my grievance. I stipulate, however, that I myself am not to be made the subject of such improvement, for then I should be precluded from profiting by their zeal. But, stay; I see it printed in an English weekly journal—which, being such, cannot lie—that "Scots do their best work in England"; so, perchance, in this regard I wrong my fellow-countrymen. It may be that they, in their modest manner, have helped anonymously to swell the volume of Southern crime, and that the key to some of those unsolved mysteries which have long baffled Scotland Yard is to be found, after all, above a Scottish door!

I

Elizabeth Nicklson or Jeffray, whose execution for double murder confers upon her high rank among homicidal dames, was, says her biographer,[1] born at Corbridge, south of Tweed, in the year 1802, of the usual respectable parents.[2] Her father was a publican; but despite the unholy nature of his calling, he did not fail to instil into the breast of Elizabeth "every principle that tends to ensure the future well-being of the child." She lost her mother early, losing also the benefit of that relationship; "but her active, well-moulded form and beautiful coun-

---

[1] *A Sketch of the Life and Trial of Mrs. Jeffray, executed for Double Murder, at Glasgow, on the 21st May, 1838; with Remarks on the Verdict of the Jury, and also upon Capital Punishments.* Glasgow: John Morrison; W. R M'Phun; Edinburgh: J. Stillie; Lanark: W. Robertson; Hamilton: W. Lyon; Wishaw: W. P ttigrew. MDCCCXXXVIII. pp. 64.

[2] I wish, with Tristram Shandy, that in this matter her begetters had been more considerate; for Elizabeth was thus by birth an Englishwoman, and only acquired a Scottish domicile in respect of marriage to a Scotsman. But she sinned and suffered in Scotland, which is sufficient for my present aim.

tenance, lighted up with the joyous hilarity of childhood, along with her innocent prattle, made her a great favourite in her father's house." These juvenile charms are hardly to be traced in her surviving portrait; but as was well observed by Mrs. Harris, that experienced matron, "Years and our trials sets marks upon us all": Elizabeth's later adventures were not calculated to have upon her expression a softening effect.

When she was seven years old her father, being unfortunate in the public line, removed across the Border to Coldstream, where he commenced schoolmaster. What were his qualifications for this learned office does not appear; but Elizabeth, averse from the change, induced her small brother to elope with her, and after long search the fugitives were captured fifteen miles on their way back to Corbridge—an instance of that force of mind whereby she afterwards became distinguished. Her father married again, and the stepmother contributed materially to the contents of his quiver; but notwithstanding the many calls, scholastic and paternal, now made upon his time, he kept a watchful eye upon his eldest child. That young lady required some looking after, as "the uncommon beauty of her person early attracted the admiration of the youth of the opposite sex." The vigilance of her parent, however, was more than matched by the ingenuity of the maid, for it was her nightly and naughty practice, so soon as the old folks were asleep and the house door barred, to "slip out by the window" to meet one of her too abundant admirers. "But she was not always successful in deceiving her parents, and she received several severe beatings from her father when he discovered her." Elizabeth, deeming the game worth the candle, continued her irregular course, until, the demise of her respected progenitor having freed her from all restraint, "night after night beheld her the object of love, and consequently of contention, amongst the numerous band of suitors who sought to win her smiles." Such reprehensible conduct could have but one end: "the fatherless girl fell a prey to the practised seducer, amidst the execrations of the neighbourhood at the titled villain." The style and title of this peccant nobleman is not disclosed. He may perhaps have been a member of that illustrious house with which the Chuzzlewit family claimed connection.

A year later, as Elizabeth with her child in her arms was standing at her father's door, there chanced to pass that way a soldier of the Berwickshire militia, "who appeared much struck with her beauty." With military promptness and decision he introduced himself, and invited the fair one to an adjacent tavern, where, after suitable refreshment, he proposed marriage. "Would you take me," frankly asked Elizabeth, "when you see that I have a child of my own in my arms?" The gallant suitor was undismayed: he did not care for that; he would take them both together. So the couple became engaged. The swain, who bore the famous name of Francis Jeffray, was a native of Bathgate; and a friend and fellow-soldier, hailing from the same village, shared also his admiration for Elizabeth. Professionally a believer in the proverb touching fairness in love and war, the friend sought to win her favour by libelling Jeffray to his betrothed; she communicated these "outrageous falsehoods" to her lover, with the result that the friends violently quarrelled. Her vanity was gratified by this tribute to her attractions, and in after-life the incident was with her a favourite anecdote. She was nineteen and he eighteen when they were married; and as the militiaman was allowed to go home, they began their joint adventure in Bathgate, where Francis plied his trade as a weaver and Elizabeth kept lodgers.

During the seven years of their sojourn there the behaviour of the young wife was far from blameless. Her neighbours viewed her with suspicion, and her biographer laments that the precepts taught her by her godly parent were forgotten, "while the debasing effect of her seducer's tuition triumphed over every virtuous principle." She took her illegitimate pleasures sadly, developing a dour, leaden-hearted callousness, and her hate and malice were readily aroused. It is characteristic of her temperament that having a grudge against a neighbouring dame, she poisoned her pig—"a large full-grown one"—by way of revenge. The episode is to be regarded as a preliminary sketch or study for her greater works, and one would like to have known more about it; but no details of the poisoning of the pig have been preserved. Other peculiarities of Mrs. Jeffray detracted from her popularity. A young couple, who set up house next door, alarmed at the unaccountable decrease of their provisions, determined to set a trap. The wife went ostentatiously out, locking the door after her, while the husband secreted himself in the kitchen. Presently the door was opened with a false key and Mrs. Jeffray entered; the husband "sprang out of his hiding-place": tableau! It was a situation of some delicacy, and as such was considered by the local authorities; "but owing to interest being used" and as it was the lady's first offence, she was dismissed with a reprimand.

Besides keeping lodgers—"one of whom," it is significantly recorded, "died suddenly"—Mrs. Jeffray ran a small cook-shop; but in 1826, by reason of the general poverty of the time due to scarcity of work, she could recover nothing from those customers to whom she had supplied goods on credit, with the result that the business failed. So angry was her husband at her mismanagement, "and also for some other parts of her conduct which were perhaps not so innocent," that he left her, secretly, in the lurch. In February 1827, in a state of complete destitution, Francis Jeffray came to the village of Carluke in Lanarkshire, where he was charitably furnished with lodging and a web, with a view to plying his old trade as a weaver. Before harvest he was joined by his lady wife, who had discovered the place of his retreat. Her presence cannot have contributed to the amenity of the ménage, for having quarelled with the landlady, she "seized a knife,

(From a contemporary lithograph.)

[*To face p.* **192.**

and threatened to rip her up." For this ebullition of temper Elizabeth was bound over to keep the peace.

It was the custom of the villagers to go in company each autumn "to the English harvest." On one such occasion, when on their way to Coldstream, the party fell in with a packman. We shall hear further of this travelling merchant. At Alnwick, though everyone else was hard up, Elizabeth boasted: "The devil may care, I have got enough to keep Frank and myself for a week at any rate." She was still in funds when they "wrought" together at the shearing at Innerleithen on their homeward trek, for she suggested that a bottle of whisky be purchased and "a spree kicked up." The liquor procured, "they drank it out of a tea cup"—probably from motives of delicacy, as in the leading case of Mrs. Gamp. It must have been above proof, for we read that "a tremendous row ensued; bowls, milk, and spoons were flying in every direction, to the astonishment and alarm of the farmer's household." Next morning the jovial crew proceeded to Peebles where they worked for a week, and so returned to Carluke. On arriving at her home Mrs. Jeffray was shocked to find that her husband's silver watch, which had been left in the house when they went a-shearing, had been stolen, and she did not hesitate to connect with its disappearance the neighbour who had looked after her house and children during her absence. But the rear guard of the shearers, arriving at Carluke, told how they had met the packman, who informed them that Mrs. Jeffray had "sold him a watch secretly"! Obviously Elizabeth was not given to stick at trifles, and in her humble way had something of the subtlety of the bewitching Lizzie in *The Eustace Diamonds*.

Nothing further of note occurs in her chronicle until Whitsunday 1837. On that date there came to lodge with Mrs. Jeffray a young man named Hugh Munro, a native of the Isle of Skye, who worked as a day labourer in the village. At the same term a room, described as "but and

13

ben"[1] with the apartment of Mrs. Jeffray, was occupied by Mrs. Ann Newal or Carl, widow of Peter Carl, sometime weaver in Carluke, an indigent and aged woman, whose declining years were to be affectionately cared for by her kindly neighbour. It was, as appears, an unlucky house: the old lady died suddenly on 5th October, after a few hours' illness; and hardly had Mrs. Jeffray recovered from the shock of her venerable friend's demise, than on the 28th young Munro was also suddenly struck down, and despite the assiduous attentions of his landlady, died early on the 31st. These happenings were the more untimely in that Mrs. Jeffray's eldest daughter, having been thrice duly "called" in the parish church, was that week to be married to the man of her choice, and the ceremony could not conveniently be postponed. The wedding—what is termed in Scotland a "penny" one, *i.e.* one at which each guest is expected to contribute to the cost of the entertainment—took place on the evening of Friday, 3rd November, the joy of the occasion being, it is to be presumed, somewhat shadowed by the tragic events of the week.

Meantime rumour had been busy about the bride's mother and her two patients. On Saturday the body of Hugh Munro was exhumed and a post-mortem examination of the remains was made, as a result of which the body of Mrs. Carl was likewise raised from its rest on the 6th, and similarly examined. On the 10th Mrs. Jeffray was arrested in her bed, and carried before the Procurator-Fiscal of Lanarkshire at the Commercial Inn. The interview not proving satisfactory to that authority, she was lodged in Lanark jail; and having emitted a declaration before the Sheriff, was in due course committed for trial upon the double charge of murder. "For a few weeks after her apprehension she was in great distress of mind, but gradually got more composed, and employed her time in reading the Bible, sewing, and dressing, which made the

---

[1] *But* the outer, *ben* the inner apartment of a two-roomed house.—Jamieson's *Scottish Dictionary.*

time hang less heavy upon her hands; and in accordance
with her declaration when she was first examined, she still
declared her entire innocence."

II

In the spring of 1838 the Lords Commissioners of
Justiciary, being upon the West Circuit, came in due
course to Glasgow. The judges for the occasion were
Lords Mackenzie and Medwyn. Robert Handyside,
Advocate-Depute, appeared for the Crown; James Craufurd (later Lord Ardmillan) conducted the defence. The
diet being called: Her Majesty's Advocate against Elizabeth Jeffray: on 30th April 1838, the prisoner was placed
at the bar, charged with the murder of Mrs. Ann Carl by
the administration to her of arsenic, mixed with meal,
water, and whisky, and also with the murder of Hugh
Munro by administering to him arsenic mixed with porridge, respectively on 4th and 28th October 1837; and
with a further administration to Munro of arsenic mixed
with rhubarb on the 30th of that month. To these charges
the pannel pleaded not guilty.[1]

After formal evidence of the emission by the accused
of the customary declaration, William Gold, weaver, pre-
centor in the parish church of Carluke, deponed to the
proclamation of the banns of marriage with the pannel's
daughter on three consecutive Sundays of October, and
the subsequent marriage of the young lady, as already
mentioned. James Graham, wright (joiner) and under-
taker in Carluke, said that a coffin was ordered for Mrs. Carl
on the day of her death. "They wished to have the
deceased buried that night"; witness delivered the coffin
to Mrs. Jeffray's house, put the body into it, and attended
the interment. Later, he received a similar order in behalf
of Hugh Munro, which he executed in the like manner.

---

[1] Swinton's *Reports of Cases before the High Court and Circuit Courts of
Justiciary*, vol. ii. p. 113.

The prisoner was present on these occasions. John Gilchrist, grave-digger, Carluke, said that Mrs. Carl was buried the day she died; he dug her grave and afterwards performed the exhumation. He had known the deceased personally for many years. Munro was also buried the same day he died. His body was likewise exhumed. Other witnesses, who had attended the funerals, spoke to the re-opening of the graves and to the identifying of the bodies.

Jane Harkness, who "carries on the business of drug-gist in Carluke," said that she knew the two deceased and remembered hearing of their successive deaths. She stated that Mrs. Jeffray, prior to those events, more than once bought arsenic from her. "The first time she got arsenic she sent a little girl, Marion Tennant, for it. She [Marion] brought a 'line,' and said the arsenic was for Mrs. Jeffray. Witness sent her niece along with the girl to see the arsenic delivered and to charge Mrs. Jeffray to take care of it, in case any accident might happen. She labelled it with the word 'Poison'; the price paid was 3d." On the Monday before Munro's death Mrs. Jeffray herself called at witness's shop and purchased another half-ounce of arsenic. She remarked that she required it for the purpose of poisoning rats: "*she had killed one rat with the first quantity, and she wanted to try again*"! She also bought 3d. worth of laudanum, "for a sick lodger who had been attacked by cholera." She returned for a further supply next day, saying she had lost what she had previously bought. Munro died that day, Tuesday. Jane Bowman, the niece, corroborated. "Pannel said the arsenic was to poison rats, with which she had 'been annoyed some nights previously."

Walter Cullens, apprentice to James Miller, weaver, Carluke, said he was a nephew of Mrs. Carl, with whom he lived "but and ben" with Mrs. Jeffray. On the Wednesday before his aunt died she was confined to bed by illness. The pannel sent him out to procure some whitening; when

he returned he met her coming out of his aunt's room.
She then "sent him away for sand"; when he came back,
Mrs. Jeffray said "she had offered the old woman a drink,
but she would not take it; and requested him to persuade
her to take it, as it would be the first thing that would do
her good." Mrs. Jeffray was then standing in her own
room, with a bowl containing a liquid of a white appearance
in her hand. She invited witness to taste it, remarking
that "it was very good." He did so; there was oatmeal
mixed with the brew; it had a sour taste and smelt of
whisky. Convinced, as appears, by its repellant flavour
that the draught was medicinal, the boy accompanied
Mrs. Jeffray into the sick-chamber, and advised his aunt
to accept the dose: she swallowed the whole contents of
the bowl and immediately vomited. Mrs. Jeffray, who
appears that day to have had many messages, then dispatched him to a farm a mile distant in quest of butter.
The boy himself was sick three times. His aunt was very
ill during the night: he became alarmed, and asked Mrs.
Jeffray to come to her. "I canna come ben just now,"
replied the landlady; "take a candle and go ben yourself."
He told her that his aunt was dying: that she was white
in the face. Whereupon Mrs. Jeffray counselled him to
be quiet, lest he should wake the lodgers. He summoned
some neighbours, who went into the old woman's room;
she was then speechless, and soon thereafter died. Mrs.
Jeffray was not present. The deceased was buried that
day at 6 o'clock, because Mrs. Jeffray said that "the body
had a disagreeable smell and she could not bear it."
Cross-examined, the pannel allowed witness to stay with
his aunt during her illness. She was generally kind to the
old woman. When his aunt was invited by the pannel to
drink of the bowl, she said there was whisky and cream of
tartar in it. In re-examination, there was no candle in
the room when the pannel came "ben" at 11 o'clock.
Deceased vomited twice during the night after she got the
drink, and again on the following morning. She com-

plained much of pain in her side. Witness himself was merely sick; he had no pain. He had swallowed about a tablespoonful of the mixture—the bowl was bigger than a tea cup. The only thing he himself gave to his aunt was a little milk.

Mrs. Miller, wife of the boy's master, said she had known the deceased for six years. She saw her in bed the morning before her death; the boy was then in the room, and she charged him to pay attention to his aunt. Witness was surprised to find that the boy had been sent out of the way. Deceased complained of thirst and pain "above her stomach." She saw the old woman again at 10 o'clock; she was then in a very low state, very pale, and apparently on the verge of dissolution. Witness afterwards assisted certain neighbours to lay out the corpse; Mrs. Jeffray was not of the party. The boy Cullens was also unwell and vomited that morning, refusing his breakfast. Mrs. Weir, widow of John Weir, mason, Carluke, whose house adjoined that of the pannel and the deceased, corroborated. She never heard of or saw any rats in the pannel's house.

Janet Meikle, who lived with Mrs. Jeffray at the time in question, said that the boy Cullens told her Mrs. Jeffray had got him to persuade his aunt to take her "medicine." Early in the morning he came to the pannel's door, crying out: "Betty, Betty, my aunt's thrawing [twisting] her mouth and rolling her eyes!" The pannel replied, "Whist, whist, you'll waken the men." She then gave the boy a candle and desired witness to go along with him. Witness asked the pannel to go too, but she refused. Witness found the old woman "almost gone." The pannel did not go in with the neighbours "to view the corpse."[1] Witness remembered the death of Hugh Munro on 31st October; Mrs. Carl died on the 5th. He lodged with the pannel, came from Skye, and worked as a miner. On Saturday,

---

[1] Such abstention constitutes in Scotland a gross breach of the courtesy due to the dead.

28th October, the last day of his life, he returned from work in good health and spirits for his mid-day meal, which was of porridge prepared by the pannel. About 3 o'clock he complained of feeling ill: sickness and pain in the stomach. He went to bed. Witness looked in to ask for him and he complained of "terrible thirst"; she gave him a drink. That night Mrs. Jeffray, with her newly married daughter and son-in-law, "went out to a tea-party and came home late." Next day—Sunday—Munro still suffered from pain, purging, vomiting, and thirst. Witness told Mrs. Jeffray she ought to send for a doctor; but she replied that Highland folk were "narrow minded," and that the patient would object to the expense. On Monday Munro was no better; Mrs. Jeffray said she had got a powder from "the Doctor" for him. James M'Kay, Munro's companion, remained up with him all night. He asked witness to make some gruel for the invalid, which she did; on taking it to the bedroom she saw Munro with his eyes fixed, froth running from his mouth, and his hands clutching his stomach.

When witness saw the state in which Munro was, she ran to the pannel's room, and told her Hugh was almost gone. Pannel trembled from head to foot, and said she thought it was the cholera, and that she would not go near him. Witness insisted on pannel going up, but she refused ; she said she was so nervous that she could not go.

She herself, with a neighbour, Mrs. Lindsay, went up to the garret where the sufferer lay; he died a few minutes later. Witness, Lindsay, and M'Kay dressed the corpse; the pannel took no part, beyond suggesting that the body should be buried forthwith, which was done. When Mrs. Jeffray's daughter was married, she got a number of new tartan frocks. We shall see where the money for the trousseau came from. Witness never heard anything about rats till after Munro's death. There was a large cat in the house.

Mrs. Lindsay, who had succeeded to the room of the late Mrs. Carl, said that she knew Munro. On the Saturday

before his death he came home at mid-day in his usual
good health. She saw him next in bed at 7 o'clock; he
complained of "pains in his belly" and a great thirst. She
spoke to Mrs. Jeffray about his condition; the pannel said
she was going to give him a glass of brandy. Witness protested that it might increase the inflammation, to which
Mrs. Jeffray replied that it was not inflammation that ailed
him, but cholera. Munro asked witness to get a doctor;
"she would have gone, had she not thought Mrs. Jeffray
would consider her rather officious." He died on the
Monday night. After his death "they were all sitting by
the fire; a bottle of spirits was sent for, and Mrs. Jeffray
told them she had been greatly frightened by a rat."
Witness never saw any rats about the house. On the
Wednesday Mrs. Jeffray informed her that Munro had died
of cholera: she said she had seen Dr. Glossart, who had
told her so, and had advised her that the house should be
disinfected.

William Lindsay, husband of the last witness, miner,
said that he "wrought" with Munro. Learning of his
illness, he went up to see him at 8 o'clock on the Saturday
night; and alarmed by his state, requested Mrs. Jeffray to
send for a doctor: "she said she would have no doctor
but Dr. Boyle, as he had attended before." On the
Sunday he revisited the patient and again asked Mrs.
Jeffray to summon medical aid: "*she said she had sent for
Dr. Rankine, but he was not to be found.*"

James M'Kay, labourer, who hailed from Skye, said he
knew Munro intimately. Munro had a brother named
Charles. Witness saw him on the Sunday; he said he
was taken very ill after eating his porridge, "and that his
trouble was inside." He saw him again on the Monday
evening, and Munro asked him to sit up with him all night,
which he did. At 10 o'clock Mrs. Jeffray brought up a
bowl, which she said contained rhubarb, and administered
it to the sufferer, who at once put his hands to his breast,
and said "he had catched something about his heart."

He continued to grow worse until he died. Mrs. Jeffray said *she had been three times for Dr. Rankine, but could not find him.* Munro had intrusted his savings to the pannel; not long before his death he told witness that he had asked her for his money, but she said "she could not give it him *in consequence of her daughter's marriage.*" She refused to see Munro while he was dying and also when he was dead. After the funeral, Mrs. Jeffray told witness that "she had given the deceased £5 to send home to his relatives."

William Harvey, miner, stated that he "wrought" in the same mine with Munro. He was quite well on Saturday morning. At 8 o'clock witness called to pay him his wages; he was sitting by the fire upstairs, "complaining." Mrs. Jeffray came up and asked if there was anything she could do for him; she said she would do anything to make him better, "as she liked him so much." Witness suggested to her that she might send for a doctor, adding that he [Munro] "had something to be doing with," *i.e.,* was possessed of means. She replied, with unconscious humour: "Yes; for he has lived very mean."

She said in a low tone that he had given her 15s. when he came home from the shearing, and that he had the pay he had received before last [*sic*], although he had sent £5 to his friends.

Witness urged her to get a surgeon, and mentioned Dr. Douglas; she answered: "No such thing! Dr. Rankine was their doctor"; but she promised to send for him. On Sunday Munro was no better; *pannel said she had sent twice for Dr. Rankine.*

James Miller, mason, who lodged with the pannel, said he saw the deceased during his illness, and described his symptoms. On Monday, between 12 and 1 o'clock, Dr. Glossart came and prescribed a powder; witness saw the powder given in a cup by Mrs. Jeffray to Munro. The doctor afterwards sent another powder, which the patient also got. Before his illness, deceased told witness that if he were to lose his job, he had £6 in the hands of Mrs. Jeffray, "which he had asked her to get up for him," as he was going home. The wages—£1—which witness gave deceased, were handed by him to Mrs. Jeffray. John Thomson and Thomas Meek, both miners and lodgers in the house, gave similar evidence regarding Munro's condition, the alleged summoning of a surgeon, and the regrettable absence of rats. William Ferguson, another lodger, concurred. It appeared from the evidence of these witnesses that a week before his death Munro had received warning from his employer; he said he did not care, as he had money and would go home. "He said that he had sought the money from Mrs. Jeffray, and she told him that she could not give it at that time."

Susan Brownlee, servant to Dr. Rankine, stated that Mrs. Jeffray did not call for the doctor either on the Saturday, Sunday, or Monday before Munro's death. Nobody called him in to the case. She was the only servant, and never was out unless the doctor was at home. James Fairie, who owned the house occupied by the pannel, stated that he never heard that it was infested with rats. William Freeland, sheriff's officer, said he apprehended the prisoner. She volunteered that she had mixed arsenic and meal in a plate and put it below the bed, with a view to the destruction of the fabulous rodents. He found no plate, rat hole, or other indication of their presence. James Currie, messenger - at - arms, corroborated. Mrs. Jeffray was arrested on 10th November; he joined in the search, but saw no plate nor any appearance of rats.

John Mackenzie, a friend of Munro, stated that he, M'Caskill, and Murdoch Mackenzie had a conversation with the deceased as to his money. He told them he had £10, and that the woman with whom he lodged had £5 of it. After the death, Mrs. Jeffray told them she had sent the money to Munro's brother. Donald M'Caskill corroborated as to this conversation. When he visited the patient and asked what was wrong with him, Munro said he "*took a fear at the porridge*." After his death, witness asked Mrs. Jeffray how much "siller" Munro had given her to keep; she replied: £5 at the end of the harvest, "and he got it from her to send to his brother to pay his rent." Alexander M'Kay, Snizort, said that for the last three years he had lodged with Mrs. Jeffray when he came from Skye to the harvest. He knew Munro well. At the last shearing, in the Carse of Falkirk, Munro told him he had left £5 with Mrs. Jeffray. He never spoke of sending home his money before going there himself. Witness never heard of any rats being in the house. Charles Munro, Snizort, brother of the deceased, said he went to the shearing with Hugh the previous year. Hugh told him he had £5 in his landlady's hands. All the money he got from his brother was 2s.; Hugh sent no money home, nor was any needed, for a cow had been sold and the rent—£3—paid with the proceeds at Martinmas.

Mrs. Tennant and Mrs. Aitken, neighbours, having described the illness and death of Mrs. Carl, to one of whom the old woman said "she wished the Lord would take her off the earth, for she was in great trouble," William Glossart, surgeon in Carluke, stated that he was called in to see Munro on 30th October at 3 o'clock. He diagnosed the case as one of diarrhœa, and prescribed a rhubarb powder, which he prepared and gave to Mrs. Jeffray for the patient. A neighbour's girl came for him; Mrs. Jeffray did not say she had sent for him. He never mentioned cholera to her in connection with the case. Robert Logan, surgeon in New Lanark, stated that as instructed by the Sheriff he made in the Commercial Inn, Carluke, a post-mortem examination of the body of Hugh Munro. He removed the viscera, part of which he reserved for chemical examination by Dr. Rankine and himself; the residue was sent in sealed jars to Edinburgh for analysis by Professors Traill and Christison. The same procedure was afterwards followed in the case of Mrs. Carl. Witness prepared two reports, which were read to the jury but are not reported. "The result of the reports was that arsenic was found in the stomachs of both Ann Carl and Hugh Munro. He (witness) had been in Court all day, and thinks that the evidence is sufficient to prove Munro's death was caused by arsenic. He bore similar testimony as to the cause of Carl's death." Dr. Rankine confirmed the reports. "The result of these reports was that arsenic was found in the stomach of Munro—and after the contents of the jars had been analysed by Doctors Traill and Christison, arsenic was found in the stomach of Carl. He had been in Court all day, and thinks that the death of Munro was caused by arsenic. He was also of opinion that arsenic was the cause of the death of Carl." Thus our authority; the reporter having done ample justice to the testimony of the village gossips, has obviously scamped the medical evidence, either because it bored him or because he deemed it too technical for appreciation by the general.

The only legal point of interest in the case arose upon the evidence of Dr. Rankine. The Advocate-Depute proposed to ask that witness whether he had been sent for by the pannel on the Sunday, as she alleged. Mr. Craufurd, for the defence, objected that it was incompetent to examine, on facts apart from his medical opinion, a witness who had been in Court during the previous part of the trial. The objection was sustained, and the question found incompetent.[1]

Thomas Stewart Traill, Professor of Medical Jurisprudence in the University of Edinburgh, deponed to receiving from the Crown Office in Edinburgh "some jars sealed, labelled, and attested by Drs. Logan and Rankine." The result of his analysis of the contents of these was embodied by him in a report, which he then read, but of which the terms are not reported. He was of opinion that

---

[1] Swinton's *Justiciary Reports*, vol. ii. p. 116 ; Dickson *On Evidence*, vol. ii. p. 961, *n.* (*a*). Edinburgh: 1887; Macdonald's *Criminal Law*, Fourth Edition, p. 506, *n.* 3. Edinburgh: 1929.

the deaths of Carl and Munro were due to arsenic, "from the contents of the stomach."

BY THE COURT.—Taking this along with the whole evidence he had heard to-day, he could not say what time the arsenic had been administered to Munro; it might have been on the Saturday, very shortly before he began to complain.

BY A JURYMAN.—The quantity of arsenic administered [? purchased], half an ounce, was sufficient to poison both.

BY THE COURT.—A person once affected by arsenic would be very quickly destroyed by a second administration. He sees no improbability as to the first quantity of arsenic, half an ounce, being sufficient to poison both persons—a part may have been retained, and administered a second time.

Dr. Christison, Professor of Materia Medica in the University of Edinburgh, identified as correct the report by him of the result of his analysis. He had heard the evidence, and was of opinion that both deaths were caused by arsenic. "Cross-examined, he could not accurately say, but thinks there would be a grain of arsenic administered to Carl. By the Court: That was sufficient to cause her death."

The Crown case closed with the reading of the accused's declarations, which are not reprinted. I can find neither in the medical journals of the time, in Dr. Christison's famous treatise on poisons, nor in his interesting *Autobiography*, any reference to this case, which is the more disappointing in view of the incompetent way in which the medical evidence is reported.

For the defence, Helen Tennant, eight years of age, stated that she remembered the death of Munro. Mrs. Jeffray sent her for "the Doctor," and she told him Mrs. Jeffray had sent her. This child was the daughter of Mrs. Tennant, a Crown witness; "the Doctor" referred to was Mr. Glossart, who prescribed rhubarb. James Tennant, father of the little girl, said that about the latter end of August Mrs. Jeffray consulted him regarding the prevalence of rats in her house; she said she had seen two rats in the garret. Witness advised her to get poison to destroy them.

He was certain that this occurred before the death of Munro. Cross-examined, witness never heard anyone else mention rats being there, nor did he himself ever see any. Mrs. Jeffray did not say that she would act upon his advice. William Outerson, mason, Carluke, said he lived "next door but one" to the house of the accused. A week after Munro's death he "saw rats," of which he killed six or seven. They annoyed him very much. John Young, who lodged with Mrs. Weir, next door to the accused, "saw some rats sometime last summer"; he believed that was before the death of Munro, but in cross-examination, he could not say whether it was before or after the death of Mrs. Carl. He mentioned the rats to Mrs. Weir at the time. Agnes Marshall, ten years of age, stated that "she saw Margaret Jeffray, the prisoner's daughter, going to Dr. Rankine's." Margaret herself—"a genteel good-looking girl, apparently about 16 years of age"—deponed that during Munro's illness her mother sent her to bring Dr. Rankine; she went to the house of Agnes Marshall and told her and her father of the errand. "Marshall undertook to go and tell Dr. Rankine, and she trusted to his doing it." Cross-examined, witness thought this happened on the Saturday; she could not tell the time of day. She only went once.

The case for the defence was here closed and counsel addressed the jury. Neither of the speeches is recorded; all we learn is that the Advocate-Depute, "after very clearly going over the facts of the case, concluded by calling upon the jury for a verdict of guilty." It must have been a powerful address, for we read that "shortly after the Learned Gentleman had commenced his speech, Mrs. Jeffray fainted away, but recovered in a few minutes." Mr. Craufurd, we are told, "in an ingenious and eloquent defence, which occupied an hour and 40 minutes in delivery, cautioned the jury about entering the regions of mystery, and allowing any doubts to influence their minds; and contending that the charges were not proved by the

purely circumstantial nature of the evidence, called upon
the jury to acquit his client." Lord Mackenzie summed
up, in a charge which occupied two hours and a half. At
20 minutes to 2 a.m. the jury retired, and after con-
sulting 20 minutes, returned their verdict, finding by a
majority the pannel guilty as libelled, but unanimously
recommending her to mercy! Lord Medwyn having proposed that she be executed on the 21st of May, Lord
Mackenzie then assumed the black cap, and in a very
solemn and affecting address, pronounced sentence on the
prisoner. The jury had unanimously recommended her
to mercy, and intimation of this would be given to the
proper quarter; but his Lordship would not hold out to
her hopes of pardon, as it was difficult to conceive how a
double murder could come within the limits of mercy.

Of the demeanour of the prisoner throughout the trial
we are told that it was firm, bold, and courageous. "Her
appearance was still prepossessing—being well made and
rather tall, her cheeks ruddy, her eyes black and prominent." During the Advocate-Depute's speech she
seemed very depressed and kept her eyes on the ground;
but when Mr. Craufurd was addressing the jury her spirits
revived, and she gave an occasional glance at the jury-box.
She received her sentence unmoved. The court was
crowded till the close of the proceedings at 20 minutes
to 3 o'clock in the morning, the trial having lasted nearly
18 hours.[1]

III

The last days of the condemned afforded for our pious
and blood-thirsty ancestors matter at once edifying and
entertaining. From the ghostly gymnastics of the Lady
Warriston in 1600, which furnished the ministers of
Edinburgh with a sort of spiritual field-day, to the godly
end of Dr. Pritchard in 1865, public sympathy has ever

---

[1] There is a good account of the proceedings in the *Edinburgh Evening Courant*,
3rd May 1838—the only contemporary notice I have been able to trace.

been moved by such ante-mortem examinations. Admirably does Miss Polly Peachum, with reference to the final performance of her lover, "voice" the popular sentiment: "I see him at the Tree! The whole Circle are in Tears!— even Butchers weep!" So naturally we find the penultimate experiences of Mrs. Jeffray recorded with a fullness and enthusiasm befitting the occasion.

"Am I not unanimously recommended to mercy?" she exclaimed on her arrival at the condemned cell; and the answer being in the affirmative, she remarked: "If I recollect aright, the Jury were not unanimous in finding me guilty." On these two strands depended the anchor of her hope.

What chiefly struck the many sympathisers who called upon the convict at this time was her extraordinary composure. "Indeed," says her biographer, "every one who visited her during her condemnation concur in stating that she was a woman of a masculine mind; and what appeared to be indifference actually arose from the absence of those weaknesses or finer sensibilities which distinguish her sex." Yet, in the circumstances, even a hardened male might, one should imagine, have been capable of some emotion. When her daughter came to see her, the prisoner shewed no feeling, and "told her not to call back again." She complained often and bitterly of the unwelcome assiduities of the local clergy, who urged her to confess her crimes. With reference to "those zealous but injudicious councillors"—the spelling is her biographer's—she observed: "I have not to learn that there is comfort in the Bible, for shortly after I was confined in Lanark Jail I procured one; and I read it constantly morning and evening, with prayer to God, and often in the forenoon. I was not above a month there till I found great comfort from these exercises; but I cannot confess that of which I am not guilty." Such was her delicacy that she did not use the power she possessed of excluding these troublesome visitors, or telling them plainly not to repeat their visits.

She stated in conversation that she had always been kind to Mrs. Carl, who was a very poor person supported by a small weekly pittance, which she received from the parish. Yet, like a Good Samaritan, she took the old woman into her own house, and in order to procure a bed for her, "went three miles to the landlord and got his consent to take down a loomstead that was in the apartment," and to set up a bed in its place. It was her daily practice, before taking her own breakfast, to take a cup of tea to the old woman: "I believe, if it had not been for my attention to Mrs. Carl, she would have died." "Many a time," continued Mrs. Jeffray, "the old woman would say that God would reward me with a blessing for the kindness I had shewn to her; but instead of a blessing, I think a curse has attended me for having anything to do with her." It certainly would have been a blessing for Mrs. Carl had she not been subject to these ministrations. Divers inquisitive folk having invited Mrs. Jeffray's views as to the arsenic found in the body of the deceased, "she said the only way she could account for it was, that after the rats had taken the arsenic placed in the garret, they had come down into Mrs. Carl's apartment and drank out of the bowl that was always placed at the bedside"; which, as an explanation of the proven facts, strikes one as pretty thin. "She described the house as being thatched with divots, and as being accessible in almost every part to the progress of rats." She also said, with respect to rats being about the premises, "that she found one dead in the garret from the effects of the first quantity of poison"; and that since she had been in jail, "a letter from her husband informed her that a neighbour had caught several rats at one time." Mrs. Jeffray's rats were of like breed to Falstaff's rogues in buckram, and had a similar power to increase and multiply after their kind.

With regard to Munro, she assured inquirers that she gave him back his £5 *in presence of her daughter*. It is remarkable that this young lady was not examined upon

14

this point, when called for the defence. As to his illness, there could have been nothing hurtful in the porridge, "for she gave half of the porridge made for him to the sow, and it was none the worse." This sow, more fortunate than the pig of her earlier experiment, was not produced in evidence. "She acknowledged that she bought a second quantity of arsenic on the Monday following, and stated she had mixed it up with meal and butter, gave a portion to the rats, and put the bowl with the remainder of the arsenic behind the dresser." At 8 o'clock on the evening of Munro's death she missed the fatal bowl, and being apprehensive of accident, "she immediately ran to Munro's bed and found the bowl standing below it." She supposed that in the bustle occasioned by his illness "some person had done it by mistake." With reference to her failure to attend the last moments of her victims, she explained that, "being naturally nervous, she was not able to stand and witness their death-struggles." It is not surprising to find that, in speaking of the deaths of Mrs. Carl and Munro, "there was always a marked caution about her manner."

The last week of Mrs. Jeffray's life was drawing to a close, and yet there had been no response to the application for mercy, based upon the jury's singular recommendation. In addition to this, there was prepared in Glasgow and forwarded to the proper quarter, a public petition for a reprieve, which is said to have been largely signed by conscientious objectors to capital punishment. On the Friday before the fatal Monday came a letter from the Home Secretary, "blasting the hope of the first application"; and on Saturday it was intimated that the petition had also been refused. On learning the result, "she exclaimed with considerable firmness: 'I am now prepared to die'—meaning that now she had lost all hope of pardon." On Sunday night her husband came from Carluke to see her for the first and last time since her condemnation. He was much affected, and urged her to confess. To which she replied: "Do you think I would confess to a thing I am not guilty of?" so the man went sorrowful away. Thereafter Mrs. Jeffray slept till 6 o'clock next morning, when being aroused by a wardress, she proceeded to make her final toilet: a black gown, a mourning cap, and a tartan shawl. At a quarter to 8 the Rev. Principal M'Farlane, the Rev. Mr. Pullar, and the Rev. Mr. Fisher—who, we read, "had been unremitting in their attentions to the prisoner," with what spiritual profit we are not informed—entered her cell and began their religious offices. These completed, the prisoner, duly pinioned by the executioner, was "conveyed to the Court Hall, which was very crowded." From thence the party proceeded to the scaffold, erected in front of the Court House, "which she ascended with a firm step, apparently nothing daunted by the fearful engine of death or the vast assemblage—not less than 10,000 persons—that encountered her gaze." [1] She even expressed a wish to address the multitude, but was dissuaded from making a speech.

The executioner's revolting preparations being completed, she stood with unshaken fortitude for about six minutes with the signal in her hand, engaged in prayer; then dropt the napkin, was instantly thrown off, and a few convulsive shudders concluded the history of this ill-fated woman.

As a public spectacle the exhibition compares unfavourably with that of which, at Edinburgh on 28th January 1829, the infamous William Burke, the West Port murderer, was the subject, the spectators whereat are stated to have been between 20,000 and 25,000. But these figures, again, fall far short of the crowd assembled at Glasgow Green on 28th July 1865, to witness the departure of the popular physician Dr. Pritchard, which was computed to number 100,000 persons—surely a generous

---

[1] "The crowd assembled was immense—perhaps the very largest we have ever seen on any similar occasion, and no accident of any kind occurred, the greatest order being kept by the police."—*Edinburgh Evening Courant*, 24th May 1838.

estimate. Perhaps, as being the last occasion when this horrid business was publicly performed in Scotland, the populace were anxious to make the most of the opportunity.

It is interesting to note that the last woman to be hanged in public in Scotland was Mary Reid or Timney, appropriately condemned by Lord Deas, and executed at Dumfries on 29th April 1862, for the illicit disposal of a successful rival in the affections of her spouse. Had Lord Deas had his way, however, this distinction would have been enjoyed by Jessie M'Lachlan, upon whom his Lordship, at Glasgow on 20th September 1862, passed sentence of death, and appointed the execution thereof for 11th October following.[1] But as the result of great popular agitation and further judicial inquiry the prisoner received a conditional pardon, so that Mary Reid or Timney retains the title. Perhaps some day I may be moved to tell her story.

Note I.—EXECUTION OF MARY REID OR TIMNEY

I am fortunate to possess the original death warrant, signed by Lord Deas, which is sufficiently curious to justify transcription:

By the Honourable Lord Deas, one of the Lords Commissioners of Justiciary.

WHEREAS by the verdict of an Assize dated the eighth day of April eighteen hundred and sixty-two, returned at Dumfries in the trial of Mary Reid or Timney now or lately prisoner in the prison of Kirkcudbright, the Jury found her guilty of the crime of murder, IN RESPECT WHEREOF I the said Lord Deas, one of the Lords Commissioners of Justiciary, Decerned and Adjudged the said Mary Reid or Timney to be carried from the Bar to the prison of Dumfries, therein to be detained and fed on bread and water only, until the twenty-ninth day of April current, and upon that day, between the hours of eight and ten o'clock of the forenoon, to be taken from the said prison to the common place of execution of the burgh of Dumfries, or to such other place as the Magistrates of Dumfries shall appoint as a place of execution, and there by the hands of the common executioner to be hanged by the neck upon a gibbet until she be dead, and Ordained her body thereafter to be buried within

---

[1] *Trial of Mrs. M'Lachlan.* Notable British Trials Series. Edinburgh: 1925.

the precincts of the said prison ; And I the said Lord Deas therefore
hereby Ordain and Require the Magistrates of Dumfries and keepers
of the said prison to see this sentence put into execution, as they shall
be answerable at their highest peril. GIVEN at Dumfries the eighth
day of April eighteen hundred and sixty-two years.   GEO. DEAS.

Note II.—RATS AS THE *RAISON D'ÊTRE* FOR ARSENIC

I know not how the fact stands in England, but it is
remarkable that in Scots practice nine out of ten persons,
contemplating the disposal of their fellow mortals by
means of poison, are moved to do so with arsenic, and to
allege as their purpose in acquiring that commodity, the
destruction of hypothetic rats.   Leading instances of this
singular obsession are furnished by the following cases:
Mary Elder or Smith in 1827;   John Lovie in the same
year;   our Elizabeth in 1838;   Christina Gilmour in 1844;
Janet Campbell or M'Lellan in 1846;   Margaret Lennox or
Hamilton in 1850;   William Bennison in the same year;
Sarah Anderson or Fraser and James Fraser in 1852;   and
lastly, in John Webster's phrase, "without wrong last to
be named," Madeleine Smith in 1857.   Of the activities of
these misguided toxicologists I have given some account
in an essay entitled "Locusta in Scotland: a familiar
Survey of Poisoning, as practised in that Realm" (*Glen-
garry's Way and other Studies*, pp. 47–118.   Edinburgh:
1922).   Most of them were commonplace folk of no
imagination, lamentably lacking in initiative.   But from
a young lady of Madeleine's education and sprightly wits
one should have looked for something more original.
True, she only adopted that hackneyed expedient after
the failure of her earlier attempt: the purchase of prussic
acid, a poison swift in action and hardly to be traced, of
which in Scotland the first recorded homicidal application
is that by John Thomson *alias* Peter Walker—the Eagles-
ham case—in the same year, a gentleman whose fancy
admittedly was quickened by the stimulating example of
Miss Smith.   So Madeleine may be claimed as, in all but

execution, a pioneer. And in this matter she resembles her American sister Miss Lizzie Borden (*Studies in Murder*, by Edmund Lester Pearson. New York: 1924), who, being denied prussic acid by a churlish apothecary, was compelled to dispatch her parents with an axe—a crude expedient from which, as a Sunday School teacher, she was naturally averse. Thus are the efforts of genius for ever frustrated by the cautious timidity of second-rate minds.

THE GREAT BURDON MYSTERY:

A CONUNDRUM IN CRIME

THE GREAT BURDON MYSTERY:

A Conundrum in Crime

What Song the Syrens sang, or what name Achilles assumed when he hid himself among Women, though puzzling Questions, are not beyond all conjecture.
—Sir Thomas Browne : *Hydriotaphia.*

IF only I were gifted with the facility of a manufacturer of detective fiction, what a fine story I should make of this case, under the appetitive title: "Who Poisoned Mrs. Wooler?" It has all the approved ingredients of a popular police romance; an undeniable murder, carried through with devilish cruelty and craft over a lengthened period, by someone ministering at the victim's bedside in that hushed house of sickness and of death; the baffled and bewildered doctors; the birth of suspicion; the strange behaviour of the bereaved husband, both before and after the event; the inconclusive inquest; the long investigation before the Darlington magistrates; the three days' drama in the courthouse at Durham, with its surprising situations and its. . . . But, soft! we are observed! Not yet must I let the cat out of the bag of mystery; that, as I understand the rules of the fictive game, would be unsportsmanlike. So I shall unfold this singular tale in the order of its original telling, and reserve for the last chapter such comments as occur to me upon the puzzle which it presents.

In no case of circumstantial evidence known to me are we supplied with more tenuous and fragile clues, which either wholly elude our grasp, or being held, break between our fingers. Only in the medical facts proved do we find satisfactory footing, and the assurance that we are on the right road; but these, unfortunately for the wayfarer, do

not lead him to a definite and conclusive end. And yet
there is no lack of guide-books. For the earlier pro-
ceedings: *Great Burdon Slow Poisoning Case. Report of
the Investigation before the Magistrates at Darlington, in the
County of Durham; including the Examinations of Dr.
Jackson, Dr. Haslewood, Mr. Henzell, and Mr. Fothergill, of
Darlington; Dr. Richardson, of Newcastle; and Professor
Taylor, M.D. of London, on the above Case; together with
the Evidence of Mr. J. S. Wooler before the Coroner at Great
Burdon.* (*Reprinted from the* DARLINGTON AND STOCKTON
TIMES.) Darlington: Published by Robert Swales. Sold
in London by Simpkin, Marshall, and Co., 1855. As regards
the subsequent trial at the Durham Assizes on 7th, 8th, and
10th December 1855, there is an excellent and full report in
the contemporaneous issues of the *Durham County Advertiser*, upon which I have relied for the evidence and
speeches; and a competent abridgment of the proceedings
is contained in the *Annual Register for the Year* 1855 (vol.
xcvii., appendix to Chronicle, pp. 375–390). Then Professor Sir Robert Christison (who was professionally
engaged in the case) contributed a valuable account of its
medico-legal aspects to the *Edinburgh Medical Journal*
(vol. i. pp. 625, 707, 759. Edinburgh: 1856); and further
references to the subject will be found in his biography
(*The Life of Sir Robert Christison, Bart.* Edited by his
Sons. Vol. ii. pp. 163, 192. Edinburgh: 1886).

So the course of our itinerary is plainly marked. A
long journey; but not I hope (at any rate for the reader) a
wearisome. I shall do my best to make straight the way
and to lighten the heaviness of the going.

I

At the time in question there lived in the township of
Great Burdon, near Darlington, in the county of Durham
and merrie land of England, one Mr. Joseph Snaith Wooler,
gentleman. All that we are told of him prior to his
appearance in the fierce light of public justice is, that

"after passing much of his early life in a mercantile capacity in various parts of the world and last of all in the East Indies," he withdrew, presumably upon a competence, from the commercial arena; and with his lady wife, whom he had married eighteen years before, to no effect as regards a family, at the respectable age of forty-five settled down in Great Burdon for good.   Jane, his spouse and senior by one year, was the daughter of a Durham doctor.   Her maiden name was Brecknell; and she had a brother, who for some undisclosed reason disliked her husband, with whom his relations were not friendly.

Though never a strong woman Mrs. Wooler seldom required the attentions of the faculty, and had no serious illness until her last, which began on 8th May 1855.   The household staff consisted of but one servant, Ann Taylor, twenty-seven years of age, who had been with the Woolers since March "a year gone."   Ann tells us that "the day Mrs. Wooler was ill she had pig-cheek, beef, and soup for dinner.   Mr. Wooler did not take any [soup]—he never does take soup at all."   Shortly after this injudicious meal the lady was seized with internal pain and vomiting, which were attributed to undue indulgence in the pig's countenance.   As these symptoms persisted, Dr. Jackson of Darlington was called in.   He first treated the patient "for influenza and disordered stomach," and continued to attend her throughout the illness.   Mr. Henzell, his assistant, saw her on 16th May, again on 4th June, and thence continually till her death.   From 8th May to 8th June the symptoms—vomiting and purging—gradually increased; and on the latter date Dr. Jackson intimated that he wou'd like further advice; at his suggestion Dr. Haslewood of Darlington was called in consultation.

These three medical men continued their attendance until the death of the patient on 27th June.   They were all equally puzzled as to the course and character of the illness, and for a fortnight before its fatal termination their attention was attracted by certain features of the case,

pointing to the influence of an irritant poison. They therefore refused to certify the cause of death; and on 29th
June a post-mortem examination of the body was made,
with the result that no signs of natural disease sufficient
to account for death were found; but there were plain
indications of the effects of poison. In portions of the
viscera removed for chemical examination by Dr. Richardson of Newcastle the presence of arsenic was unequivocally
detected. An inquest, held on 30th June, was adjourned
till 13th July to enable Dr. Richardson to complete his
experiments. The three doctors testified to their belief,
based upon the symptoms of the patient, the post-mortem
appearances, and the result of the analyses, that Mrs.
Wooler undoubtedly died from arsenic, administered in
small and repeated quantities over a considerable period.
The jury returned an open verdict: that the deceased died
by poison, but that there was no evidence as to how she
came by it.[1]

Following upon further investigations by the police, Mr.
Wooler was arrested and charged with the murder of his
wife.[2] On 4th August the body was exhumed and divers
organs were removed and sent to London in a sealed jar for
examination by the great Professor Taylor, the foremost
toxicologist of his time and still a high authority in medical
jurisprudence. Other portions of the remains were sent to
Dr. Richardson for his further and independent analysis.
Dr. Taylor reported that he found arsenic in all the matters

---

[1] The text of the verdict, delivered on 14th July, was as follows : " That the
deceased died from the effects of irritant mineral poison, but how and by whom
administered there appears no evidence to convince us ; *at the same time we
entirely exonerate the medical attendants from any blame whatever.*" The jury's
rider is important in view of the line adopted by the defence at the trial.—*Report
of Magisterial Inquiry*, p. 3.

[2] " For that he, in the month of June last past, at the Township of Great
Burdon, in the County of Durham, did feloniously, wilfully, and of malice afore-
thought, kill and murder Jane Wooler, the wife of him the said Joseph Snaith
Wooler, by then and there administering to her, the said Jane Wooler, a certain
poison called arsenic, contrary to the form of the statute in such case made and
provided."—*Ibid.*, p. 43.

submitted to him; in his opinion it had been taken in small portions, at intervals, and *in solution*—not in the form of powder. His conclusion was that the deceased died of slow poisoning with arsenic. Dr. Richardson reported that he found arsenic in all the parts of the body tested by him.

Meanwhile, in Darlington police court, on 30th July, the prisoner appeared before the magistrates. Mr. Davison of the Northern Circuit conducted the prosecution, Mr. Marshall of Durham representing the accused. The proceedings were resumed on 6th August, continued on the 11th and 24th, and concluded on the 25th. The decision of the bench was as follows: "We have given this case —a case of grave and heavy importance—the very best attention and consideration, and agree in opinion that the evidence which has been adduced during this protracted —and necessarily protracted—investigation is sufficiently strong to warrant us in sending the prisoner for trial at Durham Assizes." Whereupon the accused, by his attorney, reserved his defence. Asked whether he had anything to say, the prisoner replied: "I thank God Almighty that I can say from the bottom of my heart that I am as innocent as any of you three gentlemen sitting there; and I trust that Almighty God, before whom I stand, will bring to light the atrocious criminal who has perpetrated this foul deed." The prisoner was then formally committed for trial, and the proceedings closed.

It will be noticed that I have not dealt in detail either with the evidence at the inquest or with that at the magisterial inquiry. It was all gone over again, like a proclamation of banns for the third time of asking, at the assizes; and more merciful than the destroyer of Mrs. Wooler, I intend to give the reader but one dose. As a Scots lawyer, accustomed to our single and relatively simple means of criminal investigation: the private researches of the Procurator-Fiscal and the Crown Office, followed by arraignment before the trial judge in open court: I marvel at the exhaustive (and exhausting) methods employed beyond the Border, whereby the whole business is transacted three times in public and at large: before the coroner, the magistrates, and the judge—to say nothing of the Grand Jury, a tribunal which always, for my uninstructed mind, connotes the Day of Judgment. It may be national prejudice; but I think ours the better, as it is certainly the plainer way, and in my view much fairer to the prisoner.

I recall in this connection, in the Maybrick case, how a witness who gave very damning evidence against that lady at the inquest, failed to appear at any of the subsequent proceedings. But the bolt had been shot, the impression made; and the accused was powerless to counter it. In the present case, however, one witness testified at the inquest who by the rules of the game as then observed was not permitted to speak again, namely, Joseph Snaith Wooler; but it will be more convenient for us to hear him when we know something of the evidence which he was called upon to meet.

II

On Friday, 7th December 1855, before Mr. Baron Martin at Durham Assizes, the prisoner was placed at the bar, charged with the murder of his wife Jane Wooler, "against the peace of Our Sovereign Lady the Queen." There appeared for the Crown Mr. Edward James, Q.C., Mr. Temple, and Mr. Davison; for the defence, Mr. Serjeant Wilkins, Mr. Overend, Q.C., and Mr. Laurie.[1] The prisoner having pleaded Not Guilty, a jury was sworn; the medical witnesses were ordered out of court; and at the request of Serjeant Wilkins "his Lordship allowed the prisoner (owing to lameness) to be seated"—from which

---

[1] " Mr. Serjeant Wilkins had 200 guineas with his brief, besides consultation fees ; Mr. Overend 100 guineas, and Mr. Laurie 50 guineas."—*Durham County Advertiser.*

one infers that but for his infirmity the unfortunate man would have had, literally, to *stand* his trial.

Mr. James,[1] in opening the case for the prosecution, narrated the facts of which I have given an outline. These facts, in his submission, left no reasonable doubt in the mind of any human being that this unhappy lady came to her death by poison; the only question was: How and by whose hand was that poison administered? The prisoner at the bar had himself raised that issue; for in a letter dated 11th July he wrote: "They [the doctors] say there are symptoms of poisoning; if so, *it was given in their medicine,* for in no other way could it have got access." Undoubtedly the prisoner was there upon a grave charge; but this was a very grave charge indeed against these medical men. It went further than neglect or carelessness, because it would be proved that so early as 17th June their attention was directed to symptoms of irritant poison. Was it conceivable that in view of such suspicions they would not guard against the possibility of giving the patient anything of a noxious nature? All the bottles containing remains of medicine prescribed by the doctors were submitted to expert examination, and not the slightest trace of arsenic was found in any one of them.

The arsenic must have been administered by some person having the means and opportunity to do so. Mrs. Wooler was averse from having a nurse; she was attended by her husband and by the servant, Ann Taylor. Two friends and neighbours, Miss Lanchester and Miss Middleton, occasionally visited the sick lady, giving such assistance as they could; these, with the exception of the prisoner's brother, were the only persons having access to the deceased during her illness. To use the poison in the way it must have been used implied skill and knowledge in

---

[1] Edward James (1807–1867); barrister; M.A., Brasenose College, Oxford, 1834; admitted Lincoln's Inn, 1835; assessor of Liverpool Court of Passage from 1852; Q.C., 1853; Attorney-General of Duchy of Lancaster, 1863; M.P., Manchester, 1865–1867; died in Paris, 1867.

the subject of drugs.   It would be shewn by the evidence
of Mr. Wooler's own conversations that he possessed such
knowledge and skill.   He was about his wife during the
whole course of her illness, with the exception of one day,
20th June, on which, significantly, there was a marked
abatement of the symptoms.   Her stomach could not
retain food; injections were therefore necessary.   His hand
gave the medicines and injections.   On two occasions the
prisoner produced to Dr. Haslewood and Dr. Jackson, who
required some particular drug, a basket containing many
medicine bottles, one of which was labelled, and apparently
contained, "Fowler's Solution of Arsenic."   They spoke to
him on the subject of this arsenic.   What had become of
the bottle?   At the inquest it was sent for to the prisoner's
house; the basket of bottles was brought, but this one
could not be found.

. The injections were given by means of a syringe; the
prisoner possessed a pewter one, the elastic tube of which
got choked; so he borrowed from Mr. Fothergill, a local
surgeon, a brass syringe, which was used for the purpose
until the patient's death, when it was returned to its owner.
Mr. Fothergill put it aside, as he had no occasion to use it;
but when the question of Mrs. Wooler's death arose, he
examined it and found the pipe stopped up.   He tested it,
and found that it contained arsenic.   The other syringe,
belonging to the prisoner, was tested by Professor Taylor,
and that gentleman discovered in it also the presence of
arsenic.   The materials of which these syringes were
composed were found to be free from poison.

The conduct of the accused throughout had next to
be considered.   He expressed the utmost solicitude and
affection for his wife, but it was for the jury to say whether,
having regard to the facts of the case, these professions were
genuine or simulated.   It was not until several times urged
by Dr. Jackson that he consented to further advice being
called.   Among the undoubted symptoms of arsenical
poisoning was tingling of the hands; the doctors asked the

accused to inform them of this, should it arise.[1] On 23rd
June Dr. Haslewood ascertained from the patient herself
the presence of this symptom. Asked how long she had
felt this sensation, she replied: "Three or four days";
whereupon the accused said she was mistaken: she only
had it yesterday. But Mrs. Wooler said: "Oh, yes; I
told you of it two days before that. I particularly requested you to mention it to the medical men, but you
forgot." Mr. Henzell examined the urine before the 22nd,
and after the 23rd of June. On the former day he asked
the prisoner to send a specimen to him at Darlington,
which was done. He found that it could not possibly
belong to the patient, and that another specimen must
have been substituted. Then there was the remarkable
fact that on the 20th, when the accused was absent at
Bishop Auckland, the medicines and injections were given
by others, and that day the patient was better than on any
previous or subsequent occasion throughout the illness.
With respect to the accused's behaviour at the time of the
death, Mr. Simpson, the clergyman who was praying at the
bedside of the dying lady, came to him in his dressing-room
and told him she was at the point of death. The prisoner,
partly disrobed, was washing. "What am I to do?" he
asked; "am I to come in this state?" which indicated a
greater regard for the proprieties than for his dying wife.
"Within half an hour after the death of his wife the
prisoner was in the garden, explaining to the medical
gentlemen some facts connected with the natural history of
the bee"—his bees were hiving and a bell was rung—"and
acting otherwise in a manner altogether the opposite of a
man labouring under great grief."

During the course of her illness the accused wrote
frequently to his wife's friends and relations, describing her
symptoms and their treatment, and expressing his pious

---

[1] Why not have asked the patient personally ? Perhaps it was because Mr.
Wooler kept a note of the symptoms in a book, which he daily exhibited to the
doctors.

hopes for her recovery.[1] The correspondence, moreover, as counsel pointed out, furnishes several instances of deliberate falsehood. In some of the letters the accused described her attack as slight, in others as a supposed tendency to consumption, and after the advent of Dr. Haslewood, that she was in a galloping consumption. On 14th June, to his wife's aunt, Mrs. Rymer, he wrote: "The doctors, who attend her daily, told me this morning they could only hope to delay God's verdict—to meet her God—as she was diseased in the upper part of the lungs seriously." That, said Mr. James, was simply not true: they never told him anything of the kind. On 8th June they merely diagnosed slight old lung trouble, from which no present danger was to be apprehended. Yet three times in that letter did he call Mrs. Rymer's attention to the "fact" that the lungs were diseased. The jury would have to decide whether these letters were not written with a view of throwing a blind over the transactions, and endeavouring to impose upon others the belief that he really loved his wife and was sorry for her condition. On 26th June he wrote to his brother-in-law, Mr. Brecknell—whom he addresses as "Dear Sir"—"Her strength is so much reduced that I candidly confess I gave her up when this was told me this morning. Ann thinks as she has lasted so long she may recover. May God in His mercy so ordain it. If we could get the stomach to retain food we might have hope." On the 27th he wrote again, announcing the death of his wife on that date, and inviting Mr. Brecknell, who lived in London, to the funeral; to his other Brecknell

---

[1] It may be but a coincidence that these letters present in tone and substance a curious resemblance to those written by Dr. Pritchard ten years later in similar painful circumstances. Such a passage as this : "We now keep her alive by injecting 1 oz. of cod-liver oil, 2 ozs. of beef-tea, and one tablespoonful of rum, with $1\frac{1}{2}$ drams of laudanum every six hours. My Jane sends her kind love to you, your wife, and son, and would wish to see you and her nephew before she departs this world to inherit (I hope) a blessed crown of immortality with a gracious Saviour " : in its blend of pharmacy and piety has about it the authentic touch of the good physician of Sauchiehall Street.

brother-in-law, who lived at Gateshead, he sent no invitation.

On the 29th the registrar called to learn the cause of death, and was informed by the accused that it was ulceration of the bowels. That day the accused received from Dr. Jackson a letter, stating that an examination of the body was necessary before he could give to the registrar a certificate other than that of which a copy was enclosed, namely, that the symptoms indicated death by poison. Whereupon the accused assembled all the members of the household—Miss Brecknell, Miss Lanchester, and Ann Taylor—to whom he read the letter, and exclaimed: "Why, they say that my Jane was poisoned!" He ordered Ann Taylor to collect all the medicine bottles and put them into her box, which she did. The bereaved husband then left the house and did not return until after the funeral. So "my Jane" was laid to rest in the regrettable absence of the chief mourner.

Upon the question of motive, Mr. James frankly confessed that he could suggest none. Crimes, beyond all doubt, might and did exist although the motive urging to those crimes was unaccountable save to the eye of God Himself. It might be that was so in the present instance. That this death was caused by slow poisoning with arsenic in solution, administered from time to time in small doses, was not disputed. Possession of the means and opportunity to use it were proved; the behaviour of the accused, and the false statements made in his letters, pointed to guilty knowledge; but "whatever the result of your verdict may be, I and the country will be perfectly satisfied." Thus Mr. James, having spoken for upwards of two hours.

III

It sometimes, but too rarely happens—though fortunately the present case is one of the exceptions—that we have the benefit of the impressions of an eye-witness as to the actual conduct of a trial. At once the cold print of

the report is informed with life; the mere names of witnesses and counsel are clothed, like the dry bones of the
Prophet's vision, with the attributes of life; and the indefinite figures in the record assume, for us, the familiar
lineaments of humanity.   Now, thanks to the caustic pen
of Professor Christison, we are enabled to envisage the
truculent bulk of Serjeant Wilkins, the amiable and
anxious Dr. Jackson, the wary and resourceful Dr. Haslewood, and the competent and unshaken Mr. Henzell.
Writing to his son on 31st December 1855, Dr. Christison
remarks:—

I had a famous adventure about a fortnight ago, having been summoned to give evidence in the trial of Wooler at Durham for murder
by poison, as I got involved in the case unwarily by giving some advice
to the medical men concerned, and detecting arsenic for them in circumstances that proved material for the prosecution. I was two entire
days in Court, and returned more thoroughly knocked up than I remember to have been since the trial of Burke and Hare, when I was
twenty-four hours a hearer or actor in the proceedings. I observed
nothing better, and several things worse (by admission, too, of the
prosecuting counsel, Mr. James), in the English than in the Scottish
procedure in criminal trials. The liberty, or rather licence, allowed to
English counsel in superfluously abusing respectable witnesses, without
check or subsequent rectification by the judge, is fearful—a disgrace to
the English Bar, and of no use whatever towards the administration of
justice. Serjeant Wilkins is a strong-built, big-voiced, braggadocio-
looking man—the type of Dickens's Serjeant Buzfuz. . . .

Serjeant Wilkins made a pretty mash of one of the principal medical
witnesses, a kind-looking, good-natured, nervous, well-informed gentleman, who had been studying for his first appearance on the medico-
legal stage, but had omitted to include a few lessons in the noble art of
self-defence against impudence and perversion of truth. The Serjeant
was less successful against a clever, odd-mannered bald-head, who
elongated himself like a worm as he spoke, sometimes over one corner of
the witness-box, sometimes over the other, and who put out and drew
back his statements like his body, in quite a baffling fashion. He was
even less prosperous with a little, fair-haired, small-faced, spectacled,
quiet, boyish-looking young fellow of great intelligence, who on one
occasion did the next thing to giving the Serjeant the lie, and was found
from the judge's notes to be right, to the delight and applause of the
audience.

The knowing Serjeant, however, turned the applause to good account in his speech afterwards, by assuming it to have been malignant prejudice of the audience against his client, instead of delight at the defeat of a bully by an opponent not half his size.

He did not try it on with me : perhaps it was no object to dispute my evidence ; but others thought that he did not augur much from my monosyllabic answers and the double D of my voice, which went beyond him.[1]

The Professor is very right: no Scots judge would tolerate for a moment the swashbuckler business in which the learned Serjeant was allowed to revel; nor, I am glad to say, would any Scots counsel of repute ever think of resorting to it.

Serjeant Ballantine tells us [2] that Wilkins had acquaintance with many walks of life, having been at one time an apothecary and at another a provincial actor. Doubtless the experience acquired in these rôles was of service to him in the Wooler case. Like all bullies, he collapsed when boldly tackled: "a successful repartee threw him upon his back, and ridicule drove him frantic." Once, being opposed to Serjeant Thomas in a jury trial, he delivered his speech, as usual, "in a voice in perfect keeping with his inflated oratory." Thomas, rising to reply, began: "Now the hurly burly's done. . . ." "Wilkins waited for no more; but tucking up his gown, got out of Court as quickly as he could."[3]

Edward James, the prosecutor, is to be distinguished from his learned friend and contemporary *Edwin* James, with whom he is sometimes confounded.[4]

---

[1] *Life of Sir Robert Christison*, vol. ii. p. 192.

[2] *Some Experiences of a Barrister's Life*, vol. i. p. 100. London : 1882.

[3] *Ibid.*, vol. ii. p. 284. A full account of Wilkins' life and labours will be found in *Lives of Eminent Serjeants-at-Law of the English Bar*, by H. W. Woolrych, Serjeant-at-Law, vol. ii. p. 850. London : 1869. Woolrych completes the above anecdote with Thomas's comment to the jury—which Ballantine was too genteel to quote : " There he goes, gentlemen, *with his tail behind him !* "

[4] *Edwin* James, Q.C. (1812–1882), after a brilliant and successful career at the bar, with a professional income of £7000 a year and a house in Berkeley Square, failed for £100,000, and was disbarred for unprofessional conduct in 1861,

Of Baron Martin it is naïvely recorded that although "associated with numerous sensational trials, he invariably escaped censure; but once he made the mistake of *taking sides too soon* in a murder case, which eventually resulted in the person found guilty and sentenced to death being released with a free pardon." The trial referred to is that of Pellizžioni in 1864, known as the Saffron Hill murder case, when his Lordship "summed up dead against the prisoner," who was duly convicted. Only by the confession of the real murderer on the eve of execution was the effect of the judge's charge rendered nugatory.[1] In the present instance, as we shall see, his Lordship's predilection for "taking sides" is not less remarkably manifested. Sir Harry Poland relates of him that Baron Martin read nothing but law. Being induced, at the instigation of Mr. Justice Talfourd, a great lover of Shakespeare, to essay his favourite *Romeo and Juliet*, Martin, having perused that tragedy, indignantly protested: "I find that it is just a tissue of improbabilities from beginning to end!"[2] His Lordship, however, found no improbabilities in the complete innocence of Mr. Wooler.

And now that we know something of the players, let us proceed with the show.

IV

The first witness called for the Crown was Dr. William Haslewood of Darlington, who at this stage was examined only as to the organs removed from the body, at the post-mortem and the exhumation, for transmission to Professor Taylor. His evidence was supported by that of Dr. Jackson, of Mr. Henzell, of Dr. Taylor's assistant, and of the Darlington Superintendent of Police.

when he went to America, where he first practised at the local bar, which he later abandoned for the stage.

[1] *Some Experiences of a Barrister's Life*, vol. ii. p. 16; *Mysteries of Police and Crime*, by Major Arthur Griffiths, vol. i. p. 213. London: 1899; *Famous Judges and Famous Trials*, by Charles Kingston, p. 213. London: 1923.

[2] *Seventy-two Years at the Bar*: A Memoir, by Ernest Bowen-Rowlands, pp. 76. London: 1924.

Then Dr. Alfred Swayne Taylor, Professor of Medical Jurisprudence at Guy's Hospital, deposed to having examined these parts of the body. He tested the liver in two portions and found arsenic in each. Dr. Rees joined him in the experiments, on instructions of the accused's solicitor. Dr. Rees and witness examined the heart, the lungs, liquid from the abdomen, and the intestines. *They found arsenic in all.* Some portions of the intestines presented a black colour, which was unusual. Tested, this proved to be owing to a preparation of iron. *In the rectum they found arsenic in a larger proportion than in other parts of the intestines.* Their conclusion was that arsenic was present in all parts of the body, and that it had been taken, in solution, in small doses during life. The application of arsenic to the viscera after death could not produce the appearances observed. With regard to the intestines and rectum, the application of arsenic might give the same results on chemical analysis; but as regarded the liver, heart, and lungs, no application after death would produce the same result.[1] It is significant that Serjeant Wilkins did not cross-examine Professor Taylor.

Dr. Thomas Richardson, analytical chemist, Newcastle, deposed that he had tested portions of the body of the deceased; he recovered from the viscera half a grain of arsenic. He was not cross-examined.

Ann Taylor, the maidservant, described the illness of Mrs. Wooler on 8th May and the calling in of Dr. Jackson, who prescribed and sent the medicines.

I and Miss Lanchester used to administer them to Mrs. Wooler. Sometimes Mr. Wooler gave her medicine when I was not there, and sometimes when I was present. He did not give her any for some time before her death, because he could not lift her head from the pillow to please her. Injections were given down to the time of her death. The

---

[1] It had been suggested by the accused that the arsenic might have been placed in the body *after death.* Drs. Taylor and Rees conducted in the following year the analysis in the famous Rugeley poisoning case, and were the chief medical experts for the Crown at the subsequent trial of William Palmer for the murder of John Parsons Cook.

master administered them first, and I did afterwards, and sometimes
Miss Lanchester assisted me.

The injections began about a week after Dr. Jackson came.
A lead syringe was used till it became stopped up, and then
a brass one was borrowed from Mr. Fothergill, which was
used till the death.

I made the injections in the kitchen. I have seen Mr. Wooler
sometimes put laudanum in and have done so myself. He used to keep
the bottle from which he took the laudanum in his bedroom. It used to
stand sometimes on the washstand and sometimes on the table. The
injections were prepared in a basin. Mr. Wooler never prepared any
himself.

Her master kept no medicines, so far as she knew. She saw
a basket of medicines on the table when the doctors were
there. On the Friday after Mrs. Wooler's death a letter
came from Dr. Jackson, which her master read to her, Miss
Lanchester, and Miss Brecknell. He said: "Atrocious!
Poison! Where could it be? It could not be in the food,
Ann?" Witness replied, "No." He said again: "Where
could it be?" and witness said she did not know.

I asked where the medicine bottles were, and he said that I had
better lock them up in my box, *for I had made the food.* I accordingly
got all the bottles I could find, and locked them in my box. I took
them to the inquest and brought them back. I afterwards gave them
to Sergeant Brown, on his asking for them. They were in the same state
as when I first got them.[1]

Having given this order as to the disposal of the bottles,
Mr. Wooler went to Darlington, and did not return until
after the funeral. She remembered putting some urine,
which she got from the coachhouse, into a bottle and leaving
it on the kitchen table. Mr. Henzell or Dr. Haslewood
took away the urine themselves, except on this one

---

[1] Two baskets, containing Mr. Wooler's curious collection of drugs, were
produced at the Magisterial Inquiry : one, referred to as the Indian basket, with
34 bottles ; the other, called the oblong basket, with 9. Another basket, containing the remainder of the medicines prescribed by Dr. Jackson, was that
given up by Ann Taylor. We shall hear more of their contents when we come
to the evidence.—*Report of Investigation,* pp. 40–41.

occasion. After the injections were given, she washed the syringe, as directed by both her master and mistress. The stools and vomits were subjected to the inspection of the doctors.

Cross-examined by Serjeant Wilkins, Mr. and Mrs. Wooler were very kind to each other; they lived happily together. Mr. Wooler frequently read to her the Bible and religious books; he often prayed with her. Witness had seen him weeping bitterly at the bedside. Deceased always spoke of him in terms of affection. The excreta were placed in the coachhouse, where they were inspected by the doctors daily. At the time when the witness sent the specimen, Miss Lanchester was sleeping with her mistress. She never saw any unkindness from Mr. Wooler to his wife. He could not raise her because of his lameness, which prevented him from bending over the bed.

Dr. Thomas Hayes Jackson said he was called in to attend the deceased on 8th May, and found her "labouring under dyspepsia." Vomiting and purging continued throughout the illness, but ceased on 20th June for that day only. He first treated her for disordered stomach, but this had to be discontinued on account of the vomiting. Astringent injections were given to stop the purging; these usually gave relief, but not in this case. The vomitings averaged six times in 12 hours. These medicinal injections were made up in his surgery; there was no arsenic in any of them. Witness recommended Mr. Wooler to have further advice; "he said he was perfectly satisfied, and there was no occasion." The patient grew worse. On 8th June witness told Mr. Wooler she was in a dangerous state; he thought she was consumptive and had ulceration of the bowels. "He complained of me not informing him sooner of his wife's danger, as he was able to have the best advice." Dr. Haslewood was then called in. He found there was "a delicacy of the lungs, but that she might live many years and die of some other disease." *Mr. Wooler told them he administered the injections himself.* On 7th June the symptoms—restlessness, intense thirst, faintness, severe hiccough, in addition to the usual vomiting and purging—first led witness to suspect poison. He twice saw the Indian basket during Mrs. Wooler's illness: "it was brought out for something that I wanted." It contained over 30 different kinds of medicines, including veratria, strychnine, nux vomica, corrosive sublimate, tincture of morphia, calomel, sweet nitre, ipecacuanha, tincture of iodine, etc. "I took up a bottle labelled *Fowler's Solution of Arsenic*, and remarked to Mr. Wooler that it was good for skin diseases." Witness asked Mr. Wooler why he kept such dangerous medicines. He replied that having been twice six months on shipboard going to India, he was in the habit of keeping a large stock of drugs. He appeared to have a good knowledge of medicines. "When I saw the Fowler's Solution there was a tea-spoon, or a tea-spoonful and a half in the bottle, which was an ounce bottle." On 14th June witness administered an antidote: ammonio-citrate of iron. On 22nd June he and Mr. Henzell wrote to Professor Christison at Edinburgh; two specimens of the urine were sent to him for examination. Witness then described how on 23rd June Mrs. Wooler complained of tingling of the hands; and how Mr. Wooler had been asked by her three days before to tell the doctors, but forgot to do so. Witness never told Mr. Wooler that his wife was in a galloping consumption. After consultation with his colleagues on 29th June, he wrote the letter to Mr. Wooler. They were all satisfied it was a case of poisoning. *The bottle of Fowler's Solution was not among those produced at the inquest : it was searched for, but could not be found.*[1]

Cross-examined by Serjeant Wilkins, Dr. Jackson was taken again over the history of the illness. A year before, a patient of his, Mr. Marshall's servant, died under his hands. She had no medicine other than that which he gave her; it was prepared by his assistant, Mr. Henzell.

---

[1] "The functionaries of Darlington were plainly remiss in following up the fate of this bottle."—*Edinburgh Medical Journal*, 1856, p. 628.

At the inquest, witness gave it as his opinion that she died of arsenic. In the present case he suspected arsenic on 7th June; Dr. Haslewood came on the 8th; he diagnosed lung trouble, yet witness expressed no disagreement. At the consultation he kept back his own view. Until the 17th he never said anything about arsenic to Dr. Haslewood. He first named arsenic to Mr. Henzell on the 18th. Re-examined by Mr. James, the reason he did not communicate his suspicions on the 8th was because they were then not sufficiently strong. From the 7th to the 17th his suspicions became more confirmed from day to day, owing to the aggravated character of the symptoms. "On the 7th of June I said to Mr. Henzell that I suspected poisoning. I said: 'Poison is there, and there is some person in the house who understands the use of it!'" By the Court: "I did not take any step on the 7th, because I thought it would be imprudent; I waited till the symptoms became more developed."

George Harle Henzell deposed that he was assistant to Dr. Jackson. He first saw the deceased on 16th May. He described the symptoms under which she was then labouring. He did not see her again until 4th June, when she still suffered from vomiting and purging, accompanied by great thirst, difficulty in swallowing, dryness of the mouth, excoriation of the lips, and itching of the skin. "I was perplexed by so many symptoms conjoined together, and could not account for them. I was led to conjecture that arsenical poisoning might be the cause; but I thought that the poison must be administered in a peculiar way: over a long period of time and in small doses." He saw her at intervals up to 20th June; she exhibited symptoms of the same character. On each visit he took away samples of vomit or urine; these on examination contained a metallic deposit, which proved to be arsenic. On the 19th he communicated his suspicions to Dr. Haslewood. On the 23rd he obtained a bottle of urine which was quite different from what he had previously examined. It contained no arsenic; all that he had examined before did contain arsenic. On the 24th he asked Mr. Wooler if that specimen had come from the same source; the accused said it had, and referred him to Ann Taylor, who corroborated. Witness twice sent specimens to Professor Christison.

I saw Mr. Wooler twenty minutes after the death. He said his wife had just died. Afterwards I talked to him for a quarter of an hour in the sittingroom. I heard a bell ringing and asked him the meaning of it. He said that some bees were hiving in the garden, and that if I would go along with him I should probably be amused. I went with him, and we remained for some time watching the bees. After the hiving of the bees was completed, we walked round the garden ; he appeared at that time much as usual ; I did not observe any symptoms of distress ; he talked about his wife.

Witness was present at the post-mortem; Dr. Haslewood took notes of the appearances, in which witness concurred.

Cross-examined by Serjeant Wilkins, he first saw this lady on 16th May. He then treated her for irritation of the alimentary canal, not for influenza. On 4th June he suspected that the symptoms might be due to an irritant poison. He could not account for them on any other hypothesis. On the 7th Dr. Jackson told witness he also suspected poison. Witness began to test the urine on the 14th, and found arsenic. He used Reinsch's test. An antidote for arsenic was administered to the patient on 17th June and again on the 20th. He had heard Mr. Wooler several times complain of Dr. Jackson's conduct. He said that if his wife had been properly treated "she would have been alive now." Witness had heard him censure Dr. Jackson for not having sooner told his opinion, and say to Dr. Haslewood: "If you had had my wife under your care she would not now have been on a bed of sickness." At the beginning of the illness Mr. Wooler seemed anxious about his wife. Re-examined, he did not appear so during the last days of her life. He seemed quite unmoved when witness told him that she could not recover. He repeatedly asked: "When do you think she will die?"

By the Court, witness used no arsenic in the medicines he made up for Dr. Jackson.

Dr. Robert Christison, Professor of Forensic Medicine in the University of Edinburgh, deponed that on 24th June he received a bottle through the post. He wrote to Mr. Henzell, and received another bottle on the 29th. The seals of both were unbroken. He found arsenic in the second, but not in the first; the two specimens were perfectly different: they could not have come from the same person.[1]

The Rev. James Simpson said he knew Mr. and Mrs. Wooler. The accused complained to witness of the "very outrageous" behaviour of Dr. Jackson in not telling him sooner how serious was his wife's case. Witness suggested it was meant to spare his feelings. He never told Mr. Wooler that it would be useless to call in Sir John Fife; but he recommended Dr. Haslewood, to which the accused agreed. He then described how he summoned the husband to the death-chamber, and the accused's reluctance to go in dishabille. When he did so, he looked down at her and said: "She has been a good wife to me."

Seeing she was at her last moments, I was offering up a prayer for her, when Mr. Wooler whispered in my ear: "Are you going to Darlington to-day?" I said I could not tell. He then said: "Is she gone?" and he took a small mirror from the chimney-piece, which I put to her mouth and found that she was dead.

The accused then left the room to complete his interrupted toilet.

Dr. Haslewood was examined at great length as to the course of the illness and his treatment of the case. The chief point of interest in his evidence relates to the tingling of the hands.

I was aware that the prisoner kept a book. Mr. Wooler said to me: " You have asked me so often various questions respecting the symptoms, that in order to assist my memory I have got a slate, to mark the

---

[1] Dr. Christison's further examination was here postponed until Dr. Haslewood had been examined.

symptoms down." For this he afterwards substituted a book. I first
heard of the tingling of the hands on 23rd June; I learnt the fact from
the prisoner. He said: " My wife has a feeling of stiffness and tingling
in her hands; what can that be ? " I made no answer, but turned
sharply away to his wife's room, being struck with the remark, having
looked before for that symptom. I found that she felt tingling in her
hands, and the muscles of the forearm harder and stiffer than natural.
I went back and said it was as he reported. . . . On the following day,
the 24th, on entering the stable yard I met Mr. Wooler; I inquired how
the tingling and spasms were. He said they were rather better. I
asked how long she had had these symptoms, and he said: " Oh, only
yesterday." On going into Mrs. Wooler's room I put the same question
to her in presence of her husband, and her answer was: " Three or four
days." Mr. Wooler interposed, and said: " Oh, no; it was only
yesterday." She said: " Oh, yes; I told you to tell the doctors two or
three days ago, but you forgot." The tingling continued more or less
up to her death.

The results of the post-mortem were what he and his
colleagues expected, and confirmed their belief that the
deceased died from arsenic, "by slow and oft-repeated
doses." On 9th June, being in want of ipecacuanha,
witness asked Mr. Wooler whether he had any; he produced
a basket of bottles, containing strychnine and other deadly
drugs. There was an ounce bottle, considerably less than
half-full, labelled "Fowler's Solution of Arsenic"; the
colour corresponded to that preparation. "I said to
prisoner: 'What in the world do you do with such things?
You have enough here to poison the whole village!' He
smiled." [1] From divers conversations had by him with the
accused, witness considered that, for a non-professional
man, he was well acquainted with the use of drugs.

Cross-examined by Serjeant Wilkins, he could name no
single fact in support of that conclusion; it was based
generally on the accused's collection of drugs and the way
he talked about them. Witness never said that Mrs.
Wooler was not dangerously ill and might last for years.
He told the accused on 8th June that she was seriously ill.
On the 19th he formed the opinion that nothing but arsenic

---

[1] " The Lord Ferdinand laughs."—*The Duchess of Malfi*, Act III. Sc. 3.

would account for the symptoms, and suggested an anti-dote. He had known the Woolers since they came from Darlington; Mr. Wooler seemed always very attentive to his wife. The accused asked witness to furnish him with a correct account of the case for submission to Sir John Fife. Witness did so, mentioning every symptom then known to him, but the tingling of the hands. He did not mention that, because to do so would have been equivalent to saying it was a case of poison. "I and my medical colleagues had agreed not to divulge our suspicions at that time. I was not positive it was arsenic; I had a doubt about it till I opened the body and saw the appearances."

SERJEANT WILKINS.—And you had strong suspicions that this poor woman was at the time agonised by arsenic ?

WITNESS.—I had.

SERJEANT WILKINS.—Then I won't ask you another question.

By the Court, he stated every prominent symptom except the tingling, which had just occurred. This was on the evening of the 23rd. His reason for withholding it was, that "divulging our suspicion of poison at that time could not save the life of the sufferer; but if it came to her knowledge, the shock would hasten the fatal event."

Professor Christison, recalled, said that he had carefully considered the symptoms as detailed by Drs. Jackson, Haslewood, and Henzell: they were precisely those one should expect in a case of poisoning by repeated doses of arsenic. He had heard the notes of the post-mortem read: the appearances were such as arsenic might produce. Combining all the facts: the symptoms, the appearances, and the results of Professor Taylor's analyses: witness could come to no other conclusion than that the deceased died from poisoning by arsenic, administered in repeated doses.

SERJEANT WILKINS.—I ask no question.

After evidence by two local chemists, who produced their books shewing all prescriptions made up by them for

Drs. Jackson and Haslewood, none of which contained
arsenic, the will of the accused, dated 12th June 1855, was
proved and read. He left his whole estate to his wife,
Jane Wooler, for life; after her death the property was to
go to his brother, Octavius Borrowdale Wooler, subject to
an annuity of £40 to Miss Lanchester.

Miss Lanchester deponed that she kept a school at
Haughton, half a mile from Great Burdon. She had known
the Woolers intimately for seven years. During the last
month of Mrs. Wooler's illness she stayed in the house every
night. She occasionally gave her the medicines, and twice
assisted Ann Taylor in giving an injection. She was
present when Mr. Wooler read Dr. Jackson's letter, refusing the death certificate, but she did not know whether
Mr. Wooler told Ann Taylor to put the bottles in her box.
Cross-examined, she was over 40. The Woolers lived
cordially and happily together; he was a kind husband.
He manifested great anxiety for her recovery; he read
prayers every night and morning, and daily read the Scriptures to her. Witness had often seen him in tears during
the illness. By the Court, the accused's affection for his
wife appeared to be sincere.

W. H. Chapman, London, stated that he was a manufacturer of elastic tubes for syringes, and that no arsenic
was used in their manufacture.

SERJEANT WILKINS.—And so you have come all the way from
London to tell us that ! Well, you need not attend on Monday (laughter).

Sergeant Brown, of the Darlington police, described the
arrest of the accused, and the search of the house. Ann
Taylor produced the medicine bottles from a locked box in
her room, of which she had the key. He found a syringe on
a shelf in the store-room. He delivered them all to Superintendent Robson. That officer stated that on 14th July,
on the adjournment of the inquest, he searched the house
particularly for a bottle of Fowler's Solution of Arsenic.
He found an Indian basket, containing many bottles, of

which he took possession; the Fowler bottle was not among them. Cross-examined, he searched the whole premises; he saw no broken medicine bottles. The "night soil" was examined as well, but nothing was found. Re-examined, between the inquest and 27th July the house was in the possession of the prisoner.

Miss Middleton stated that she lived at Haughton and was a friend of the Woolers. During the illness of Mrs. Wooler she called every day and occasionally gave the medicines. She was never present at the administration of the injections. Cross-examined, she never saw anything but the greatest kindness between them. Mr. Wooler was exceedingly kind to his wife, who appeared to have every comfort a woman in her station could desire. Dr. Valentine Devey stated that he had professionally attended Mrs. Wooler at Wolsingham in 1854. He had conversed with Mr. Wooler on the subject of drugs and chemicals; he seemed to have a knowledge of them. Ann Brecknell stated that she was a sister of Mrs. Wooler and lived in London. She went to Great Burdon on the Monday before the death. She recollected the reading of Dr. Jackson's letter; Ann Taylor was present. Cross-examined, she had remained in charge of the house since her sister's death. She went at the request of Mr. Wooler. He was reading the Bible to his wife the greater part of the night before she died.

A niece of Mr. Wooler and a brother of Mrs. Wooler having given evidence as to the good relations of the parties, and the Registrar of Deaths having stated how Mr. Wooler registered the cause of death as "ulceration of the stomach and bowels, not certified," Mr. John R. Fothergill stated that he was a surgeon in Darlington and a member of the Royal College of Surgeons, Edinburgh. He knew the prisoner, with whom he had a conversation about a week before his wife's death. "He desired me to lend him a syringe; I lent him one; the syringe now produced is the one I lent him; it was new at the time. He said his own

16

apparatus was stopped up.   He afterwards told me that my
syringe acted admirably, and he was much obliged to me."
On its return to him, witness placed it in a drawer.   Having
heard · "something about arsenic," he tested the tube,
using Reinsch's test.   He detected arsenic.   He afterwards
found that the muriatic acid he used was impure; so
he tested again, and discovered arsenic in less quantity
than before.   He made a comparative analysis.   Cross-
examined, he gave his evidence at the inquiry before he
ascertained that his first test was impure.   He told Mr.
Henzell at once.   They did not agree to keep the matter
secret.   He informed the magistrates of the fact a fortnight later.   By the Court, "Why did you not go at once
and state your error before the magistrates?"   Witness:
"I was making my comparative analysis."

Professor Taylor, recalled, said that he had listened
attentively to the account of the symptoms up to the time
of the patient's death.   His judgment was that she met her
death by arsenical poison.   He had examined 125 cases of
arsenical poisoning.   The symptoms anterior to the tingling
of the hands might have been produced by other causes.
The analysis of the urine and the post-mortem appearances
confirmed his view: that she died from arsenic, administered in solution in small doses.   Referring to his own
experiments with Dr. Rees, witness said that all their tests
were perfectly pure.   He found arsenic in both syringes.
Cross-examined, assuming a blunder or mistake in the
making up of the medicines, the chemical results of the
examination might be the same.   Four drachms of Fowler's
Solution, given over five days, would destroy life: there
was a recorded case of a woman poisoned by that quantity,
the smallest known.   By the Court, it was possible that
the poison could be administered by injection.   This concluded the case for the Crown, and the defence adduced no
evidence.

Before submitting ourselves to the eloquence of Serjeant
Wilkins, in his impassioned address to the jury in behalf of

his client, it may be of interest to hear what Mr. Wooler had to say for himself when he was examined as a witness at the inquest.

V

Before the Coroner, at Great Burdon, on Saturday, 14th July 1855, Joseph Snaith Wooler, sworn and examined, described the illness of his wife and the calling in of Dr. Jackson to attend her.

I drew Dr. Jackson's attention to the nervous excitement the liver was undergoing ; she vomited quarts of pure bile, and otherwise emitted it. I never saw anything like it, except on board ship. He said he understood she had been a long time in India, and that he had made a mistake in treatment.

Dr. Jackson suggested the calling in of Dr. Haslewood: "I said I had no objection, as I thought he was talented."

Dr. Jackson in the meantime had apprised me that he conceived Mrs. Wooler consumptive, and that from the first he had doomed her. I said : "God bless me ! Dr. Jackson, why have you not apprised me before ? I have means, and would have had the first advice in the kingdom."

In order to ascertain the extent of the lung disease, Dr. Haslewood suggested that Mr. Henzell be consulted, "as his ear was accurate."

We waited a long time for Mr. Henzell ; at last a note came from Dr. Jackson to the effect that it was not professional etiquette for his assistant to attend before him. I was too agitated to write ; and said : " Good God ! Dr. Jackson has told me my wife is in great danger, and can he stand upon any foolish etiquette ? " I said I could never overlook it, and was very angry. This was on the 8th of June. After some time Dr. Jackson made his appearance, and they saw Mrs. Wooler. Dr. Haslewood tested the upper portion of the lungs, and told me he did not think there was that danger I had apprehended from Dr. Jackson, and cheered me up again. Mr. Henzell and he a day or two afterwards made a thorough examination of the chest. Mrs. Wooler said : " Joseph, dear, I am not consumptive ; why do they test my chest ? "

The vomiting still continuing, Dr. Haslewood put her on a very small allowance both of food and medicine. Witness kept an account of the symptoms in a book. Mrs. Wooler gradually grew worse, "until we relied almost on injections for her support."

Dr. Jackson having, as I conceived, acted in so gross and unfeeling a manner, when Dr. Haslewood was called in I repeatedly mentioned that I wished to put the case into his hands. I told Dr. Jackson, in the presence of my brother Octavius, that I had ample means, and he ought not to have kept me in the dark until the symptoms had become so formidable; that I had just cause to feel hurt to think he knew I had ample means of calling in the first advice in the kingdom. Had it cost me a thousand pounds I could have afforded it; and I had reason to feel hurt to find the symptoms so aggravated before I was aware there was danger. . . . She never got any better, except occasionally. On one occasion, when I sent some urine to the town, the doctor said, if genuine, it was that of a person in good health. I caught at straws, and never realised till two days before her death that I must lose her.

[*Cross-examined.*]

Q.—How long was Mrs. Wooler ill before Dr. Jackson was called in? *A.*—Only a few days; she was first taken unwell on the Thursday night and could not continue the prayers; I read them through for her.

Q.—Had she taken any medicines before? *A.*—No, I don't think she had. I don't know whether she had one of Dr. Dixon's tonic mixtures or not, but it was very little if any. It was an old recipe of Dr. Dixon, of Gateshead.

Q.—Kept in the medicine basket? *A.*—No; the medicine basket was never opened until it was opened by Dr. Jackson. I did not know where it was.

Q.—You were not aware it was in the house? *A.*—Not at all. As for Mrs. Wooler, she knew nothing of the properties of the medicines, nor did I.

Q.—Did Mrs. Wooler vomit before Dr. Jackson was called in? *A.*—Yes; she had taken some soup and pig-cheek. I never take soup the servant and Mrs. Wooler had it.

Q.—Who generally administered the medicines? *A.*—First one person and then another. I never could, because I could not hold up Mrs. Wooler's head; it required a person to go underneath and hold up her head.

Q.—Did they pass through your hands before being administered? *A.*—I brought nearly all the medicine from Dr. Jackson; I used to ride down for it.

Q.—But after it was poured out? *A.*—It is a thousand to one that frequently I have had it in my hand, but only to pour it out before Mrs. Wooler, and give it to the person who administered it.

Q.—Who administered the injections ? *A.*—The girl and myself.

Q.—We are told of some arsenical preparation : where was it got from ? *A.*—I cannot tell that I got it ; if there was a solution of arsenic, I have had it in my possession since 1840. Dr. Jackson never told me there was a solution of arsenic in the basket.

Q.—Dr. Jackson has also spoken to some other poisons ? *A.*—I don't know of them. It was Mrs. Wooler's basket, that she brought from India, and the medicines had been all packed away until I brought them down to Dr. Jackson on the occasion referred to. I didn't know that they were there.

Q.—Where were they kept ? *A.*—Under lock and key.

Q.—Who kept the key ? *A.*—Mrs. Wooler.

Q.—Had any person access but Mrs. Wooler ? *A.*—No one ; unless she sent anyone, or myself, if I ever went.

Q.—You never used arsenic for anything ? *A.*—No, never ; I don't know what it is when I see it.

Q.—Did you ever speak to Dr. Jackson about arsenic ? *A.*—Never.

[A letter was then read from the accused to Dr. Dixon, with reference to the suggestion that he should visit his old patient, in which the accused said that he thought the gentlemen already attending her would do all that could be done.]

Q.—Were you satisfied at that time with the medical attendants ? *A.*—I had Dr. Haslewood and Mr. Henzell; after Dr. Jackson's behaviour I almost altogether appealed to them ; so much so that I conceived I was really acting offensively, and tried to school myself to act differently.

Q.—About the same time you made your will ? *A.*—Yes; I ordered Octavius to make it in the beginning of June.

Q.—Had you at that time any reason to suppose Mrs. Wooler was in a dangerous state of health ? *A.*—Why, on the 8th of June Dr. Jackson told me he had doomed her from the first time he saw her !

Q.—Have you any insurance upon her life ? *A.*—Not a halfpenny.

Q.—Were you ever separated ? *A.*—Never. She told me on the 16th of June I had been a devoted and unexampled husband ; and hoped if ever she had, though unwittingly, offended me, I would forgive her.

Q.—Did she ever shew that she was afraid of you ? *A.*—Never. We had an established rule, from marriage, that if she wanted anything and I objected, she had only to put her arms round my neck, and she had it. That rule was acted upon, and she always carried the day.

Q.—Do you recollect going into the garden immediately after her

death ? *A.*—Yes ; I had been up all night, and had only washed before
she died.

Q.—For what purpose did you go into the garden ? *A.*—For relief to
my feelings. My sister [*sic* : Miss Brecknell] had fallen on my shoulder
and said : " You will be better in the open air. Bear up ; you have
had a long trial, but my sister has made a blessed change." Mr. Simpson
assured me of his full conviction that she was an angel in heaven.

Q.—Did you go with the doctors to see the bees swarming ? *A.*—No,
it was not for that purpose. My sister suggested that I should be
relieved in the open air, as I am of a weakly constitution.[1]

The gentlest reader will perceive upon how many matters
of fact Mr. Wooler, in his evidence before the Coroner, has
the misfortune to differ from the sworn testimony of the
witnesses at the trial. The disparities of the respective
statements, and the inferences to be drawn therefrom, may
profitably be considered.

VI

On Monday, 10th December 1855, being the third and
last day of the trial, "a solemn silence prevailing throughout
the densely crowded building," did Mr. Serjeant Buzfuz—
I beg pardon—Wilkins rise in his wrath to denounce the
iniquities of the prosecution and to shew what he could do
for his 200 guineas.[2]

Gentlemen of the Jury : I will endeavour to remove the whole of the
irrelevant and, as it seems to me, immaterial statements by which the
real merits of this case have been clouded, hidden, and disguised ; and
I think before I have done, without arrogance and without self-sufficiency,
I may venture to say that the prisoner under his trial is the last man in
this wide world who ought to have stood before you on this occasion.
And but for that disgraceful and disgusting prejudice which has exhibited itself out of doors and indoors with reference to this trial, a
prejudice as disgraceful to this country as it is inimical to the interests
of justice—but for that, I should have addressed you without any

---

[1] *Report of Investigation*, Appendix, pp. 44–47.

[2] Charles Wilkins (1800–1857) ; barrister, Inner Temple, 1835 ; defended
William Henry Barber, 1844 ; Serjeant-at-law, 1847 ; Patent of Precedence,
1851 ; retained to defend Dr. Palmer, but unable to appear (being then at
Boulogne, " which he dared not quit, through fear of arrest for debt "), 1856 ;
died at Queen's Bench Walk, Temple, 1857.

apprehension, and confining myself exclusively to the merits of the case, should have anticipated without any fear a favourable verdict at your hands.

Having characterised the Press comments upon the case as "multifarious and scandalous publications designed to poison the public mind," the learned Serjeant glanced at the matter of which we have heard from Professor Christison, namely, when Mr. Henzell in the witness-box drew blood from his mighty adversary, amid the applause of the audience. He reminded them (the jury) how, "bending under the weight of responsibility upon him," seeing a fellow-man upon his trial for the wilful murder of his own wife, while they had to decide the eternal as well as the temporal interests of the accused, he (counsel) "saw in that court room a man, who ought to have known better, exhibit such an unseemly course of conduct as to applaud what he thought was an answer disparaging to the prisoner and aiding the case for the prosecution. I did feel shame for that man; I did feel shame for those who followed in his wake; I did feel shame when I found that a man calling himself an Englishman. . . ." But we need not farther pursue the stream of the learned Serjeant's invective, which flowed from the fact that his unwarrantable attack upon the witness had been foiled.

Gentlemen, do you wonder that prejudice should have taken root in the minds of men when you have listened to the infamous conduct— I use the word advisedly—of the medical men in this case ? I repeat the word : their infamous conduct ; and I do not hesitate to say that, but for that infamous conduct, this poor woman Mrs. Wooler might have been still living and this trial would never have taken place. When you find a man applauded for the manner in which he gave his evidence —only for the manner ; it could not possibly be for the matter ; when you find a man extolled as a man of extraordinary skill, placing himself in an attitude be'ore ^r. Taylor, so childish, so silly, so utterly devoid of sense, as to ask him for information and advice : whether it was not his duty to publish at once the fact that Mr. Fothergill's test was imperfect, what then will you think of this Mr. Henzell—*I think that is his name* ?

This witness, "who three or four years ago was a grocer's

apprentice," knew from Fothergill that "they had sought arsenic by means of arsenic." "They slept upon it [that knowledge], they ate upon it, they drank upon it, and I daresay they said grace upon it!"

MR JAMES pointed out that his learned friend was in error.

HIS LORDSHIP begged that learned counsel be not interrupted.

SERJEANT WILKINS.—God knows I have been harassed enough in this case.

He asked the jury to consider the situation of the accused.

Who can tell the hours of mental agony that man has gone through within the walls of his prison ?   Let your sympathy go as far with him as it may ; let your imagination take wings ; and in some measure you can appreciate his position. " But yesterday," he might have said, " I was respected by all who knew me. But yesterday my society was courted by my friends. But yesterday my reputation, dearer to me than life, was untarnished. Where am I today ? With the prospect of the confiscation of all I possess ; my wife, whom as a husband I esteemed more than most men can boast of—my wife ! even her body has been mangled in order to further the tests they have applied—that body which I almost worshipped has been submitted to inspection to meet the requirements of justice ! " [1]

But let them take a quiet and sober view of the case.

It has been, I assure you, for me, without flattery and affectation, a great happiness to witness your demeanour during this trial. I have now been for about twenty years or more in the habit of addressing juries ; but never, since I had the honour of appearing at the bar, did I witness such sobriety of demeanour, such closeness of attention, such an anxiety to arrive at the truth, as I have observed on the part of the jury whom I have now the honour of addressing ! [2]

What were the grounds upon which this accusation was made? First, that Mrs. Wooler died in consequence of being poisoned with arsenic. That he was not going to dispute. He accepted the judgment of one of the highest

---

[1] For forensic flowers such as these one must go back to Serjeant Buzfuz and his description of the bereavement of Mrs. Bardell.

[2] "Counsel always begin in this way, because it puts the jury on the very best terms with themselves, and makes them think what sharp fellows they must be."—Report of the memorable Trial of Bardell v. Pickwick.—The Pickwick Papers.

authorities in Europe: Professor Taylor. By that admission he did his client no damage, because one of the medical witnesses [1] had stated that not twelve months before a patient of his, *who received medicine from no one but himself*, died from arsenic. It was quite possible that Dr. Jackson or his assistant had made a mistake; such a supposition was far more probable and compatible with the evidence than that Mrs. Wooler died by the hands of her husband.

But I do say this; that but for the conduct of Dr. Jackson, of Mr. Henzell, and of Dr. Haslewood—conduct which I say advisedly was infamous in the extreme—my client would not have been placed at the bar and you would not have been engaged in this inquiry today. Whether it arose from professional jealousy, from misgiving among each other, or from what, I don't know; but one thing is clear: if on 7th June, when Dr. Jackson says he suspected poison, that suspicion had been mentioned and acted upon, the mistake might have been discovered and the whole catastrophe prevented.

The second ground was that the person who administered the arsenic must have been a person of skill. A greater absurdity was never uttered. "Anything so abominable or disgraceful to a court of justice as the way in which these three gentlemen were allowed to give their evidence—their opinions, rather—before the magistrates is not to be found in the annals of British law." Although he was not instructed, and did not seek to accuse anybody, he would put various hypotheses to shew that the prisoner was the last man in existence who ought to have been charged with that offence. The prosecutor's argument applied to each and every one of these doctors. They were persons of skill; they had the means; they had access to the deceased. Suspicion might rest upon any one of them rather than upon Mr. Wooler. "Why should I not accuse them? It may be said they had no motive; no more had the prisoner: all his motives were the other way." The third ground was that the accused shewed indifference to his wife's death.

[1] Dr. Jackson.

Why, the very symptoms which so superficial a gentleman
as the Rev. Mr. Simpson took as proofs of indifference,
might be quite the reverse. Mr. Simpson saw Mr. Wooler
with part of his person uncovered, yet thought it extraordinary that.he should ask whether he was in a fit state
to go into a room where were Miss Lanchester, Miss Middleton, and Ann Taylor! It said little for the Christian
charity which the reverend gentleman preached, that he
should have formed so hasty and injurious a conclusion.
After the death he said to Mr. Wooler "he hoped he [the
accused] was comforted, because he believed she was
happy."

Well, then, if Mr. Simpson is a respectable clergyman, if he is incapable of hypocrisy, if he is incapable of falsehood, he did grieve for the
prisoner's loss and hoped he would derive consolation. Is it true what he
tells us ?   Did this poor man stand by his wife's deathbed ; did he fix
his eyes upon her ; and did he, after fixing his eyes upon her for a time,
make use of the expression : " She has been a good wife to me " ?

But it might be said he whispered in Mr. Simpson's ear:
"Are you going to Darlington today?". No doubt he did;
he was not in a fit state to go himself, and he had at Darlington a dear brother to whom the intelligence of his wife's
death was important.[1] What did his wife's sister, his own
niece, and Ann Taylor prove? All those who were about
him say that he was full of grief, his anxiety was great, and
his kindness and affection for his wife prevailed on all
occasions. It was said that he was unwilling to call in
medical aid. Who called in Dr. Jackson and Mr. Henzell?
These two wiseacres differed as to her complaint, but they
agreed that the same remedy would do! Who called in
Dr. Haslewood? On the 7th Dr. Jackson believed that
she was being poisoned; on the 8th he told Mr. Wooler she
was consumptive!

Consumptive ! Do you believe that the agony under which she was
labouring—the red tongue, the feeble pulse, the pain in her stomach,

---

[1] Octavius Borrowdale Wooler, the residuary legatee.

the coldness of her extremities—were the symptoms of consumption ? You cannot be such idiots. I. say there is no man in the world will believe that Dr. Jackson was not deceiving, and wilfully deceiving, that man when he told him that falsehood about consumption.

Why, if he were poisoning her, did the prisoner ask for Dr. Jackson's opinion? Generally speaking, a criminal is a coward; if there is any one whose observations he wishes to escape, it is the man who may detect him. What does the prisoner do? He tells Dr. Haslewood that if he had come to his wife she would have been well, and he dismisses Dr. Jackson for the incompetent manner in which he had treated her. He courted investigation.

Look at the conduct of Dr. Jackson, good, amiable, humane man. On the Monday of the inquest he writes a letter to Mr. Wooler, beginning " Dear Sir " and ending " Yours faithfully." It is the last link in that chain of hypocrisy. He believed the prisoner was a poisoner of the deepest dye, that he had been guilty of the foul crime of murder, and that the murder of his wife—and he writes to him as " Dear Sir " ! and then following the rules of society, he calls himself " Yours faithfully " ! [1]

On the other hand, the learned Serjeant had the hardihood to maintain that every statement made by the accused in his letters with reference to his wife's illness was "consistent and creditable [? credible]." As for the alleged suppositious specimen, Miss Lanchester slept in the same room, and it was likely enough that the vessels had been inadvertently changed. With regard to the collection of poisons in the basket produced by the accused to the doctors:

If he wished any concealment, why bring that basket forward and shew the poison ? Do you find the murderer who has killed his fellow-man produce the bloody dagger that would prove his guilt ? Do you find the assassin produce his weapons of destruction ? No. Why bring the basket that contained Fowler's Solution instead of bringing what was wanted, and not produce the whole contents ?

But there was no proof that there was in that basket a drop of Fowler's Solution; the bottle was so labelled, but

---

[1] This pleasantly recalls the exegetical feat of Serjeant Buzfuz in the matter of Mr. Pickwick's letters to Mrs. Bardell.

it was not examined and they knew not what it contained. The learned Serjeant then dealt at great length with the absence of motive and the accused's devotion to his wife.

Do you believe that, like a demon, he agonised her whom for hour after hour, year after year, season after season, he had cherished with the greatest fondness, whose every wish to gratify was his joy? Do you ask how any man could thus give agony to the object of his love, not only for a moment, but day by day adding to that torment? Do you believe that he was so perfectly an atheist that he habitually prayed for the relief of that suffering which he himself had caused? [1]

As good men they could not believe it; as good men they would not believe it. "You may come to the conclusion that there is a great mystery which you cannot fathom; but that you will say that the prisoner is the person who poisoned his wife is what I am certain you will never do." It was said that the accused was well acquainted with drugs; but that was a two-edged weapon. There was no poison so vulgarly and commonly used as arsenic, none more easily detected. Why use it, when he had strychnine, than which there was no poison more difficult of detection? Would he have been such an egregious fool, having given her arsenic, as to supply the doctors with vomits and furnish them with stools? The case had been reported throughout the length and breadth of the land, yet no one had come forward to say that the prisoner ever bought arsenic. It was suggested that he had destroyed the Fowler bottle, but there was no evidence whatever to connect him with its disappearance. The verdict of the Coroner's jury was the only one to which, as conscientious men, they could come.

In the name of Him whom we revere as our God, in the name of our

---

[1] However the fact may stand as regards Mr. Wooler, certain it is that this passage accurately foreshadows the deeds of Dr. Pritchard, an affectionate and pious husband, who tortured his wife to death with antimony for four months and entered in his diary a prayer for her eternal welfare, all without discoverable motive, in the year 1865. Indeed, the Doctor went one better; for his wife died in his arms, and he had the coffin opened that he might kiss her for the last time.

common country, in the name of humanity, and by the majesty and purity and honour of our law, never let prejudice be found there ! If there be one spot in the land dedicated to reason and truth, let that spot be the jury-box. I speak in the name of my country and fellow-men, and I implore you, for the cause of truth and honour and justice, not to let passion or prejudice guide you. Yield to nothing but reason, let it have its sway, and I shall not have spoken in vain. Though that man's sufferings be greater than I can describe, this lesson, severe and bitter as it is, may teach him wisdom and righteousness and humility ; and he may have reason in his last hour to thank God that affliction overcame him, that he was chastised and persecuted, when it was demanded for the cause of justice and of truth.

"With this beautiful peroration Mr. Serjeant Buzfuz sat down," and Mr. Baron Martin began his charge to the jury.[1]

VII

The charge of the learned judge embraced a review of the whole evidence, which it were wearisome to recapitulate; so I shall refer only to such particulars as appear to me to call for notice.

We have heard that his Lordship was prone to "take sides," and in the Wooler case that judicial peculiarity is plainly visible. There could be, he admitted, no question that this lady died from the effects of arsenic, the only one for their determination being: Was there any evidence to satisfy them that the prisoner was the person who administered that poison? "This is the first case where the poisoning is alleged to have extended over a long period; and I believe you will, for the first time in the annals of the jurisprudence of this country, be called upon to give a verdict in such a case." Dealing with what he termed the most important point in the case: the possession by the prisoner of Fowler's Solution of Arsenic: his Lordship observed that the prisoner produced the bottle "openly,

---

[1] Sir Samuel Martin (1801–1883) ; Baron of the Exchequer ; M.A., Trinity College, Dublin, 1832; Hon. LL.D., 1857 ; barrister, Middle Temple, 1830; Q.C., 1843 ; Liberal M.P. for Pontefract, 1847 ; Baron of Exchequer, 1850–1874 ; knighted, 1850 ; died, 1883.

publicly, and without concealment." By the time of the inquest it had disappeared.

Now, the strong observation which arises upon that is : Why was the prisoner not asked what had become of it ? There is supposed to be missing the genuine agent by which the crime was committed, and yet no person appears to have taken the trouble of asking the prisoner if he knew what had become of it. *And really we do not know, if the question had been asked, that the man might not have said : " I used it for so and so, or I put it away."* But it does not appear to have entered into the minds of one of these people to say a single word to him upon the subject. Nothing of the kind was asked ; and all you are told upon the subject is, that at the inquest, when the bottle was wanted, it could not be found.[1]

The next point made by the prosecution was that the accused did not take sufficient steps to procure medical attendance. His Lordship did not think that there was anything in that. As to the keeping by the accused of a book detailing the symptoms, while it was an extraordinary thing to do, it was done at the request of the medical men themselves. He thought that there was nothing whatever in that circumstance to tell against the prisoner. Had the accused suppressed the tingling symptoms, it would have been strongly suspicious;[2] but it appeared from the evidence that the doctors first learned of their existence from him. The conduct of the medical men had been very reprehensible; if the account which they gave of their proceedings from the time their suspicions were first aroused was correct, that conduct was undoubtedly not what it should have been. His Lordship, however, believed that they were wise only after the event. If they suspected that arsenic was being injected into their patient, they should have gone to Mr. Wooler and told him so, and have inquired into the matter. He would even go farther: they should have gone before a magistrate, rather than see this

---

[1] The strength of his Lordship's observation is somewhat abated by the fact that Mr. Wooler, being questioned at the inquest about this bottle, not only did not admit possession of it, but denied that the conversation regarding it, to which the doctors swore, had ever taken place.

[2] He *did* suppress them for three days.

woman murdered by inches beneath their eyes. The conclusion to which his Lordship came was that, in fact, they did not entertain so strong a suspicion that she was being poisoned as they believed they did, before her death. With regard to the substituted urine, Ann Taylor was the person responsible.

MR. JAMES pointed out that his Lordship would find that it was the prisoner who sent the bottle.

What benefit could arise to the accused from any person sending a spurious specimen, when the other samples had been so frequently examined? As to the behaviour of the accused after his wife's death, the jury must judge for themselves whether or not it was that of a man affectionately and devotedly attached to her. One man might exhibit very little feeling; another might give way to excessive grief. Having dealt with the reception of Dr. Jackson's letter by the accused and his direction to Ann Taylor to lock up the medicines, his Lordship said the jury must ask themselves whether there was in all that anything to indicate consciousness of guilt.

It was his duty to call their attention also to the circumstances in the prisoner's favour. In the first place there was no motive in the world for the commission of this murder. The learned counsel for the prosecution told them in plain terms that he could suggest no motive. They must therefore ask themselves, as twelve sensible men, whether the accused was likely to be guilty of the crime laid to his charge. . . . The law required that, in cases of presumptive evidence, it should be clear presumption—not surmise, suspicion, or imagination, but plain natural inferences, following upon ascertained facts. It was for them to say whether it was possible that anybody could act upon such proofs— they scarcely deserved the name—as had been adduced in this case to shew that the prisoner murdered his wife. It was a case wrapped up in mystery. His Lordship had endeavoured, perhaps more than he ought to have done, to come to some conclusion, but had been unable to do so. He would not say, if he were called upon to find a verdict, that anything like proof had been adduced, because he did not think there was any. *He could only say for himself that if he were making any surmises or were allowing his imagination to take scope,* THERE WAS A PERSON UPON WHOM HIS SUSPICIONS WOULD REST OTHER THAN THE PRISONER.

The jury retired to consider their verdict; and returning to Court in three or four minutes, announced their decision: NOT GUILTY. Baron Martin, in dismissing them, said that both the country and himself were indebted to them for the manner in which they had performed their duty. "At a very early part of the case," said his Lordship, "he acquired a strong opinion upon the case. He would have interfered sooner, but he thought it more satisfactory to allow it to be fully heard."

The prisoner was then discharged, and the Court rose.

VIII

Not the least remarkable feature of this singular case are the concluding words of the judge's charge. It was admitted upon all hands that this lady had been murdered. Mr. Wooler, by self and counsel, accused the medical men of the crime; they, in turn, accused Mr. Wooler. The Coroner's jury expressly found that the medical attendants were in nowise to blame for Mrs. Wooler's death; the jury at the trial acquitted the prisoner of the charge. And now, at the eleventh hour, to make confusion worse confounded, the learned judge indicates that he has in his eye the actual criminal!

Who, then, was the object of this judicial vision? It must have been someone within the four walls of that sickroom. If we eliminate the doctors and Mr. Wooler—both officially pronounced blameless—there remain the servant, the two lady friends, the clergyman, Mrs. Wooler's sister, and Mr. Wooler's niece and brother. These are the only persons who ever visited the bedchamber, and that —excepting the servant—but occasionally. Upon which of these did his Lordship's suspicions rest? Even the reckless imputations of Serjeant Wilkins insinuate nothing against Ann Taylor. She was 27 years of age, she bore an irreproachable character, and she can hardly have possessed the knowledge and skill required for so nice an operation.

Did Miss Lanchester slay her friend for the £40 legacy? Did Octavius Borrowdale Wooler, the residuary legatee, feloniously accelerate his succession? Supposing they had the will to do so, they lacked the opportunity; for it must be borne in mind that this was a long-drawn-out murder, perpetrated by means of small doses of poison, given over a tract of time, constant and methodical in its execution.

Upon the matter of what, with due respect, may be termed the judicial red herring, Professor Christison, writing after the trial, remarks:—

I cannot agree with him in this. I believe I know the whole evidence brought forward, not merely on the trial, but likewise at the Coroner's inquest, and at the inquiry before the magistrates. I even know a good deal of the dark tales and guesses of the neighbourhood—a kind of information of which Baron Martin probably knew nothing. Nevertheless, if any specific individual may be understood to have been in the judge's eye, *I can only say I have no idea who is pointed at*.[1]

The *Times*, in an able leading article on the result of the trial, observes with regard to the persons in the case, other than Mr. Wooler: "It would be preposterous to presume that they had either the opportunity or the will to do her [Mrs. Wooler] injury."

Now, it was her husband who administered the remedies during these fifty days—even the injections. One day he was absent, and the strength of the symptoms abated. He was known to dabble in poisons. He had an Indian basket in the house, containing many phials, with various drugs and deadly poisons, among others a small portion of Fowler's Solution of Arsenic. It was stated that in one of the syringes which he had used traces of arsenic were found. He was accused of concealing from the knowledge of the medical men for three days a symptom indicative of arsenic, namely, tingling of the hands. Many other slighter circumstances of suspicion were urged against him, which we cannot from considerations of space set out here in detail, nor are they of much account, as they were satisfactorily explained away. The case, upon its leading features, weighed most heavily against him. There did not appear, however, that high degree of proof which the law requires.

---

[1] *Edinburgh Medical Journal*, 1856, vol. i. p. 711. My copy of the *Report of Investigation* belonged to Professor Christison, to whom it was presented by Dr. Jackson, who has annotated it with his own hand.

The presumption seemed that the verdict would be Not Guilty, in the
face of every man's belief.   On the other hand, we are bound to state
that there were many and violent presumptions in favour of the hypothesis of Mr. Wooler's innocence. . . . Thus, then, for the present, the
case must remain enveloped in yet deeper mystery from the very fact
of Mr. Wooler's clear acquittal.   The concluding words of the judge
must not, however, be forgotten.   *Suspicion rests upon another person,
whom we do not think ourselves justified in naming at this stage of the
proceedings* ; but these words were not spoken to idle ears.   This is,
upon the whole, one of the most remarkable cases in our criminal records,
both from the circumstances and manner of the murder, and from the
mystery which yet surrounds it.[1]

The local organ, in a leading article on the trial, con-
gratulates its readers on the termination of this painful case,
perhaps of all trials for murder the most complicated and
extraordinary; but regrets that the result of the proceedings "leaves the great sea of dark conjecture as stormy
and shoreless as ever."   With reference to Baron Martin's
chimerical criminal, that journal remarks:—

Are such words to drop like seed upon stony places ?   Is a person
expressly referred to by a high judicial authority as more apparently
obnoxious to judicial censure than the late accused—a person whom
the keen disciplined intellect of one of our ablest judges avowedly fixes
as the guilty being—the administrator of that cruel arsenic—is that
person to walk the smooth paths of social life covered with secrecy as
with a garment, and compassed with safety as with a girdle ?   We ask
this question with such feelings as few other questions could excite ;
and we are convinced that whoever reposes faith in Judge Martin's
surmises of fancy (as who will not ?), *and agrees with us that no finger of
accusal points to the surmised person from out the whole mass of evidence
on the trial,* will also agree with us that something has transpired beyond
the limits of the County Court on which the eye and the hand of justice
solemnly demand to be fixed.[2]

Yet despite the dictum of the learned judge, the
esoteric wisdom of the *Times*, and the moral certitude of the
Advertiser, the guilty party, habited and girdled as above,

---

[1] *Times*, 12th December 1855.
[2] *Durham County Advertiser*, 14th December 1855.

continued to walk unmolested the social paths, nor, so far
as I am aware, was any official notice ever taken of his
unconscionable ambulations.

. . . .

Well, I have put all the cards on the table, and the
reader—having paid his money—can take his choice.   If he
is interested to learn my private opinion, I confess that,
pace the learned judge and the model jury, I have my
suspicions as to the efficacy of Serjeant Wilkins' spells.   In
this I am no doubt biassed by reason of my old aquaintance
with Dr. Pritchard, between whose case and the present one
I cannot help fancying I perceive in certain features some
resemblance.   But that, of course, like "what the soldier
said," is not evidence.   It is far from my purpose to im-
pune the verdict; I merely set forth the mystery.

Note I.—Serjeant Wilkins

The late J. B. Atlay, in his admirable *Famous Trials of
the Century* (London: 1899), devotes a chapter, entitled
"A Miscarriage of Justice," to the case of the unfortunate
William Henry Barber, convicted in 1843 of forging wills
in order to obtain unclaimed stock in the public funds,
sentenced to transportation for life, and his innocence
fully established in 1848.   Barber's defence was conducted
by Wilkins, of whose capabilities Mr. Atlay gives the following account:—

This gentleman was one of the leaders of the Old Bailey Bar, who,
after a somewhat mysterious career, owed a large practice less to acquaintance with the law than to a wide and extensive knowledge of human
nature, great fluency of speech, and a dauntless audacity, which had a
tendency to degenerate into brow-beating.   He was thoroughly at home
in the ordinary run of criminal work, and had dragged many a prisoner
out of the dock in the teeth of facts and reason ; but in a complicated
case, which required close analysis, and the careful handling of a mass of
detail, together with dexterity and tact, he was apt to lose his head, to
miss the bearing of essential points, and to trust too much to the effect
upon the jury of his sonorous platitudes.

Note II.—Professor Christison on the Wooler Case

In an "Account of a late remarkable Trial for Poisoning with Arsenic," contributed by Dr. Christison to the *Edinburgh Medical Journal* as already mentioned, that high authority observes:—

There has seldom been a criminal trial in this country which has involved so many points of interest to the medical profession. . . . There is perhaps no trial on record in which the general or moral evidence is so contradictory. Not so with the medical evidence of death by arsenical poisoning. . . . Not one word of approbation was bestowed throughout this long trial on the most elaborate, difficult, and conclusive medical investigation and evidence hitherto produced upon any criminal trial in Britain. The proof of poisoning by arsenic was so perfect, in very nice and difficult circumstances, that even the prisoner's counsel evidently surrendered that point, without attempt at dispute, from the very beginning. . . . Death having been caused by repeated small doses of arsenic, what was the agency by which the poisoning was brought about ? Was this accident ? Was it design on the part of the lady herself ? Was it the work of another ? and of whom ?

Having demonstrated that, in the circumstances of this case, accident and suicide were equally "so very improbable that it is needless to spend time in splitting hairs on the question," the learned author proceeds: "There remains the third view: Was she murdered?" As to which he is not in doubt.

But is the direct evidence adequate to prove murder against a party, either known or unknown ? The question is impossible to review with the necessary freedom in the present contingency. The prisoner was found by the jury Not Guilty ; and I agree with their verdict. The judge held him proved to be innocent ; and that opinion I shall not gainsay. . . . It is plain that nothing can be made at present of the question of crime or a criminal ; and that nothing further will be made of it, unless Providence shall be pleased to lift by force of new facts the veil which now envelops it.

With regard to the judge's strictures on the conduct of the medical men, Dr. Christison deals at length with the duty of a doctor who suspects that his patient is being poisoned, and advises that "when the medical attendant is satisfied of the fact of the poisoning, he should communicate his conviction *to the patient himself*. Should he do so to the person suspected, the guilty agent abandons his purpose for the time; in the most favourable event his victim escapes destruction; and a monstrous criminal is let loose into society, and without punishment." Ten years after the Professor thus wrote, the question was raised in an acute form upon the famous trial of Dr. Pritchard. Dr. Paterson, who had been called in to Mrs. Pritchard's case by her anxious husband, formed the opinion that she was being poisoned by antimony. He maintained that to have acted upon that opinion would have been contrary to medical etiquette, in the particular circumstances of the case; a view which earned for him a most severe rebuke from the presiding judge, the Lord Justice-Clerk (John Inglis).

Professor Christison concludes with a dignified protest against Serjeant Wilkins' scandalous attack upon the three leading medical witnesses, which he holds to be "unparalleled on any similar occasion in a British Court of Law."

No matter how manifest a scoundrel he [counsel] may have for a client, or how estimable a member of society for a witness, he may, in his cross-examination and address to the jury, make the two exchange characters, to the best of his ability and the utmost of his liking. . . . The medical profession will look to the Bench for protection against superfluous, undeserved, unmeasured abuse. I feel certain they will not look in vain in Scotland. Certainly, on the trial of Mr. Wooler, the judge very feebly repelled the unwarrantable assault of the prisoner's counsel.

And he points out the very grave results to the administration of justice which must follow upon the adoption and countenance of such practices.

Note III.—THE CASE IN FICTION

Since the foregoing account was written I find that the Wooler case has recently formed the subject of a magazine article, entitled "In Some Manner Unknown," by C. J.

and Annie O. Tibbits (*The Premier Magazine*, February 1930). The facts of the case are well and truly stated, much being made of Mr. Wooler's predilection for Bible-reading and bees. Of these partialities, by the way, the former was shared by Dr. Pritchard; not so the latter: that erratic practitioner kept no bees—unless, indeed, as some have surmised, there was one in his bonnet. The writers suggest that Mrs. Wooler may have been the author of her own tragedy:—

Had Mrs. Wooler poisoned herself—by accident ? She had been in the habit of taking medicine of her own. Could she have taken some secret preparation of arsenic that had culminated suddenly, as arsenic will, and flooded both her own life and Joseph Wooler's, too, in a storm of horror and disaster ?

It is one of the questions that arise over this queer case, but it is only a possibility. All the evidence went to point to crime—to some mysterious person about that quiet house who had administered the poison in some manner unknown.

But as a matter of fact the manner of administration *is* known: it was proved to have been effected by means of a syringe—of which ungenteel weapon the writers, in their narrative of the circumstances, make no mention.

THE EDGE OF CIRCUMSTANCE:

A PROBLEM IN PARRICIDE

THE EDGE OF CIRCUMSTANCE:

A PROBLEM IN PARRICIDE.

The line between suspicion and fact might be thin as a hair, but it was deep as the grave.

—THE LORD JUSTICE-GENERAL.

THE crime of parricide is relatively rare in Scotland. Until the historic example of Philip Stanfield, convicted and hanged in 1688 for the slaughter of his sire, there are upon record but three other cases of this terrible offence. Strangely enough, however, our own times have furnished as many instances of the accusation. On 3rd February 1911 a young man of twenty-four, named John James Hutchison, an assistant chemist, deeply in debt through gambling on the stock exchange, put arsenic into the coffee served at his parents' silver-wedding party at Dalkeith, near Edinburgh, with the result that the guests became violently ill, and one of them, together with his father, died. He fled from justice; and on his arrest in the Channel Islands, whither he had sought safety, committed suicide. On 26th August 1924 William Laurie King, a student of chemistry, aged twenty-two, was indicted before the High Court of Justiciary at Edinburgh, charged with the murder of his mother and the attempted murder of his father—by a curious coincidence, also at the domestic supper table and by means of the same poison. He was, after trial, unanimously acquitted of both crimes. On 1st February 1927 John Donald Merrett, aged eighteen, was charged in the High Court at Edinburgh with the murder of his mother by shooting her with a pistol, and with uttering forged cheques upon her bank account. The first charge was, by a majority, found Not Proven; convicted unanimously on the second count, he received sentence of twelve months' imprisonment. On 12th December of the same year James M'Kay was tried before a Circuit Court at Glasgow for the murder of his mother, whom, having killed with a hatchet, he dismembered, and cast the residue into the Clyde. He was found guilty and executed.

The latest case in this connection, of which I now propose to give a sketch or outline—that of Robert Swift Willox, aged twenty, tried at the Glasgow Circuit in December 1929, for the crimes of uttering, robbery, and the murder of his father—presents in certain of its circumstances an interesting parallel, on a lower social plane, with the case of Merrett above mentioned. In each there is the near relationship between the parties: parent and child; the fiscal irregularities of the son; the imminence of discovery; and, finally, the opportune removal by violence of the parent defrauded. Of course, in the Merrett case there were other alternatives before the jury: accident or suicide; in this case these were wholly excluded, and the issue was a single one; for in view of the nature of the injuries inflicted, the fact that murder had been done admitted of no dispute.

But the present case has its peculiar puzzles and perplexities. Such are, *inter alia*, the unusual domestic conditions, at once unnecessary and discomfortable, under which the pair elected to live; the acquiescence by the son in a state of affairs so unnatural to his age and sex, and fraught with such prejudice to his future prospects; and the attitude of aloofness and reserve maintained by the father in relation to his neighbours. As regards the commission of the crime there are many mysteries. The practical immunity from bloodstains of the accused's clothing in a murder unquestionably bloody, no less than the coolness exhibited by him that evening, particularly in playing a good game of billiards shortly after he had smashed his father to death with a hammer; the failure of the people in the adjacent rooms to hear any sound of so furious an assault—though, as appears, voices were plainly audible in the respective houses; the economy of time exercised by the boy-murderer in the actual attack, and the subsequent cleansing of his person, raiment, and weapon from the damning traces of the deed—all done, according to the evidence, in a matter of minutes; the scientific controversy as to what the learned Judge at the trial termed the vital question whether or not that night the dead man had his supper; and with further reference to the *time* of the murder, the presence and duration of *rigor mortis* and the clotting of the blood.

The result of the trial, too, is unsatisfactory and inconclusive. The narrow majority upon which the verdict turned: nine to six—the same proportion, by the way, that determined the doom of Oscar Slater—coupled with a recommendation to mercy, singular in a crime of such atrocity; the dismissal, with manifest difficulty and anxiety, of the appellant's case by the Court of Criminal Appeal; and the commutation, in record time, of the death sentence to penal servitude for life, are among the features which make this case remarkable, and worthy the consideration as well of the expert in criminology as of the student of human nature.

The evidence adduced by the Crown, upon which a verdict was secured, was what is commonly called purely circumstantial, and the guilt of the accused is only to be inferred from a series of separate facts and circumstances, which, being assembled and weighed, are held sufficient to warrant his conviction. "Circumstances cannot lie," Lord Deas told the jury on the celebrated trial of Jessie M'Lachlan in 1862; yet they may upon occasion be found susceptible of terminological inexactitude. And while I am by no means to be taken as holding the verdict of the jury one which is, in the statutory sense, unreasonable or incapable of support, having regard to the evidence, I confess, had I been a member of that assize, seeing the edge of circumstance is here so exceeding fine, my vote would have been "Not Proven."

My friend and fellow-worker, Mr. Edmund Lester Pearson, "if this should meet the eye of," will perceive in the present case divers points of resemblance—I had almost said, a family likeness—to his own most excellent study of parricide: "The Borden Case," America's best and brightest murder.[1] Not that I would claim for my Glasgow lad equality with his incomparable spinster of Fall River; the fact that she disposed of *both* her parents and, in the popular phrase, "got away with it" after all, secures for her the palm. So far as nerve, audacity, and luck are concerned, the Lady with the Axe is admittedly in a class by herself. Should this passing tribute to her charms move the reader to cultivate her acquaintance, I shall have done, Boy Scout-wise, my one good deed for the day.

PART I.—QUESTIONS AT ISSUE.

Murder most foul, as at the best it is ;
But this most foul, strange, and unnatural.
                                        —*Hamlet*, Act I. Sc. v.

I.

At 9.20 on the evening of Monday, 4th November 1929, the occupants of the third flat of No. 79 Grove Street, in the Cowcaddens district of Glasgow—a stark range of tenements, consisting of small shops and flatted houses inhabited by working-class tenants—were alarmed by loud cries from the landing and a violent banging upon their several doors. Going out to see what was wrong, the three neighbours found young Bertie Willox, who lived alone with his father in the fourth house of the flat. He appeared to be in great distress, and kept on crying out: "Look! look! look!" as he pointed to the open door of his home. The

---

[1] *Studies In Murder*, by E. L. Pearson, pp. 3–120. New York : The Macmillan Company. 1924.

gas was lighted in the house, and from the landing the
neighbours could see the figure of the father, Robert Willox,
prone upon the threshold of the kitchen, his feet in the
lobby and his body in the kitchen, the arms extended, the
legs slightly drawn up, and the head lying in a great pool
of blood. The ghastly spectacle told its own tale; no one
ventured to enter the kitchen, and the boy was advised to
run for the police. At 9.30, in a very excited and exhausted state, he reached the 'Northern Police Office and
called to the officer on duty: "Send an ambulance, send
an ambulance; my father is bleeding!" Asked what was
the matter with his father, he made the strange reply:
"My mother died some time ago," and fainted. On
recovering, he explained that the injuries were to the head;
"he [the father] could not have done it himself." Two
constables accompanied the boy back to the house. By
the way, "he appeared to swoon a wee bit." He informed
the officers that his father must have fainted and fallen
against the iron bed-couch, cutting his head, "because the
blood was coming from the head." *He further volunteered
that he and his father had their supper ; and that he washed
the dishes and set the table for breakfast.*

They came to the house. The dead man, dressed in
the uniform of the Commissionaires' Corps, of which he was
a member, lay bleeding on the floor, upon his left side,
his head horribly injured. The table appeared to the
officers to be set for a meal which had not been consumed:
cups, plates, knives, etc. were clean; a piece of boiled beef
was on the table, and upon the gas range was a pot
practically full of soup. Inspector Cooke, arriving on the
scene, asked the boy when he had last seen his father alive.
He said: about 6.30, when he left him alone in the house.
"I then tried to comfort him, as he was still excited," says
the officer; "and I laid my hand on his shoulder and said:
'Now, son, try and control yourself. Were you and your
father on good terms, or has there been any trouble?' and
in answer he said: 'Yes; he is a good father'; then he

swooned and slipped from the chair on to the floor before I could prevent him." When restored, he was taken into Mrs. Mackenzie's house next door. There Detective-Inspector Stewart, who came at 10.30 to take charge of the case, had an interview with him and got from him a statement regarding his father's circumstances and habits, his own brief history, and in particular, how he spent his time that evening between 6 o'clock, when his father came home from work, and his discovery of the crime on his own return at 9.20. As the police were in possession of the house, it was arranged that the boy should go to an old friend, Mrs. Smith, No. 5 Canal Street; a constable took him to that address and explained the situation to the lady, with whom he stayed the night.

Next day, Tuesday, 5th November, Bertie Willox called twice by appointment at the police office. Inspector Stewart, who had meanwhile made inquiries as to the truth of the boy's story, on the second occasion informed him that "he [Stewart] had found certain errors in his previous statement." He said he was sorry if he had made any mistake; but if so, was quite prepared to correct it. The inspector, having in mind what he had learned that afternoon, cautioned the boy that anything he might now say could be used in evidence against him; but despite this warning, he elected to make a further statement, which was taken down by Stewart at the time on a typewriter, and of which the substance is as follows:—His mother died on 23rd January 1929. "A week after mother's death it was arranged between father and I that I would leave off work altogether and that I would keep house for him." On 4th November his father left for his work as usual at 4.45 a.m. He came home that day at 6 p.m. "I had his tea ready for him when he came home, or rather his dinner, of *soup, rice pudding, and a drink of milk. He had no tea.* He never takes tea in the evening, not even on Sunday. When father came in that night he took off his coat and cap and hung them on the peg in the lobby. . . . Immediately

after dinner father said to me: 'How much do I owe
Daly?' I replied: 'I think over £2.' Father replied:
'Well, you'll better pay him and Mrs. Duffy to-night and
get them off the map.'" Thereafter the son washed the
dishes and prepared to go out. His father gave him
£3, 3s. 6d. for Mrs. Duffy and £3 for Daly: six single one
pound notes, half a crown, and a shilling. When he left
the house between 6.30 and 6.45, his father had sat down
and was cleaning the buttons on his tunic. At the corner
of Scotia Street and Grove Street he met his "pal," James
Turner, with whom he went to Sinclair's billiard rooms at
St. George's Cross, where they played for half an hour.
After the game they went together to No. 91 Hopehill Road
and paid Daly; thence to No. 532 St. George's Road and
paid Mrs. Duffy; and finally to No. 490 St. George's Road,[1]
where they parted company, Turner going home and
Willox going up to visit his friend Alfonso Jacovelli, with
whom he spent the evening, and who, when he left later,
accompanied him part of the way home. Before going up
to his own house he looked into Meehan's shop, on the
opposite side of the street, and spoke to the girl there; she
smiled, but made no reply. He then opened his house
door, discovered the murder, and alarmed the neighbours.
He knew nothing of what money his father had; "when
he was giving me money he always did it in a secret
manner," *i.e.*, turning his back and taking it from his
pocket. It was his father's practice, on entering the house,
to leave his keys dangling from his pocket-chain until he
had hung up his coat and cap in the lobby, *when he always
put them into his pocket.* "I do not possess any money
myself. I have at present 2s. 11d., which is the remainder
of the £3 which I got to pay Mr. Daly. I got 5s. 1d. change
from Mr. Daly, and I have spent 2s. 2d. to-day for food and
cigarettes." *He did not know who set the table as it was*

---

[1] It is interesting to note that Oscar Slater lived at No. 69 at the time of Miss
Gilchrist's murder.

*when he returned ; probably his father, whose nightly custom
was to lay it for breakfast next morning.*

Now, apart from other discrepancies, the police had
ascertained that Daly had been paid, not in coin and the
exact amount, but with a £5 note, and had given in change
£2, 5s. 1d.: a penny, 5s. and £2 in notes. Asked to shew
what money he had on him, the boy produced 2s. 11d.
The inspector noticed, sticking out of his vest pocket, a
small leather wallet, and by inspiration—for he had not
till then suspected the boy—took it out and examined it.[1]
The contents were £4 in notes—three Treasury and one
National Bank of Scotland—and four pawn tickets. As
the inspector afterwards explained: "This was a case
where I was searching for a possible criminal; and it
suddenly dawned on me that *this* might be the criminal.
I did not want to lock him up unless I got some proper
evidence, and that evidence I was to find upon him."
The boy then stated that he got *all* the four notes from
the *Weekly News* people in respect of permitting them to
interview him, giving them his father's photograph, and
allowing himself to be photographed for that journal. He
denied that he had paid Daly with a £5 note, whereupon
he was detained on suspicion. Mr. Daly, summoned to
the office and confronted with the boy, repeated his statement as to that payment. "I did not," retorted Willox;
"I never gave you a £5 note." Charged subsequently at
the bar of the police office with having assaulted and killed
his father and stolen £8 from the house, the accused
replied: "I have nothing to say meantime," and was
duly committed to prison.

II.

Robert Swift Willox, at the time of his trial a fair, pale-
faced lad of slim build, looking much younger than his age,
well educated, and exceptionally intelligent for his years

---

[1] There is no proof as to whom this wallet belonged ; it is assumed that it was
the father's property.

ROBERT SWIFT WILLOX.

(*From the photograph taken for the " Weekly News" the day after the murder.*)

[*To face p.* 272.

and station, was born on 15th May 1909 at No. 122 Cambridge Street, Glasgow, where his parents lived before they removed to Grove Street. His scholastic career was singularly varied, for he attended no fewer than four schools, two Catholic and two Protestant, before leaving to begin the world at the age of fourteen. For his religion, in spite of these divergencies, he appears to have remained officially of the Roman faith. When he left school he started as a message boy; became an apprentice engineer with Messrs. A. & J. Inglis, the firm of shipbuilders for whom his father worked; and his last job was with Messrs. Simpson, Lawrence & Co., yacht outfitters, Glasgow, where he was earning 16s. a week. Upon the death of his mother, as already mentioned, his father kept him at home to run the house, his remuneration being from 2s. 6d. to 4s. 6d. a week at the father's pleasure. One should have expected that a boy thus situated would naturally and inevitably go wrong; but his character, hitherto good, continued such; and his reputation was that of an amiable, quiet lad, who had no bad companions, was given neither to drink, gambling, nor going about with girls, and surprisingly in these times, he did not dance. The leisure permitted by his household or domestic duties was employed by him in walking about the streets with his "pals," playing billiards, and frequenting "the pictures."

Of the father, Robert Willox, a mysterious figure, less is known. Fifty-five years old at the time of his death, he is said to have been a native of Aberdeen and to have been employed as a young man on the staff of a local newspaper. He is further reported to have disappeared suddenly from that city, leaving behind him for his creditors nothing but a painful memory; and thenceforth his relations heard no more of him, until they read in the newspapers the tragic tidings of his fate. He joined the army in 1898 at the age of twenty-four, and served throughout the South African War in the Royal Scots Fusiliers. He was mentioned in dispatches, and won the Queen's and King's medals. In

18

1906, being transferred to the reserve, he joined the Corps of Commissionaires in Glasgow. In 1908 he married Margaret Swift, then engaged as a stenographer in that corps. Called up during the Great War, he was wounded at Mons in 1914.[1] After demobilisation, be became a gatekeeper with Messrs. A. & J. Inglis, shipbuilders, Pointhouse, Partick. His wages were 50s. 3d. per week and he was in receipt of a War pension of 2s. 6d. He seems to have had no friends; so unsociable was his disposition that even the occupants of the other houses on the same flat only knew him "to pass the time of day"; and his neighbour William Watt, who worked for the same firm, had no further acquaintance with him, though they had lived next door to each other for ten years.

Such were the protagonists in this strange drama, of whom one dreadfully died and the other hardly escaped hanging for his murder.

III.

Far into the night doctors and detectives were busy about the flat. Never was the *locus* of a crime more diligently investigated than were that little lobby and kitchen by the electric torches of the searchers. Dr. Campbell, the casualty surgeon, was upon the scene by 10.20, and Professor Glaister, who occupies the chair of Forensic Medicine in Glasgow University, arrived at midnight. Both gentlemen carefully examined the body; we shall hear the result of their observations later.

The Yale lock of the outer door was intact. The furniture of the kitchen—three chairs, table, bed, and bedcouch—was undisturbed, except that one of the chairs was overturned in front of the body, and that the table cloth at the corner nearest to the head was slightly pulled down, but not so as to disarrange the dishes. If the boiled beef and broth suggested dinner, the sugar bowl, cups, and

---

[1] For these particulars regarding the father's history I am indebted to the research of the *Weekly News*, 9th November and 28th December 1929.

marmalade were indicative of tea. *There was no sign of any rice pudding.* In his first statement to Inspector Stewart the boy had said: "I gave him his tea"; and being asked of what that meal consisted, he replied: "*He had soup and then tea.*" All the table utensils were perfectly clean, the beef was apparently uncut, and the broth pot full to within 1¼ inches of the top. From the fact that vegetables were visible upon the beef it was manifest that it had been boiled with the broth; but it does not seem to have occurred to anyone to put the beef back into the pot, to see whether its presence would bring the broth up to the level. The remaining room of the house was unfurnished.

The inspector had asked the boy that night whether there was in the house any "likely" weapon; and he said "there was a heavy coal hammer, used for breaking coals, and that there were initials on the hammer."[1] In the course of his search that officer found in a cupboard of the kitchen the implement in question: a two-pound engineer's hammer, 11½ inches long, with a double head measuring 4¾ inches, the diameter of the larger striking surface being 1½ inches, and that of the smaller, one inch. It was comparatively clean, quite dry, and wholly free from coal dust. On the cross bars below the table were a pair of shoes, very wet, belonging to the boy, who at that time was wearing boots. In the pocket of the dead man's overcoat, hanging in the lobby, were found two of that day's newspapers, unopened, together with his spectacles. A search of the clothing on the body produced from the tunic pocket some Army papers; and from other pockets 2½d., a pencil, knife, and scissors. A bunch of keys, attached to the deceased's trouser button by a chain, lay on the floor behind the body.

The linings of *both* trouser pockets were bloodstained, "showing," in the opinion of Professor Glaister, "that a

---

[1] These initials are described by the witness as "A & I I"; but, having seen the hammer, I suggest that they are "A & J I": plainly A. & J. Inglis, the firm with whom both father and son were employed.

hand with blood on it had been thrust into each of them."
There were marks of blood—spots and splashes—upon the
lobby walls, the uprights of the kitchen doorway, the outside of that door itself—which was fully opened back to
the kitchen wall and against which the body lay; and on
the skirting and walls of the kitchen, on both sides backwards from the body; while towards the table and the fire-
place in front the blood had flowed out upon the floor,
forming a large pool. It was plain that very extensive
spattering had followed the assault, and that the assailant
must necessarily have been to some extent exposed to this
sanguineous shower. We shall learn more particularly as
to the disposition of these bloodstains when we come to
the trial.

But there were two specific stains as to the presence of
which the evidence affords no light. On the upper panel
of the *inside* of the kitchen door—which was flat against
the wall, the body lying on the outer side—was an irregular
mark of blood 6 inches long, "containing clotting of a
smear-like character," as if a wet, bloody surface had
brushed against it. There is no explanation of how this
mark was caused. It was noted by Professor Glaister
when the door was taken to his laboratory, as aftermentioned; but Inspector Stewart said he did not see the
mark when he looked at the door after the event. Then,
again, on the top or wooden surface of the table was "an area
of red staining, measuring $1\frac{1}{4}$ inches by a quarter," which
on examination was found to contain mammalian blood.
*There was no corresponding stain upon the white table cloth
which had covered it*, the only marks thereon being a few
spots at the corner that had been pulled down near the
floor, within a short distance of the body. Mr. Sherlock
Holmes, had he been consulted in the matter, might have
inferred from this fact that the table was bare at the
moment of the murder, and that the cloth was laid subsequently, with a view to "staging" a meal.

The inspector, in the course of his observations, found

that the fire was out, though the grate was yet warm. The sink presented to his skilled eye nothing suspicious. A damp towel, hanging hard by upon a nail, and a dishcloth folded up but very wet, on the side of the sink, seemed to him equally innocuous.[1] If the hammer produced were in fact the weapon used in the crime, it must surely have been washed and dried at that sink; and it is strange that the authorities did not extend their researches to the waste-pipe, which, on that assumption, might have been expected to yield traces of blood. An interesting "find" was a loose leaf from a scribbling tablet on the dresser, containing a memorandum of the boy-housekeeper's orders for that day: "Monday.—Bone, vegetables, $\frac{1}{4}$ stone potatoes, $1\frac{1}{2}$ pints milk, $\frac{1}{2}$ dozen eggs, 1 lb. of b. b." "b. b." is interpreted by the best commentators to signify boiling beef. The inspector also discovered in the kitchen—and by the way, *there were no lockfast places in the house*—passbooks between the deceased and (1) the Household Supplies Company and (2) Messrs. Gunn, grocers; and two collecting books between Willox senior and junior and the Hearts of Oak Assurance Company, together with relative policies of insurance upon the lives of father and son.

The boy had but two suits: one brown; the other black, with a white stripe. When seen by the police and others on the night of the crime, he was wearing the black jacket and vest, with the brown trousers. The brown jacket and vest were afterwards said to have been found hanging behind the door of the unfurnished room—according to the police evidence; but I am informed that the boy always maintained that they were hung by him *behind the kitchen door*. Whether, if so, the fact bears any relation to the mysterious smear, I cannot tell. He was also wearing a rainproof coat and a cap, neither of which is of importance. Upon his arrest next day all his clothing was confiscated,

---

[1] These articles were not included among the forty-four productions from the house sent to Professor Glaister for examination, and so were never tested for blood.

and later the police took away in a lorry from the house everything removable, even unto the kitchen door; and sent to Professor Glaister a selection of their spoils.

IV.

On Monday, 16th December 1929, at a sitting of the High Court of Justiciary held in the North Court, Glasgow, began the five days' trial of Bertie Willox for the murder of his father. Public interest in the case was shewn by the fact that the accommodation available was at every hearing taxed to its utmost limits, while outside the courthouse long queues waited patiently throughout the dark winter hours in the hope of gaining admission. The presiding judge was the Honourable Lord Hunter; Mr. D. P. Blades, Advocate-Depute, assisted by Mr. A. M. M. Williamson, advocate, appeared for the Crown; Mr. A. C. Black, K.C., with Mr. W. Ross M'Lean, advocate, represented the accused.[1]

At the first or "pleading" diet on 6th December, when the accused in due course of law was brought before the Sheriff, a special defence of insanity had been intimated; but his examination by alienists having negatived the possibility of maintaining that plea, it was not persisted in at the trial, and he formally pleaded Not Guilty to the charges. These were four in number. The first related to certain false entries and forged receipts by him of weekly payments in two passbooks between the deceased and the Household Supplies Company on divers specified dates, and his exhibition thereof to his father as evidence that he had made such payments. The second, to similar fraudulent entries in a passbook with D. A. Gunn, Limited, bearing a forged receipt: "Paid with thanks. 2/9/29. J.M."

---

[1] It says much for the fairness, nay, generosity of Scots justice that in this, what is technically termed " poor " case, the penniless prisoner was defended by eminent and able counsel, who gave ungrudgingly of their time and talents, working as hard in his behalf as though, like for example John Donald Merrett, he had all the resources that money could provide for his defence.

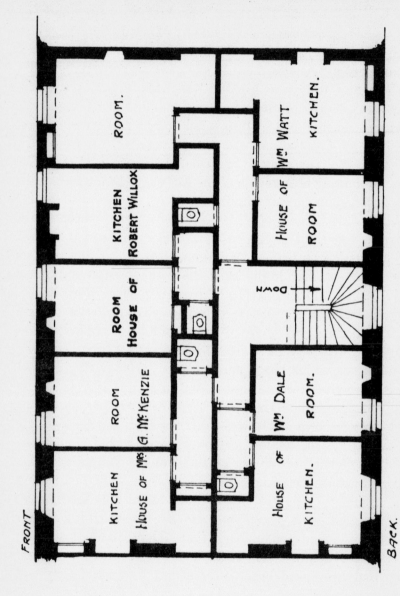

PLAN OF THE THIRD FLAT OF No. 79 GROVE STREET, GLASGOW.

(*From the original produced in Court.*)

[*To face p.* 279.

The third had reference to two entries in a premium receipt book, issued by the Hearts of Oak Assurance Company, of pretended payments, certified by forged initials. The fourth, that on 4th November 1929, in said house at 79 Grove Street, he did assault the said Robert Willox, his father, and did beat him on the head and face with a hammer or other blunt instrument, rob him of £8 of money, and did murder him. Appended to the indictment were lists of 56 productions and 54 witnesses. An objection taken to the relevancy as regarded the form of some of the charges having been repelled, the Advocate-Depute adduced his proof upon the fourth charge.[1]

The first witness was Mrs. Florence Watt, whose house door was at right angles to that of the deceased. As will be seen from the plan of the premises, there was a partition wall between her lobby and the kitchen of Willox, her lavatory extending into the lobby and kitchen of his house. She had known the deceased for ten years; he was a very reserved man and spoke to none of his neighbours. On Monday, 4th November 1929, being at her own door, she saw him enter his house about 6 p.m. Her husband came home shortly after. About 6.40, "or a little after half-past six," a man named Harrington called to see her husband.[2] After letting him in, she went into the lavatory for a couple of minutes, and while there overheard in their house the "angry voices" of Willox and his son.[3] She thought the father was "chastising" the boy, by which she explained she meant "going for him." She heard the father say: "*You won't get a penny from me!*" On returning to her kitchen she told her husband that "they [the Willox pair] were cross again." He remarked: "Never heed them." She had overheard other altercations between father and

---

[1] For the following account of the evidence my authority is the official short-hand-writer's notes, taken at the trial.

[2] William Harrington, a witness for the defence, said he arrived at Watt's house about 6.37.

[3] Although there is some confusion in her evidence, on this point it is quite clear : " *That* [the lavatory] *is where I heard the voices.*"

son on the preceding Friday and Saturday. She next described the alarm raised by the boy at 9.20, as before narrated. William Watt, her husband, corroborated. Harrington was in his house only three minutes, and left about 6.45. He, too, deponed to the "wailing howl" of young Willox on the landing, the discovery of the body, and the sending of the boy for the police. William Dale, another neighbour, gave similar evidence.

The movements of Bertie Willox that evening after he left the house are minutely set forth in the testimony of the several witnesses. His "pal" James Turner, aged nineteen, who had known him since their school days, said he met the accused casually on the night in question at half-past six. They had no appointment. Willox was then coming out of Haddow's shop with a packet of cigarettes.[1] He suggested they should go and have a game of billiards in Sinclair's rooms at St. George's Cross. They went first into Meehan's shop to try to get a pass for the Empress Picture House, but failed to do so. Eugene Meehan, who lived in the flat below the accused and carried on business on the other side of the street, said that he saw Willox and Turner in his shop about 6.30. He left the shop shortly after they did, overtook them, and asked if they were going to the Empress. Turner said, "No; *they had no money.*" Margaret Maguire, his assistant in the shop, put the time at 6.35. She explained that in respect of shewing a theatre bill, they (Meehan's) sometimes had free tickets. Felix Carey, who knew both lads, saw them outside a barber's shop in Grove Street at 6.40. He "passed a joke to Bertie about the girl in the shop [Maguire]." A few minutes earlier he had seen Turner in Meehan's, and Turner said: "*Can you change me a pound, Felix?*" Witness replied that he could not do so; he saw the money: a green £1 note.[2]

---

[1] Isabella M'Kinney, assistant in Haddow's shop, said Willox was there at 6.25. All the shops referred to are in Grove Street, close to the house of the accused.

[2] Turner in his evidence denied that this incident occurred : 1s. 2d., he said, was all the money he had that night. He also, for some unaccountable reason, denied that he accompanied the accused to Mrs. Duffy's.

Angus Duff, manager of the billiard rooms, said that Bertie Willox played there nearly every night. He and Turner were playing that night from 6.35 to 7.5. He produced the play sheet for Monday, 4th November, on which those hours were marked at the time. Bertie paid for the game: 9d., tendering a 2s. piece and receiving 1s. 3d. change. Mrs. Margaret Duffy, who lived in St. George's Road where she followed the occupation of agent for a firm of credit drapers, said she was a friend of the late Mrs. Willox and had known Bertie from boyhood. In January he borrowed, "for Dada," a pound from her "to get the doctor for his mother"; a fortnight later he called, not to repay the pound, but with a memorial card for his mother, who had died. In March or April he brought from "Dada" 6s. towards the reduction of the debt; and in September called to inquire whether she had safely received "the 15s. which was sent to her from Rothesay." This remittance had failed to reach Mrs. Duffy. He then proposed to borrow a further £2, 10s. "to lift his father's medals," which were in pledge.[1] She lent him that sum, and saw no more of him until about 7 o'clock on Monday, 4th November, when he called to repay the debt in full. "He gave me £3, and a half-crown, and 1s."; and she gave him 6d. "to himself." Witness now identified the three £1 notes in question, which had been commandeered later by the police. It was raining hard that night, and the boy was very wet. Denis Daly, salesman with the Household Supplies Company, said that when in January Mrs Willox died she was £4 in their debt. Up to June certain payments to account were made by the accused, but after that date nothing was received till 4th November. About 7.15 that night he called at witness's house and squared the account: £2, 14s. 11d. He tendered a £5 note—which witness identified (it had a name and address written on the back) —and received in change £2 in notes, 5s., and a penny.

---

[1] It is more than likely that " Dada " knew nothing of these transactions.

First of all, he took £2 out of his pocket and laid that in his cap, then he took some silver; and when I told him it was £2, 14s. 11d., he said, "Can you change me a fiver?" and I said, "Certainly." He put the other money back in his pocket, took the £5 out of his pocket, and handed it to me.

Next day witness heard of the murder; and having taken counsel with his employers, communicated with the police, to whom he delivered the note.

It is to be noticed that all these witnesses, knowing the boy well and seeing him thus within half an hour of the crime, saw nothing unusual in his appearance or manner.

Alfonso Jacovelli, aged twenty-one, married, and living in rooms in St. George's Road—Bertie Willox had been his best man—said he had known the accused intimately for eight years and was often at his house. Bertie had been unemployed since his mother's death and was always complaining about being short of money. Witness gave him sundry small loans. He was in the habit of pledging clothing and other articles from the house. Between 1 and 2 o'clock on 4th November witness went up to see him in his house, and invited him to come and spend the evening; he said he would come at 7.30. Witness noticed that the table was set for a meal: there were two plates "*with a small piece of pudding on them*"; some cold meat "on the bunker," and a pot on the gas cooker.[1] Bertie remarked that he was hard up. That evening, as arranged, he arrived at witness's house at 7.30. He said he would not stay long, as he was tired and wanted to get to bed. "He was quite cheery; some moments he was quiet": witness had seen him so before. They amused themselves with a gramophone; and Jacovelli, noticing a small leather case sticking out of his guest's waistcoat pocket, "made a grab for it" in fun, but was "prevented" by Bertie.[2] He

---

[1] Why should the table be thus spread and furnished between 1 and 2 o'clock for a meal to be consumed at 6?

[2] Inspector Stewart was more successful in his raid upon this wallet, which, as the reader may recollect, contained the four £1 notes.

accompanied his friend on his way home to the corner of
Grove and Scotia Streets at 9.30. Bertie was then wearing
his brown trousers, with his black jacket and vest. In the
afternoon he had on his brown suit. So far as witness knew,
he and his father were on good terms with each other.

It will be remembered that young Willox, in his statement to the police, said that before going up to the house
he looked in at Meehan's and spoke to the girl Maguire;
but that young lady in her evidence denied that he did so.
This is all we hear of the boy's doings on the fatal night.

V.

Into the details of what may be termed the food forgeries
—those in the household accounts—it is unnecessary to
enter, seeing that the accused was unanimously found
guilty of their fabrication. He had, as appears, pilfered
the housekeeping money and made false entries in the passbooks to conceal the fact from his father; but from time
to time he did make small efforts to reduce the deficit. It
is remarkable that on the last weekly call of Messrs. Gunn's
representative on 28th October, the accused asked him *not
to call on the following Monday, 4th November*, as he would
himself come and make the payment on the 6th. His
dealings with the life insurance premiums are of more
importance. The three members of the family were in-
sured with the Hearts of Oak Assurance Company, and in
respect of his wife's death Robert Willox received £49, 1s.
As he had no bank account, his master cashed the cheque
for him. Henry Cox, agent for the company, said he
personally collected the monthly premiums; he usually
saw young Willox. The last payment was on 7th
September. He got no payment on 7th October: accused
said his father had spent too much upon the Autumn
Holiday, and the two payments would be made together
on *4th November*. Cox called for them on Saturday, the
2nd, when accused said his father had not left the money,

as he thought it was not due till the 11th. It was arranged that Cox should call again on Monday. He did so, at 1 o'clock. Accused said his father was "just away" to his work—he had left at 4.45 a.m.—and that he wanted to see witness regarding an "endowment." Cox said he would come back that night; but accused said his father was then "going to the doctor's." As we know, it was the doctors who came to him! Finally, they agreed that Cox should return on Tuesday night; but by that time he had learned that the father's policy had become payable. Shewn the premium receipt book found in the house, containing entries of two payments on 7th October and 4th November, initialed "H.C.," witness said those entries were not made by him and his initials were forged. Michael Martin, district manager of the company, stated that the two payments referred to were never made, and the entries regarding them were false. The premiums were 6s. 4d. a month: 5s. for the father and 1s. 4d. for the son. £48, 15s. was the sum payable on the death of Robert Willox. The policy was still in force if the premiums were not more than two months in arrear. A statutory notice, giving 28 days to pay, was required before the policy became void, which in this case had not been given.

When Bertie Willox was arrested the night after the murder, there was found upon him, in addition to divers pawntickets, a message in his handwriting, apparently intended for a relative in America:—

Mrs. Wm. E. Dreyer, 63 South Seventh Street, Newark, N.J.

79 Grove Street, Glasgow, 5/11/29. Father met with an accident last night and died. Will send details later.

ROBERT WILLOX, JUNR.

This, in any view of the case, was a strangely euphemistic version of the occurrence. He also wrote after his arrest a letter to his friend and neighbour, Mrs. Mackenzie. These two documents having been submitted to James Brown, expert in handwriting, for comparison with the forged entries in the passbooks and premium receipt book, that authority reported, and in the witness-box confirmed his opinion, that the whole were in the handwriting of the accused. With regard to the pawntickets, Alexander M'Leod, pawnbroker, stated that the accused had since September pledged his mother's rings, his father's War medals, trousers, shirts, sheets, etc., all of which were still unredeemed. On 4th November accused called between 1 and 2 o'clock and wanted to pledge a pair of shoes. Witness said they were worn out, and declined them. They were emblematic of the boy's fiscal resources that afternoon. These are the shoes found later, wet, beneath the table in the kitchen. With reference to his pawning proclivities, his friend Turner stated in the witness-box: "He [Bertie] did not want his father to find out"; so that the money was raised for his own purposes.

Miss M'Kinney stated that the morning after the murder young Willox came into Haddow's shop at 7 o'clock, "very flurried and upset looking." Aware of the tragedy, she put to the boy the pertinent question: "Are you sure, Bertie, you didn't do it?" "Oh, no," he replied; "my father has been good to me." He added that she would "see it all" in the papers, that he had been through a terrible ordeal, and that "he had made one slip." It would be instructive to learn the nature of this indiscretion. "He said something about vengeance—'I will have my revenge on whoever did it !'." J. R. M. Christie, reporter on the staff of the Weekly News, stated that at 11 o'clock that forenoon he saw the accused and arranged to interview him later in the day regarding the crime. He got from him his father's photograph, and permission to take a photograph of himself.[1] For these favours he paid the accused £3 in notes: two Bank of England and one Treasury, which witness identified as three of the four found later in the wallet by Inspector Stewart. Thomas Duff, hairdresser, stated that the same day the accused—

---

[1] This photograph is reproduced herewith.

probably in view of his appointment with the *Weekly News* photographer—came to have his hair cut, a shampoo, and a shave. He remarked that his father had been murdered the night before and that he had last seen him alive at 6.30. Being then in funds, he gave witness a tip of 6d.—the only occasion on which, though a regular customer, he had ever been so generous.

VI.

The two chief difficulties presented by the evidence relate to the question of time and to the comparative freedom of the accused from bloodstains. Upon the first point, Hector Kennedy stated that in connection with the municipal election on 5th November, his father being a candidate for the Ward, he had occasion to canvass in Grove Street. At 8.30 on the evening of the 4th he called at Robert Willox's house, but could get no answer. He entered on his card: "Not in." So it may be presumed that the man was then dead or incapable of reply.

When at 10 p.m. Inspector Cook examined the body, he found "the hand was cold to the touch." Dr Campbell, the casualty surgeon, came at 10.20. "I detected," he says, "no *rigor mortis*" (post-mortem rigidity). He would expect to find it within 4 to 6 hours of death, according to the circumstances. Professor Glaister, arriving at midnight, found the limbs "quite flexible"; he would expect *rigor mortis* to set in from 5 to 6 hours after death. For the defence, Professor Sydney Smith, who occupies the Chair of Forensic Medicine in Edinburgh University, but who did not have the advantage of seeing either the body or the *locus*, held that upon these data death had probably occurred within 4 hours of Professor Glaister's examination, namely about 8 o'clock; and Dr. Garry, medical officer in Duke Street Prison, having examined the bodies of many persons who had met with sudden and violent deaths, stated that he invariably found *rigor mortis* present within 2 hours thereafter.

Then, again, Dr. Campbell said that, as regards the condition of the blood, he expected to find the clotting process further advanced than it was. On his conclusion that the man had been dead not less than three hours, if there were not some peculiarity in the blood, that process was more delayed than he should have anticipated. Professor Sydney Smith stated that the clotting process would begin in about 10 minutes; and as the blood continued to ooze from the wounds, that would tend to delay coagulation.[1]

At the post-mortem examination of the body, conducted by Professor Glaister and Dr. Anderson, "*the stomach was found to be entirely empty, no vestige of food being found therein.*" From that fact the Professor inferred that the man had his last meal about 5 hours before his death, "and a very light meal at that." If such a meal were taken, the stomach would be empty in from 5 to 6 hours; if a heavy meal, from 6 to 8 hours. On the other hand, Professor Sydney Smith stated that an ordinary full meal would disappear from a healthy stomach in about 4 hours; a light liquid meal, say of milk and soup, might pass out in 20 minutes. In this clash of skilled opinion, it must have puzzled the jury to know how long they would retain the benefit of their lunch!

If Bertie Willox slew his father, he must have done so between 6 and 6.30; for by 6.35 he indisputably began his game of billiards in Sinclair's rooms, and was not lost sight of throughout the evening. Yet Mrs. Watt, who as to the hour is supported by her husband and by Harrington, heard the "angry voices" of father and son about 6.40, "or a little after half-past six"; while the girl in Haddow's shop says the accused was there at 6.25, and Turner swears

---

[1] Professor Glaister said : " I think the man must have lived for at least a considerable number of minutes after he received the violence, although practically unconscious, during which time the action of the heart and the blood-vessels would send out the blood." I am advised on high medical authority that the injuries sustained by the deceased *may not have been immediately fatal*, and that the man may have lived for some time ; and of course the longer he lived, the more would both *rigor* and coagulation be postponed.

they met in the street at 6.30! Unless Mrs. Watt's time was unconscionably "fast," it seems a very pretty alibi. The Crown theory, as I understand it, was this: the man was struck down by a blow with the hammer in the lobby so soon as he had entered the house and hung up his coat, and fell through the kitchen doorway, the subsequent blows being delivered on his head as he lay upon the floor [1]— which implies an assault shortly after 6 o'clock. This would be a matter of minutes; but the murderer had still to search the body and secure the money; to clean and dry the reeking hammer; to free his person from the "filthy witness" which we know his hands, like Macbeth's, bore against him; and if Professor Glaister's view be accepted, partially to wash his trousers.

This brings us to the other vexed question: the blood-stains. There is no doubt that this was, in the literal sense, a bloody crime. Inspector Stewart counted 100 spots of blood on the skirting and south wall of the kitchen, some being 3 or 4 feet from the floor; [2] Professor Glaister found 29 bloodstains, due to forcible bespattering, upon the kitchen door alone; there were splashes on the south and east walls of the lobby, and upon the sides of the kitchen doorway; there was upon the floor a great pool and three streams of blood, and the end of the bed-couch nearest to the body was saturated with blood. It is obvious that the person who produced these shocking conditions, using the short hammer as alleged by the Crown, must have bent over or knelt beside his victim as the man lay on the floor; and all the experts admitted that in doing so he must necessarily have been exposed to the spirting blood as it followed upon the blows, and that his clothing could hardly escape contamination.

---

[1] Professor Glaister thought that the first blow was struck from behind, " probably on the back of the head " ; Professor Sydney Smith favoured a frontal attack, producing the single wound between the eyebrows.

[2] Others are described as resembling in shape an inverted lemonade bottle, the splash having struck the wall and run down 8 or 9 inches.

As regards the presence of blood upon the accused's clothing, Professor Glaister stated that he found on the shirt three small spots, "the size of a millet seed": two on the right sleeve and one on the left shoulder. Cross-examined, he thought these were "exaggerated flea-bites"; he admitted that the exposed front, not covered by vest and jacket, was unstained, and *the cuffs entirely free from blood.* On the brown jacket were two small spots of similar size to the above: one on the front of the right shoulder, the other on the left lapel. In cross-examination, *both sleeves were quite free from stains.*[1] On the brown vest, two: one on the right front of the breast opening, another at the bottom of the right front. On the brown trousers were (1) "on the front of the left thigh, 5 inches down from the fork, three separate stains of different shapes"; and (2) "indefined staining and stiffening." These stains were found to be "faintly positive of mammalian blood." In cross-examination, witness explained that he used the term "because he believed the stains to have been washed by rubbing with a wet cloth, and some blood left in the interstices of the fabric." On the damp pair of shoes were several small spots of blood, the majority on the side of the right shoe, nearest the body. These were on the uppers; *the soles were unstained.* It was ingeniously brought out by Mr. A. C. Black in cross, that the shoes being found beneath the table, placed roughly at right angles with the line of the body and with the toes pointing towards the east, the spots might have been received during the assault, for a few spots had reached in that direction the corner of the table cloth.[2]

As in the notorious case of Oscar Slater, the condition of

---

[1] On the *black* jacket was found a stain " doubtfully positive of the presence of blood." It seems unlikely that the boy wore both jackets at once. If he committed the crime, the probability is that he was in his shirt sleeves and that these were, in the course of his household duties, rolled up.

[2] With respect to the *dampness* of the shoes, it is in evidence that the night was very wet ; on the other hand, Professor Glaister stated that the dead man's boots were perfectly dry.

the hammer, the alleged weapon, was all-important; *but in neither instance was the metal head removed from the wooden shaft.* Professor Glaister said he found small stains on the wood (*a*) at the junction of the head and shaft, (*b*) at the top of the shaft between the heads, (*c*) on the neck of the smaller head, and (*d*) in debris from the sunken letters on the side of the head. Scrapings from all these contained mammalian blood, and in (*c*) there was a minute clot.

For the defence, Professor Sydney Smith stated that if the head of the hammer had been thoroughly washed and dried, it was impossible that a clot of blood could have remained upon the metal surface. I lack space to follow this expert in his weighty criticism of the post-mortem report, the medical evidence for the Crown, and the various tests employed. It is sufficient here to note that he could discover no blood in the several stains upon the clothing left untested by Professor Glaister for the benefit of the defence, and that he could see on the trousers no signs of washing. In view of all the circumstances, he held that the assailant would certainly be thoroughly splashed with blood: "I do not think there can be any question about that." If his hands were bloody, witness would expect to find blood upon the cuffs. When the boy fainted and fell on the floor, it was reasonable to suppose that some blood would get on to his trousers; or that might have happened as he was carried unconscious out of the kitchen.[1] The wallet and notes, all tested by witness, were found to be completely free from bloodstains.[2]

The defence case closed without the accused availing himself of his statutory right to enter the witness-box. The Crown cannot, the Court in its discretion may, comment upon such abstention. Here the learned Judge did not do

---

[1] The area of the kitchen floor was only 10 feet by 13 ; in so small a shambles anything might have become contaminated.

[2] The presence of bloodstains inside the pockets of the victim indicate that the hands of the murderer were copiously stained with blood, and if these hands abstracted the wallet and money from the pocket of the deceased, then detectable stains should have been discovered on either the wallet or the notes.

so. There is little doubt that, as a general rule, the failure of an accused to tell his own story weighs against him with a jury. In the present case the accused had pleaded "Not Guilty"; his whole tale had been already told through the medium of the police, and he could add nothing to it. It may be that, having committed forgery, he was afraid to face cross-examination; but it is difficult to understand how any consideration could withhold a son, conscious of his innocence, from the fullest opportunity to refute the fearful charge of parricide. Personally, I should like to have heard from him more about his relations with the father whom he twice describes as "good," what was the nature of the "slip" which he made to the police, and the authentic history of that £5 note.

VII.

The addresses of the Advocate-Depute for the Crown and of Mr. A. C. Black for the defence are, unfortunately for me and my readers, not reported; but the learned Judge, in charging the jury, took occasion to compliment both counsel on the ability and fairness with which they had presented their respective cases. With reference to the first three charges, his Lordship observed that if the conclusions reached by Mr. Brown—and he was not cross-examined— were sound, was there any other explanation of those documents found in the deceased's possession, than their having been presented to the father in order to vouch payments of money, which the accused received to make in his father's behalf and which he had spent on himself? But although the jury were satisfied that the accused forged those entries, it by no means followed that he killed his father. Whoever did so must either have possessed the means of entry to the house or had been admitted by the deceased. It was his habit to take his evening meal at 6 o'clock. Did he do so that night or not? The table was set for a meal which had not been eaten; there was beef, and a pot practically full of broth. The dead man had not taken off his boots and his

newspapers were still in his pocket. The evidence indicated
that he had been attacked in the lobby. There was the
significant fact that his stomach was entirely empty.
Having reviewed the conflicting medical testimony regarding the process of digestion, his Lordship pointed out that
there was nothing except the statement of the accused to
shew that the deceased had taken only a light meal of soup
and tea, instead of the ordinary meal he might have been
expected to take after his day's work. With regard to the
time when Mrs. Watt said she heard the "angry voices,"
witnesses often went astray upon questions of time; but
if her evidence on this point was accurate, it would be
impossible to accept the Crown theory.

But if you reach upon the vital points of the case a perfectly clear and
definite conclusion, then you have to take into account the question as to
the probability of mistake being made. Because if these two facts are
brought home without reasonable doubt to your minds—you must judge
of them—that the deceased had no supper upon that night and that
quarrelling took place between him and the accused, it becomes a matter
of very great difficulty indeed to draw any other conclusion than one
adverse to the accused.

The witnesses who saw the accused after he left the house
differed as to the exact time of his movements; but there
were always discrepancies when a number of people were
speaking as to time. With regard to the accused's statement that his father gave him money to pay the sums due
to Daly and to Mrs. Duffy, as the passbook bore to be completely discharged by Daly, why should the deceased make
any payment to him at all? and as to Mrs. Duffy, was her
account an account incurred by the deceased, and if not,
why should he pay it? The accused said he received the
exact sum to pay Daly, yet he paid him with a £5 note and
denied that he had done so. After going through the conflicting medical testimony regarding articles alleged to be
bloodstained, his Lordship observed that the jury would
probably incline to a view that was favoured by the real
evidence, without attaching too much weight to the theories

or speculations of experts. That there were upon these articles traces of human blood, his Lordship understood Professor Sydney Smith did not dispute; and there was no explanation of their presence. There was a further conflict of scientific testimony as to the questions of *rigor mortis* and the coagulation of blood. As to the theory of how and where the first blow was struck, the jury were in as good a position to form an opinion as either of the experts. If a stranger called and struck the deceased at the door, it was peculiar that he should fall into the kitchen, which was somewhat to the right. It was also peculiar that the coal hammer should be found quite clean.[1] His Lordship directed the jury that it was not necessary that premeditation be proved; if the accused used violence to his father that caused his death, he was responsible for the consequences of the act. As several blows were struck, the suggestion of culpable homicide was out of the question. Upon the matter of motive, although the jury might not think it proved that the accused had a preconceived design to kill his father that night, if in a moment of passion he lost control of himself, and killed his father because some request which he had made was not acceded to, it would still be murder. Since his mother's death the accused had done no work beyond keeping the house, for which he received from his father a small sum; much of his time was spent in billiard rooms; and he had pawned a very miscellaneous assortment of articles. That morning he said he had not the money for a game of billiards; in the afternoon he complained to Jacovelli that he was hard up. In view of his postponement of Cox's call, it might be that, because of his impecunious state, he realised that he must make a desperate effort to get money to meet the difficulties in which he was placed. If the jury reached that conclusion, while the moral responsibility attaching to premeditated

---

[1] If the family hammer were in fact the weapon, the " strange " murderer must have been uncommonly tidy and considerate to have taken the trouble to wash it so thoroughly and to replace it in the cupboard.

murder might be lessened, his Lordship could not direct
them in law that it would justify any other verdict than one
in accordance with that which the Crown asked of them.

The jury retired to consider their verdict at 3.15 p.m.,
and returned at 5.5 p.m. with the following finding:—

> The jury unanimously find the pannel guilty as libelled under charges
> 1, 2, and 3 ; by a majority find him guilty of murder as libelled under the
> 4th charge, and, unanimously, strongly recommend him to mercy on
> account of his youth.

The Advocate-Depute having moved for sentence on the
4th charge, Lord Hunter pronounced sentence of death.[1]

PART II.—APPEAL UNTO CÆSAR.

> Let us meet,
> And question this most bloody piece of work,
> To know it further.
>
> —*Macbeth*, Act II. Sc. iii.

I.

In the good (or bad) old days before the passing of the
Criminal Appeal (Scotland) Act, 1926, no more would have
been heard of Bertie Willox, except a paragraph announcing his ultimate annihilation in Duke Street Prison on
Friday, 10th January, in terms of his sentence.   But availing himself of his right under that statute, the prisoner
lodged an appeal against his conviction.

There has been so much to say about the five days' trial
at Glasgow that I have but little space left in which to do
justice to the importance of the three days' hearing on
appeal in the High Court of Justiciary, Edinburgh, on 14th,
15th, and 16th January 1930.[2]   The Lord Justice-General

---

[1] " Hardly had Lord Hunter placed the black cap on his head and completed
pronouncing sentence than Willox, who had been standing while the Judge
addressed him, collapsed in the dock into the arms of one of the police constables
beside him.   Immediately about half a dozen policemen rushed towards him and
he was carried unconscious downstairs."—*Glasgow Herald*, 21st December 1929.

[2] The appeal proceedings are reported in the *Glasgow Herald* and *Scotsman*,
15th, 16th, 17th and 18th January 1930.

(Lord Clyde), with Lords Blackburn and Morison, occupied the Bench; Mr. A. C. Black, K.C., and Mr. Ross M'Lean appeared once again for their client; the Lord Advocate (Mr. Craigie Aitchison, K.C., M.P.) and Mr. Blades, Advocate-Depute, represented the Crown. The appellant, who had asked and obtained permission to be present, on counsel's advice withdrew his request. He was, however, in custody within the precincts of the Court.[1]

For the many members of the legal profession among the audience, not the least interesting feature of the proceedings was the appearance of Mr. Aitchison as chief law officer of the Crown, in view of his long-recognised pre-eminence as the leader of our criminal bar. One recalled in that courtroom, in 1927, his successful defence of John Donald Merrett, charged with the murder of his mother; and in the following year, his even more notable achievement: the quashing of Oscar Slater's twenty-years'-old conviction. The impressive dignity and restraint with which on this occasion his Lordship conducted the Crown case, is a signal instance of the diversity and amplitude of his powers.

The grounds of appeal were (1) that incompetent evidence was wrongfully admitted by the presiding Judge, the Hon. Lord Hunter; (2) that the jury were misdirected by the presiding Judge; and (3) that the jury's verdict was contrary to the evidence and involved a grave miscarriage of justice.

Mr. A. C. Black, whose devotion to his " poor " client's interests, no less than his admirable handling of his case, merits the highest praise, argued that the direct evidence completely exonerated the appellant. Mrs. Watt thought she heard the "angry voices" of father and son on the subject of money at a time when it was conclusively proved that the son was outside the house. The other evidence

---

[1] I had the opportunity of a word with him : a well-spoken, pleasant-mannered lad, of rather effeminate type—most unsuitably cast, one should think, for the rôle of First Murderer.

was purely circumstantial. It was remarkable that while
the floor, walls, and door of the kitchen were covered with
bloodstains, the only things that escaped the shower of
blood were the appellant's clothes; yet the assailant must
have bent over his victim for some minutes. Equally
remarkable was the fact that this boy went out and played
billiards at 6.35, under a bright light, and with nothing
unusual in his appearance or demeanour. There was no
sign in the house of an attempt to destroy anything, or of
the cleaning by washing of any article. None of the notes
traced to him was bloodstained. When the boy fainted
and fell off his chair to the floor, he might well have got
some stains upon his trousers. With so short a weapon
there must have been on the assailant's clothing an appreci-
able quantity of blood. The medical evidence was not
inconsistent with the view that this man met his death an
hour after the boy had left the house. The Crown case was
that the appellant had some dispute with his father about
money. If he showed his father the discharged accounts,
then the father was pacified and there was no reason for any
further difficulty. There was no proof that anyone was
pressing him for immediate payment of any outstanding
balance. After dealing fully with the evidence relating to
the first three charges, counsel argued long and learnedly
as to the competency of admitting as evidence the statement taken from the appellant by the police before he
was charged, which was in the nature of a precognition. He
(counsel) had made strong objection to its admission at the
trial, but this was overruled by the presiding Judge. To
use the statement for the purpose of facilitating police
inquiries was one thing; co read that statement to the jury
was quite different. Having criticised certain passages
in the Judge's charge, counsel submitted that the jury's
minds were allowed to be influenced by evidence which was
improperly admitted; that the jury did not reasonably
come to a conclusion upon the circumstantial evidence;
that the Judge in his charge failed to put before the jury

certain matters which told in favour of the appellant; and that the conviction should be set aside.

The Lord Advocate, in his reply for the Crown, submitted that the evidence, although entirely circumstantial, if analysed and assembled, was sufficient to justify the inference of guilt and the verdict which the jury, by a majority, returned. The case started with one fact that was not in controversy, namely, that for months before 4th November the appellant was guilty of criminal conduct in relation to his father's money matters. On that date discovery of the fraud was imminent: it was vain for the appellant to say that there was no pressure or urgency on that day. The jury were entitled to draw the inference that that afternoon the appellant had made up his mind to get money somehow, and had fabricated an entry in a receipt book. He was hard up that afternoon; at 6.30 or 6.40 Mrs. Watt overheard an altercation between him and his father, during which the father said: "You won't get a penny from me!" and later the same evening the son was in possession of several pound notes. Where did he get that money? There was only one answer: it came from his father. Did he get it honestly? The jury were driven by the evidence to the conclusion that the appellant had possessed himself dishonestly of money belonging to his father. The whole discrepancy as regards time was within the compass of five minutes. The jury were entitled, in determining what weight attached to Mrs. Watt's evidence, to rely on their ordinary knowledge of the way in which people spoke of time. The actual commission of the murder would not take above half a minute. There was no proof that the deceased's pockets were picked; he might have left the money on the table.[1] The medical evidence proved that there was not a vestige of food in the man's stomach, and the inference was plain that he had not taken his evening meal. The jury were entitled to infer that he met his death before he took his supper. The weapon

---

[1] What about the bloody hands in the trouser pockets?

fitted the wounds, and was found on examination to contain human blood. The fact that the hammer was found in the cupboard disposed of the suggestion that the crime was committed by a stranger. The argument that the assailant would be covered with blood proceeded on the assumption that blood was spattered in all directions, which was not the case. The question was pre-eminently one for a jury, and they did not arrive at a hasty conclusion, being absent for over two hours. On the other hand, they were not unanimous. On the whole matter, his Lordship submitted that the evidence was sufficient to warrant the inference which the jury solemnly drew. With regard to the statement made by the appellant to the police, there was no evidence that it was made under any promise, threat, or inducement whatsoever. It was entirely voluntary; the boy was not under arrest and had not been charged. He was warned; but in his Lordship's opinion, no warning need have been given. In conclusion, he submitted that the appeal failed and should be dismissed.

The Court reserved judgment.

II.

When the Court of Criminal Appeal reopened on 17th January, the Lord Justice-General pronounced judgment. His Lordship observed that this must have been a peculiarly difficult and anxious case for the jury, who convicted only by a majority of 9 to 6. The case was no less difficult and anxious from the point of view of the Court of Criminal Appeal, but it was necessary to keep in mind the very different functions belonging to the jury and to the Appeal Court. The jury's business was to make up their minds, on the materials presented to them, whether the accused was guilty or not guilty, or whether the case was not proven. The function of the Appeal Court was not to set the jury's verdict aside because they formed the impression, however strong, that had they been performing the jury's function they would have returned a verdict different from the jury's, but to upset it only if they came to the conclusion that the verdict was unreasonable or could not be supported, having regard to the evidence. Reasonable men might differ, each with reason on his side. Their Lordships could only interfere if they were satisfied that the verdict was not consistent with reason and was incapable of support by the facts proved.

His Lordship then reviewed the evidence regarding the appellant's movements on the night in question; and remarked, with respect to that relating to the "angry voices" heard by Mrs. Watt, that if that testimony was correct, all the three witnesses were at least half an hour wrong as to time; for the quarrel about money must have been the preliminary, not the sequel, of the assault, and if the witnesses were in any reasonably approximate sense correct as to the time, the deceased's quarrel about money could not have been with the appellant. The difficulty of the case was thus apparent from the outset.

Having dealt with the appellant's manipulation of the household accounts and insurance premiums, his Lordship said that these circumstances were obviously consistent with a quarrel about money between father and son on the evening of the crime. The appellant was hard up that afternoon, and when he left the house was in possession of £5. He must either have robbed his father, or been given the money by him. With regard to the condition of the house, obviously something had happened to prevent the deceased taking his usual meal. Either the son had quarrelled with, and assaulted his father; or having succeeded, after high words, in getting the money he required, he left the house; and before the father had taken his supper, some other person called and committed the crime. With regard to the weapon, human blood was found upon the hammer; assuming it to have been used, its use was consistent with intimate knowledge of the contents of the house.

After dealing with the expert testimony as to the minute spots found upon the appellant's clothing and the conflict of scientific evidence as to whether or not the assailant must have been bloodstained, his Lordship concluded as follows:—

There were undoubtedly facts proved which inferred grave suspicion on the appellant. But that was not enough. There must be reasonable grounds, founded on evidence, for the inference in fact, that he was his father's murderer. The line between suspicion and fact might be thin as a hair, but it was deep as the grave. Using the best judgment he had, his Lordship could not say, whatever his own verdict might have been had he been a juror, that the inference drawn by the majority of the jury was either unreasonable or incapable of being supported on the evidence. It must therefore stand ; although his Lordship felt bound to add that if the verdict had been one of "Not Proven," he would certainly not have said it was unreasonable either. The appeal could not therefore be sustained.[1]

Lords Blackburn and Morison concurred.

III.

Application was forthwith made in behalf of the convict to the Secretary of State for Scotland, praying for the exercise of the Royal prerogative, in respect of the narrowness of the majority verdict and the jury's strong recommendation to mercy. On 22nd January the Lord Provost of Glasgow received from the Scottish Secretary the following reply:—

With reference to the case of Robert Swift Willox, now lying under sentence of death in His Majesty's Prison, Duke Street, Glasgow, I have to inform you that, after full consideration, I have felt justified in advising His Majesty to respite the execution of the capital sentence, with a view to its commutation to penal servitude for life.[2]

The decision was at once communicated to the person most nearly concerned, "who appeared relieved and grateful." The postponed ceremony of which he was to be the

---

[1] *Glasgow Herald* and *Scotsman*, 18th January 1930.
[2] *Glasgow Herald*, 23rd January 1930.

subject had been fixed for 4th February, so he was put out
of suspense as speedily as possible.

Among the inventories of estates lodged during the trial
week with the Sheriff-Clerk of Lanarkshire at Glasgow, was
that of the late Robert Willox. The inventory, which
showed an estate of £57—made up of £9 due from the Corps
of Commissionaires and £48 of an insurance policy—was
attested by the dead man's son. It is recorded of Miss
Mary Blandy, who suffered at Oxford in 1752 for the crime
of parricide, that she had been heard to say, in extenuation
of her offence: "Who would grudge to send an old father
to hell for £10,000?" In the present case the consideration seems inadequate.

.   .   .   .

In reading the other day, not for the first time, a certain
inestimable Chronicle, I came upon this passage: "My
dear," said the eldest Miss Prettyman to poor Grace
Crawley, "in England, where the laws are good, no gentleman is ever made out to be guilty when he is innocent."
It is my patriotic hope that this Act of Providence applies
to Scotland.